Italian Political Cinema

ITALIAN POLITICAL CINEMA

Figures of the Long '68

Mauro Resmini

 University of Minnesota Press
Minneapolis
London

This book is freely available in an open access edition thanks to TOME (Toward an Open Monograph Ecosystem)—a collaboration of the Association of American Universities, the Association of University Presses, and the Association of Research Libraries—and the generous support of the University of Maryland. Learn more at the TOME website, available at: openmonographs.org.

Portions of chapter 1 and a different version of chapter 2 were published as "The Worker as Figure: On Elio Petri's *The Working Class Goes to Heaven*," *Diacritics* 46, no. 4 (2019): 72–95; copyright 2018 Cornell University, published with permission by Johns Hopkins University Press. Portions of chapter 7 were published as "Asymmetries of Desire: *Salò, or The 120 Days of Sodom*," in *Unwatchable*, ed. Nicolas Baer, Maggie Hennefeld, Laura Horak, and Gunnar Iversen, 160–64 (New Brunswick, N.J.: Rutgers University Press, 2019).

Copyright 2022 by Mauro Resmini

Italian Political Cinema: Figures of the Long '68 is licensed under a Creative Commons Attribution-NonCommercial-NoDerivatives 4.0 International License (CC BY-NC-ND 4.0): https://creativecommons.org/licenses/by-nc-nd/4.0/.

Published by the University of Minnesota Press
111 Third Avenue South, Suite 290
Minneapolis, MN 55401-2520
http://www.upress.umn.edu

▣ Available as a Manifold edition at manifold.umn.edu

ISBN 978-1-5179-1137-9 (hc)
ISBN 978-1-5179-1138-6 (pb)

A Cataloging-in-Publication record for this book is available from the Library of Congress.

The University of Minnesota is an equal-opportunity educator and employer.

A Viviana e Camilla

Contents

Introduction: Cinema/Politico   1

1. "A Dance of Figures": For a Figural Theory of Political Cinema   15
2. The Worker: Subjectivity within and against Capital   35
3. The Housewife: Figuring Reproductive Labor   81
4. The Youth: The Dialectic of Enjoyment   127
5. The Saint: An Ethics of Autonomy   165
6. The Specter: Totality as Conjuration   183
7. Apocalypse with Figures: The Tyrant, the Intriguer, the Martyr   223

Epilogue: The Cinema of '68, the '68 of Cinema   253

Acknowledgments   259

Notes   263

Index   289

Introduction

Cinema/Politico

Italian political cinema (*cinema d'impegno,* "engaged cinema," "civil cinema") most commonly designates a set of films made between the mid-1960s and the early 1980s that are informed by a resolutely progressive, if rarely radical, agenda and that explicitly deal with either contemporary or past political events or issues, such as factory strikes, political terrorism, state violence, Mafia conspiracies, and the pervasiveness of capitalist speculation—but also antifascist resistance and, more generally, episodes in the history of leftism in the twentieth century. Elio Petri, Francesco Rosi, Damiano Damiani, Carlo Lizzani, Florestano Vancini, and Giuliano Montaldo are among the most notable directors broadly associated with this trend. With its explicit focus on politics as content, political cinema is then understood as a genre among many others within the domain of Italian cinema writ large—a cinema about politics.[1]

Against the traditionally held notion that political films are simply expressions of political contents, this book begins from the following hypothesis: what if instead of signaling a connection between cinema and politics, political cinema actually designated a nonrelation between these two domains? Further, what if, for this exact reason, the link between cinema and politics could never be decided in advance but had to be reinvented anew with each individual political film? The starting point of *Italian Political Cinema* is a refutation of political cinema as a general category based on a relation between cinema and politics whereby the latter is represented by the former. Moving beyond the idea of political cinema as a cinematic representation of politics opens up the possibility of reading political films differently—not as serialized instances of a genre but rather as singular responses to an original nonrelation. From this starting point, the book advances a fundamental thesis: to find provisional solutions to this nonrelation, films invent *figures*. The figure may be understood as the material support of a dialectical interaction between one element and its opposite, for a figure is, in its very essence, always a figure of the Two: order and chaos, form and formless, figuration and disfiguration. The figure should therefore not be defined as a stable and immediately legible entity but rather as the movement of one thing toward another across the nonrelation.

The figure provides the organizing principle of the book's structure. Each chapter is centered on a single figure, tracing its appearance across a number of films made during the Italian long '68. These figures conjure a multifaceted, complex portrayal of Italian society and of the currents of antagonism and repression that constituted the sociopolitical fabric of the country from the mid-1960s to the early 1980s. To gain a better understanding of this crucial historical passage, this book puts cinema in dialogue with the radical political thought of the time. As many critics have argued, from the 1960s to the late 1970s, Italy was a political laboratory for imagining and theorizing new forms of collective struggle. In the past few decades, contemporary philosophy has rediscovered this rich intellectual legacy, as we have witnessed the work of thinkers such as Mario Tronti, Antonio Negri, Sergio Bologna, Silvia Federici, Mariarosa Dalla Costa, Bifo Berardi, and Paolo Virno garnering international recognition. *Italian Political Cinema* shows how Italian cinema of the long '68 thought in its own way some of the same problems and questions as philosophy and political theory of the same period, which coalesced most notably around the *operaismo* of the 1960s, the Autonomia archipelago of the 1970s, the antiauthoritarian demands of the student movement, and the rise of new forms of feminism.

The films discussed in this book belong to both popular and art cinema. They help us locate cinema's engagement with politics across a wide array of genres, including comedy and noir, realist drama and the grotesque. Through a detailed analysis of films by Elio Petri, Francesco Rosi, Lina Wertmüller, Ettore Scola, Liliana

Cavani, Bernardo Bertolucci, Marco Bellocchio, Pier Paolo Pasolini, Michelangelo Antonioni, Marco Ferreri, and others, this book aims to provide a critical account of Italian political cinema with all its historical and geographical specificity, while simultaneously offering a figural paradigm for a radical rethinking of the concept of political cinema tout court, beyond the confines of a specific national context. Indeed, a global, comparative approach to political cinema in the second half of the twentieth century might prove crucial in our attempts to map cinema's engagement with our contemporary political horizon—a horizon that descends genealogically from the negation of the political possibilities opened up in the transitional phase of the long '68.

The Impurity of Italian Political Cinema

The perspective articulated in this book opens up the possibility for a radical reconsideration of what constitutes Italian political cinema. Because no objective ontological criteria decided in advance can account for the singularity of the solutions to the nonrelation that each political film invents, political cinema is not beholden to any imperative of idealistic purity. Recalcitrant as it is to any attempt to establish its true essence once and for all, political cinema escapes existing categorizations, be they production oriented (mainstream, independent), aesthetic (genres, styles), or biographical (the militant pedigree of the director). Political cinema, irreducible to a single genre, instead opens itself up to generic interpolations. It traverses the territories of all film genres, appropriating whatever materials and forms it may need to bring its figures into existence.

As a consequence, this book challenges long-held assumptions about the canon of Italian political cinema. It restricts its reach while moving past it to include films that are foreign to it. While the analysis that follows prominently features the work of staple directors of the *cinema d'impegno* (Petri, Rosi), some of the other films that I will analyze decidedly exceed the boundaries of Italian political cinema proper. Examples include works of mainstream directors like Mario Monicelli and Ettore Scola; Lina Wertmüller's farce-melodrama *The Seduction of Mimì* (*Mimì metallurgico ferito nell'onore,* 1972); Salvatore Samperi's erotic tale *Come Play with Me* (*Grazie zia,* 1968); and even more auteurist works by Pier Paolo Pasolini, Marco Bellocchio, Bernardo Bertolucci, Liliana Cavani, Michelangelo Antonioni, and Marco Ferreri.

This forcing of the canon runs counter to one of the most deeply rooted characterizations of *cinema politico*—namely, its essential *medietas,* or midpointness. Because this *medietas* has been understood differently in different historical contexts, I will provide two examples. One kind of *medietas* is the one lamented by critics in the 1970s and early 1980s. According to their vision, *cinema politico* is just average, when not plain mediocre, filmmaking. In English, the derogatory aspect of this *medietas* is perhaps best defined as middlebrow; too derivative of Hollywood cinema to really challenge dominant formal paradigms, it is also too steeped in the dynamics of mainstream film production to be truly subversive.[2] These limitations are taken to be immediately political: who can realistically expect a revolutionary consciousness from a cinema that is thoroughly petty bourgeois in inspiration and intentions? The second example of the use of *medietas* to describe the films of *cinema politico* is more recent. It deploys the term to indicate a character of virtuous mediation—not only between high culture and low culture, but also in the sense of a deliberate eclecticism capable of combining political reflection with the patterns of recognition and enjoyability of popular film genres.

These two conceptualizations of the *medietas* of political cinema are exemplified in the critical assessments of Elio Petri's *Investigation of a Citizen above Suspicion* (*Indagine su un cittadino al di sopra di ogni sospetto,* 1970), discussed in chapter 6. Lorenzo Pellizzari, writing in 1981, calls the film a

> perfect "commodity" [*prodotto*], insofar as it is enjoyable on different levels and layers of reading. It finally creates a "phenomenon" [*caso*] and becomes one of the pinnacles of the trajectory of "political cinema," while the authors and their following remain unaware of the fracture that occurs between the smooth and benevolent representation of a "pathology of power" ... and the much more harrowing reality ...

that precisely in those years . . . the young students and the not-so-young militants lived in squares, police headquarters, and prisons, where they faced a much more immediate and lucid resolve on the part of the State to destroy dissent and turn itself into a fascist institution.[3]

Structures might not walk in the streets, but according to Pellizzari, films should. In properly superegoic fashion, his reprimand sets for the film a standard it will never be able to meet: on what basis is one supposed to compare a political film to a student protest or a strike? The disavowal of the nonrelation between cinema and politics in the discourse of militant criticism often ends up producing an unduly superimposition of the two, in which one term (cinema) is held accountable according to the principles that pertain to the other (politics).

Contrary to the militant position of Pellizzari, Claudio Bisoni writes exactly thirty years later that the midpointness of a film like *Investigation* reduces politics to a type of fishing "baits that, intentionally or not, [the film] throws into the socio-political imaginary of the decade."[4] For Bisoni, the film's political relevance is as tenuous as it is fortuitous, and that is to be regarded as a virtue. The implication here is that Petri somehow intercepted and gave form to the vaguely defined social anxieties that floated on the surface of the Italian public discourse between the late 1960s and the early 1970s. From Pellizzari's imposition of politics as an unattainable horizon to Bisoni's diminishment of politics as mere bait—in either case, this idea of *medietas* assumes a certain transitivity between cinema and politics, where the latter is cast as either an ultimate goal (Pellizzari) or a reified trace (Bisoni).[5]

If we are thus to define a corpus of political films in Italian cinema according to the logic of the nonrelation, we need to transgress the historically consolidated confines of the category of *cinema politico* and extend the reach of the concept of political cinema beyond the prison of its *medietas*—that is, both upward to so-called art cinema and downward to popular, even exploitative genres. In other words, a rethinking of the concept of political cinema must embrace a certain impurity. In this book, political cinema emerges as an inherently transversal category oblivious to the criteria that separate high culture and low culture and that separate different genres from each other.[6]

The aversion of militant critics toward *cinema d'impegno* is indissociable from a rejection of the political project put forward by this cinema. These critics' drive to delineate a properly antagonistic form of cinema was one with the harsh denunciation of the supposedly reformist politics of filmmakers such as Rosi and Petri.[7] What was in question for many militant critics were the pedigrees of these directors as members or former members of the Italian Communist Party (PCI)—a party that for all intents and purposes abandoned any revolutionary identity after World War II and that in the early 1970s began to seek an alliance with the dominant center-right party, the Christian Democrats (DC).

Yet this judgment, however politically well intentioned, is anchored in the assumption that cinema's primary goal should be inherently pragmatic—that is, a direct intervention in the existent political struggles. It is the trope of cinema as a weapon, as old as cinema itself and famously appropriated throughout history by revolutionaries and reactionaries alike. Yet the intervention that political cinema makes is not reducible to the dissemination of some positive content or program. Italian political cinema is not only impure; it should also be regarded as politically impractical, in the sense of nonpragmatic. Political cinema should not be mistaken for the site of the affirmation, however mediated, of political ideas or strategic solutions to the woes of the times. On the contrary, the militant dimension of political cinema resides precisely in its being wholly impractical, in its refusal to be judged according to utilitarian standards of political effectiveness.

By the same token, neither the political allegiances of the directors considered here nor the political agendas that they were supposedly pushing in their films are of any consequence to the argument presented in this book. The sheer variety of political backgrounds of the filmmakers I discuss attests to that. They include party intellectuals (Scola, Rosi, Moretti), former members of the PCI (disillusioned, like Petri; excommunicated, like Pasolini), supporters of the extraparliamentary left (Bellocchio, Caligari), communist sympathizers (Bertolucci), and political opportunists

(Samperi). This assortment hardly conveys the sense of a unitary political program. Instead, what brings the work of these directors together is the way they experiment with the nonrelation between cinema and politics by inventing figures.

One cannot but admire the uncompromising partisanship that animated the militant criticism of the long '68, especially in their most theoretically sophisticated iterations in the journals *Cinema&Film* and *Ombre rosse*. Their writings are nothing if not a subjective decision to take sides in a time—the late 1960s and 1970s—when neutrality would have been the worst kind of betrayal of the event that was unfolding. Radical film critics not only understood this in the most lucid of ways but also actively contributed to further expand the reach of revolutionary politics well beyond its strictly political domain—a gesture that was as necessary as it was inherently flawed, as one of the most prominent militant voices in Italian film criticism, Goffredo Fofi, demonstrates in the following description of another film by Petri, *The Working Class Goes to Heaven* (*La classe operaia va in paradiso*, 1971), discussed in chapter 2. The film, he writes, is "neither sufficiently sociological nor sufficiently psychological, neither comedy nor drama, and above all, absolutely not political other than at the most distant levels."[8] This series of negations, which is obviously meant as a ruthless takedown, instead gives us an ideal definition of political cinema. It is "neither . . . sociological nor . . . psychological" because it does not aim to represent a social or psychological condition but rather creates a figure of the worker; it is "neither comedy nor drama" because it cannot be placed into a preexisting genre taxonomy; and it is "not political other than at the most distant levels" because in its very act of inventing a figure, it is mindful of the nonrelation that separates cinema and politics. Surely one couldn't hope for a more precise description of the concept of political cinema articulated in this book!

Con-Figurations

My preoccupation in the chapters that follow is anything but philological. I have no ambition to bring to completion the geography of Italian political cinema by simply adding what is missing.

The project of this book is not (or not primarily) to unearth forgotten films that would expand the dominant definitions of political cinema while leaving the essence of these definitions unaltered. Rather, the aim is to add what is not missing, a supplement that would introduce incompleteness, thwarting the very project of an exhaustive geography. The approach articulated in this book aims to impose a shift in the way we look at and think about political cinema, revealing it to comprise potentially infinite attempts at improvising singular solutions to the nonrelation—as infinite as the number of figures that may be invented with these attempts.

A figure is never established once and for all; each iteration is different, and each iteration contributes to the figure's outline. Emerging from the multiplicity of its concrete manifestations, the figure comes into existence as a set of compounded contours—or, better, as something *con*-figured. Along these lines, Jacques Derrida considers the logic of the nonrelation (aporia) to be "plural," in the sense that its manifestation coalesces around multiple "figures": "A plural logic of the aporia thus takes shape. It appears to be paradoxical enough so that the partitioning [*partage*] among multiple figures of aporia does not oppose figures to each other, but instead installs the haunting of the one in the other."[9]

It is remarkable how this idea of a con-figuration of multiplicity traverses accounts of the concept of the figure, though it is typically mentioned in passing and always in a rather autarchic fashion, as the faint trace of a potential conversation that never actually occurred. Georges Didi-Huberman, for instance, captures the propagative aspect of the figure's con-figuration: "Figures are made to proliferate: they generate one another, spread, and trace labyrinthine trajectories, like a gigantic dream work."[10] As for the specific modalities of the creation of figures in cinema, both Nicole Brenez and Alain Badiou, in a surprising mutual reverberation, argue that a certain fragmentation and dissemination are essential to the figure as such. "A figure," writes Brenez, "exists only to distribute itself onto various characters."[11] While the figure escapes capture in a single character, its silhouette is outlined by a set of characters that contribute to its con-figuration. Similarly, Badiou argues that because of this irreducibility to a character, the figure as con-figuration poses a direct challenge to characterization. Con-figuration, then, names this abstracting gesture whereby the existence of individual characters is at once preserved and surpassed in favor of a more general idea of the figure.[12]

This logic of con-figuration explains the emergence of figures across multiple works. In this book, I trace figures as configurations that traverse heterogeneous sets of films made by different directors and belonging to different genres. "Figure" then returns to one of its early meanings, the "constellation" that Erich Auerbach found in Manilius's *Astronomica* and that Walter Benjamin adopted in his theorization of the dialectical image in *The Arcades Project*.[13]

Eight Figures

Italian Political Cinema is composed of seven chapters. Chapter 1 provides the theoretical framework of the book, reconceptualizing the category of political cinema according to the logic of the nonrelation and establishing the fundamental principles of a theory of the figure. The chapter interrogates the unspoken assumptions of established models for thinking the relationship between cinema and politics (with a particular focus on ideology critique) to then propose a different framework: instead of a situation of mutual transitivity between cinema and politics, what political cinema points to is, in fact, a nonrelation. Of course, this does not mean that no linkage between the two terms is possible. Rather, it means that any linkage improvised by each individual film exists without recourse to a predetermined form, for each film invents the form of its linkage in the guise of a figure. The defining trait of political cinema, then, would not be reducible to a specific stylistic or thematic feature or set of features. Rather, it has to do with a fundamental willingness to wrestle with the angel of this nonrelation, with each film inventing a new way of bridging the gap between the two domains. This principle of singularity (the endless reinvention of a tie in the face of a nonrelation) informs the book's general theoretical approach. The figure is the point where this linkage between cinema and politics occurs. Figures exist in opposition to simple representation; they do not convey preexisting political ideas or a militant call to arms. Rather, the dynamic dialectical unfolding of the figure provides a dramatization of the field of possibility—or impossibility—of subjectivities to arise within the material and structural conditions of the historical sequence of the long '68.

Chapter 2 centers on the figure of the worker, focusing on *The Working Class Goes to Heaven*, *The Seduction of Mimì*, and *Trevico-Turin: Voyage in the Fiat-Nam* (*Trevico-Torino: Viaggio nel Fiat-Nam*, Ettore Scola, 1973). A largely understudied film, *The Working Class Goes to Heaven* constitutes the centerpiece of the chapter. The analysis of the film unearths the figure of the worker in the historical sequence of the long '68 as simultaneously a protagonist of radical political struggle and a victim of an irreversible crisis as a result of capitalist restructuring. In this figure, we locate the snapshot of the decline of a once-hegemonic figure that is slowly losing its centrality with the advent of a new form of capitalist organization. But what makes the worker in *The Working Class Goes to Heaven* a paradigmatic incarnation of the figure is the mapping it provides of the various moments of political subjectivation. This is played out in a dialectic between the existing capitalist structure and an antagonistic force of the proletariat bent on transforming it—or destroying it altogether. To the paradigmatic articulation of political subjectivity in Petri's film, the chapter juxtaposes the exploration of the limits of subjectivation undertaken in *The Seduction of Mimì* and *Trevico-Turin*. What happens, the films ask, when the process of subjectivation remains incomplete? In *The Seduction of Mimì*, the dialectic between structure and force is resolved in favor of the structure, as the figure of the worker indexes a futile antagonism unmoored from any true realization of the worker's condition of exploitation. *Trevico-Turin* pictures the opposite predicament: the alienation of the southern migrant working at the FIAT assembly lines in Turin becomes all pervasive, suffocating any possibility of collective antagonism.

Chapter 3 turns from productive labor in the factory to reproductive labor at home, centering on the figure of the housewife. In the Italian cinema of the long '68, the housewife is easily recognizable as a figure, but she rarely stands out, relegated instead to ancillary roles that put her on the backdrop of any given scene.

Omnipresent yet invariably marginalized, the housewife is what we might call a receding figure. The chapter traces the presence of this receding figure in one of the films discussed in the previous chapter (*The Working Class Goes to Heaven*), with the aim of highlighting the unique nature of the housewife's figurality. Then the chapter goes on to investigate domestic labor, surveying the field of the subjective possibilities of the housewife in the cinema of the long '68. By analyzing films by Ferreri, Scola, and Antonioni, the chapter interrogates housework as simultaneously a cause of the exhaustion of all radical subjective possibilities (the repetition; the physical and mental fatigue) and as the possible site of new forms of struggle and antagonism. To that end, the chapter combines the analysis of the films with a discussion of the Wages for Housework international movement in the 1970s, with a specific focus on the work of authors such as Silvia Federici, Mariarosa Dalla Costa, and Leopoldina Fortunati.

Building on the dialectic of the figure outlined in previous two chapters, chapter 4 focuses on the figure of the (predominantly male and bourgeois) youth as one of the most elusive, yet central, actors on the social, cultural, and political scene of the long '68. Largely a twentieth-century invention, the youth is not defined by the central position he occupies in the direct process of production (as with the worker); nor is it a receding figure (like the housewife). With this figure, the chapter argues, antagonism undergoes a process of generalization and dissemination into the fabric of the social, aiming to overthrow the institutions to which the perpetuation of the status quo is entrusted (the state, the education system, the church, the party, the family, and so forth). This diffused antagonism no longer constitutes itself in the universalist collectivity of the working class. Instead, it finds its roots in the irreducible singularity of the individual's desire. The political wager that defines the youth is that of attempting to establish a dynamic of mutual determination between the liberation of individual desires from the yoke of capitalism and the necessarily collective dimension of political action. The figural reading of the films discussed in this chapter unearths the ways in which this desiring force finds itself in dialectical tension with the reactive feedback of the structure. Accordingly, the chapter unfolds as a discussion of the youth as a figure of desire in films by Bellocchio, Bertolucci, Cavani, and others, with each incarnation articulating a specific variation of the relation between desire and law that marks the terrain of the youth as a possible revolutionary subject.

Following from the previous chapter, chapter 5 centers on the figure of the saint. The figural dialectics of the youth identified a tension between the liberation of one's own desire and the collective dimension of militancy. The saint pushes this dialectic to its limit. As the outcast that is at the same time produced by and excluded from the (supposedly) functioning mechanisms of society, the saint makes the unyielding pursuit of desire into an ethical imperative that ultimately leads to self-destruction. The rare but crucial figure of the saint features most prominently in two of Pasolini's films: *Teorema* (1968) and *Pigsty* (*Porcile*, 1969). Through a discussion of the Pauline conception of sainthood in Pasolini and Badiou, the chapter outlines the revolutionary potential of this figure, while also contending with the relentless attempts by the structure to co-opt its antagonism to its own advantage.

Chapter 6 looks more closely at the figural logic of the structure by focusing on the specter. At the most basic level, the figure of the specter evokes the intangibility and omnipresence of a threat. The collectivity that this figure relays is no longer class based (as for the worker) or generational (as for the youth). Its contours are blurred, its identity and extension obscure. This spectral collectivity is an entity that never fully manifests itself—an absent presence whose peculiar regime of visibility is that of haunting, and that assumes the form of the conspiracy. It is well known that Italy in the long '68 was an arena for competing plots and intrigues, with the state the center of the action. The chapter looks at the relationship between the state and conspiracy in films by Rosi and Petri through the lens of the spectral conjuring Jacques Derrida remarks on in *Specters of Marx,* highlighting the inherent political ambivalence of conspiracy as an agent of both rebellion and authoritarianism. However, the specter does not limit itself to signaling a network of interlocking conspiracies. True to its nature as a revenant, the specter lingers even as conspiracies dissolve and the very idea of collective struggle becomes a thing of the past. What happens, the chapter asks in its coda, when a specter is all that is left? Through an analysis of Marco Tullio Giordana's *To Love the Damned* (*Maledetti vi amerò*, 1980), we investigate the spectral persistence of antagonism in the historical moment of *riflusso* (ebb) that followed the end of radical experiments of struggle in the 1970s. The specter, then, is not just a figure of the defeat of radicalism; perhaps more poignantly, it also carries a certain melancholic inability to come to terms with it.

In the final chapter we focus on the exhaustion of Italian political cinema—an exhaustion that cannot be reduced to mere historicochronological factors (such as the collapse of a genre) but that demands to be understood figurally, in accordance with my overarching project here. To grasp this conclusion of Italian political cinema, chapter 7 focuses on three of the most singular, not to mention controversial, films in Italian cinema: Marco Ferreri's *La Grande Bouffe* (*La grande abbuffata*, 1973), Pier Paolo Pasolini's *Salò, or The 120 Days of Sodom* (*Salò, o Le 120 giornate di Sodoma*, 1975), and Elio Petri's *Todo Modo* (1976). The panicked reaction with which these films were met by censorship is, if nothing else, a testament to the fact that they managed to touch on some uncomfortable truths of Italy in the 1970s. Namely, these films mark the reaching of a historical turning point whereby the master signifiers that had organized Italian society after World War II (the triad of state, church, and capital, allied in their promise of social order and economic progress) found themselves caught in an irreversible crisis, thus signaling the end of the sovereignty of the bourgeoisie born from the ashes of World War II. The moment of crisis is depicted in starkly similar terms in the three films, with the recurring motifs of seclusion and the establishment of what we might call a state of exception, in which the rule of law is suspended and substituted by a new, ritualistic set of norms. The chapter, following Walter Benjamin's figural taxonomy in his analysis of German baroque drama, identifies three distinct figural variations generated by this crisis of sovereignty: the tyrant, the intriguer, and the martyr. Each of these figures corresponds to a specific pathological position: the pervert, who willfully submits to an absolute law (the tyrant in *Salò*); the obsessional neurotic, who tries to stave off the collapse of the law by way of repetitive, ritualistic actions (the intriguer in *Todo Modo*); and the psychotic, who openly confronts the breakdown of the law by giving himself over to the death drive (the martyr in *La Grande Bouffe*).

As a potentially infinite set of singular responses to a fundamental nonrelation, political cinema as such cannot end. However, it may reach a point of exhaustion at the end of a given historical sequence. In the book's epilogue, I pose the question of how to think about the exhaustion of something that is grounded in a nonrelation, as opposed to some positive transcendental condition. No doubt the periodization of Italian political cinema of the long '68 that I propose in this book hints at a certain moment of closure. Yet the potentialities of thought and subjectivity articulated in the films analyzed in these chapters live on well beyond that conclusion. My hope is that this book will be able not only to reactivate these potentialities for our present moment but also, and perhaps immodestly, to inscribe itself in them in an act of fidelity to what the political cinema of the long '68 was able to think.

1 "A Dance of Figures"

For a Figural Theory of Political Cinema

> The absence of relation does of course not prevent the tie [*la liaison*], far from it—it dictates its conditions.
> —Jacques Lacan, *The Seminar, Book 19, . . . Or Worse*

> Cinema is an art of figures.
> —Alain Badiou, *Cinema*

Nonrelation

In the history of film studies, the question of the relationship between cinema and politics has generated a wide array of critical discourses, testifying not only to the rich complexity of the topic of political cinema but also to the volatility of a term like "political cinema" in the first place. Whether made explicit or not, the shared assumption of most of these discourses on political cinema is that there exists a certain correspondence between the domains of cinema and politics. Notwithstanding the occasional noise or interference, the two terms are assumed to communicate, and political cinema is the name of this communication. Political cinema therefore signals above all the existence of a relationship between cinema and politics, which in some cases is conceived as a simple mirroring and in others as a more complex and mediated interaction.

This book begins from a contrary assumption, setting out from the idea that the term "political cinema" points not to a relation but rather to a nonrelation between politics and cinema. Political cinema designates not a positive presence but its opposite: the negativity of an obstacle that prevents us from simply assuming the existence of a transitivity between politics and cinema. To borrow a term coined by Jacques Derrida, political cinema refers us to an aporetology, or a study of the way in which political cinema comes into existence as an aporia. Etymologically, aporia is a site of nonpassage between two domains (from the Greek word *aporos*, "without passage," "impassable").[1] At its most basic level, starting a discussion of political cinema from this nonpassage means positing that political cinema names first and foremost a problem, a difficulty or resistance, that cuts through the aura of apparent self-evidence that has historically enshrouded the designation.

As we outline the contours of the aporetic aspect of political cinema, it is important to bear in mind that the obstacle presented by the aporia cannot simply be ignored or bypassed; nor can it be likened to a definitive dead end. If the latter were the case, we would be forced to postulate an absolute reciprocal autonomy between cinema and politics.[2] But what if political cinema is neither the proper name of an entity grounded in the relation between cinema and politics nor a mere sophism that muddies the waters, obscuring the fact that cinema and politics are completely independent from each other? I propose to look at political cinema as a problem that neither a theory of transitivity nor one of autonomy can fully solve. In fact, what political cinema names is an aporia, a lack of a passageway between its two domains that must nevertheless be traversed.

The existence of a nonrelation does not automatically translate into the fact that no link whatsoever can be constructed between cinema and politics. Rather, it means that the nonrelation is the condition that makes possible and structures any improvised attempt at a linkage. In her discussion of the concept of aporia in Plato's dialogues, Sarah Kofman argues that any aporia must be understood dialectically, for although it certainly marks a nonpassage, it also elicits a desire to overcome its impassability. Irreducible as it is to a simple paralysis, the aporia for Kofman (and Plato) is configured as a productive negativity: there is no way around this obstacle (so it cannot be ignored), but the disorientation the aporia generates becomes the spur to find a way—a passage, a *poros*—through it. In Greek mythology, Poros is the son of Metis, and Kofman observes that this kinship connects the idea of passage (*poros*) to a certain guileful wisdom, flexible and effective (*metis*, of which Odysseus's cunning would be the prime example). Specifically, *poros* in Greek refers to a sea route, a passage opened by the sailors' *metis* across the tumultuous vastness of the sea: "In this infernal, chaotic confusion, the *poros* is the way out, the last resort of sailors and navigators, the stratagem which allows them to escape the impasse and the attendant anxiety."[3] This anxiety is the dialectical pivot of the aporia. It denotes a state of suffering (aporia is anxiety producing), but because this situation is untenable, it incites one to devise a way out. However, any attempt to cross the "infernal, chaotic confusion" is necessarily tentative and singular. Nothing guarantees in advance the viability of a certain *poros*, which "has to be found anew each time, in each case. It has to be traced, woven, in some new way, and that involves an element of risk."[4] Improvisation is of the essence: to figure out a way across the sea, one sets sail and invents the route as one goes. Charting a passage through an aporia thus always involves a wager that exceeds any assurance of success that the general objective coordinates of the situation might provide. It is only at the end of the journey, on the other side of the wager, that the correctness of the *poros* can be adjudicated.

In this sense, the films that constitute political cinema are a multitude of *poroi*. Each finds a singular way to traverse the nonrelation between cinema and politics—a nonrelation that, however, is never solved once and for all. Yet this does not translate into a pure plurality either. The films do not experience the luxury of unimpeded becoming, forever anchored as they are in the aporia that made them possible in the first place. Because the nonrelation between cinema and politics cannot be ignored or finally solved, individual films can only experiment and improvise with this nonrelation. Political cinema thus comprises a nontotalizable set of attempts at crossing the aporia.

In the history of film studies, this aspect has often been overlooked. Italian film scholar and critic Alberto Farassino appropriately called political cinema a fetish category (*categoria-feticcio*).[5]

True to the nature of the fetish, it presents itself as an object on which desire fixates while it dissimulates its own inadequacy to satisfy that very desire. This fetish category has always enjoyed a distinct fortune in the critical discourse, thanks not only to its halo of obviousness but also its flexibility. Yet fetishes are also defense mechanisms, diversions. The fetish has a pacifying function; it crystallizes desire and stops its endless shifting from one object to the other by making lack, the negative cause of desire, disappear. As a fetish category, political cinema operates on a similar logic. It purports to dissimulate the deadlock of a fundamental nonrelation into the reassuring consistency of a self-identical category. In the scholarly discourses about the place of politics in the field of cinema, the fetish of political cinema has often functioned as a sort of critical blockage, positing the relation between politics and cinema as a given and thus preventing the possibility of actually interrogating it. As a result, the nonrelation between politics and cinema has often been erased, and with it the possibility of thinking the two terms together, but not as one. It is in this sense that the question of political cinema needs to be posed anew, mobilized as a problem rather than fixated, or fetishized, as a solution.

Similarly, the nonrelation between cinema and politics that defines political cinema should not itself be fetishized or reified into a positive given that exists before the individual films. If there is a transcendental condition of political cinema, then it must be located in the negativity of the nonrelation. This negativity exists solely in the multiplicity of individual filmic attempts to devise a path through it. The universal nonrelation between cinema and politics can only be inferred from the singularities of the films—or, more precisely, from the singular linkage between politics and cinema that each film invents in place of the nonrelation. As a way to work through the aporia, each individual political film is structured by the nonrelation that is constitutive of political cinema as such. This, however, is not a simple reflection, as political films bring the nonrelation into existence only by way of the *poroi* that they open up to traverse it. These passages, like the seafarer's *poros* in Kofman, are never given; they must be invented, then invented again with each new film. For all intents and purposes, then, this means that the condition of political cinema itself is reconceived anew with each political film. Every singular attempt at linking politics and cinema frames, displaces, and mobilizes the nonrelation in new ways.

This leaves us with a curious paradox. The potentially infinite set of political films does not amount to a systematic and coherent solution for the problem of the nonrelation of political cinema; nor does the category of political cinema endow political films with an a priori guarantee for the success of their attempts at tying together cinema and politics. Instead, as films put their *metis* to the test and improvise their way through the nonrelation, each singular *poros* intervenes on the nonrelation itself and redesigns its contours. This dialectical tension never coalesces into a proper synthesis; the sort of parallax view between political cinema and political films is precisely the split that keeps the nonrelation alive. Once a crossing has been attempted, the aporia changes its complexion only to remain as daunting as before, calling for a new path to be charted through its impassable expanse.

The constitutive nonrelation between politics and cinema is precisely what other theories of political cinema foreclose. Let us now consider one such theory in detail: ideology critique. Arguably the most comprehensive and sophisticated attempt in the history of film studies at thinking the relation between cinema and politics, ideology critique puts many questions that are central to our argument under meticulous scrutiny.

"A Noticeable Gap"

Among the most potent analytical tools for investigating political cinema, ideology critique stands towering. Serving broadly as the conceptual link between economic structure and cultural production, ideology offers the ideal terrain for testing one possible way of thinking cinema and politics together. In what arguably constitutes the conceptual manifesto for this intellectual project—the programmatic 1969 essay "Cinema/Ideology/Criticism"—*Cahiers du cinéma* editors Jean-Louis Comolli and Jean Narboni posit not merely a relation but rather a correspondence between cinema and ideology in which the former is construed and analyzed as an expression of the latter. "The film," they write, "is ideology presenting itself to itself, talking to itself, learning about itself."[6] The essay, which is essentially a translation of Louis Althusser's theory of ideology into the domain of film, set the intellectual course of *Cahiers* for the following decade, with a strong emphasis on the militant imperative that should inform any critical endeavor.[7]

Among the many far-reaching consequences of the critical stance defended by Comolli and Narboni was the drastic expansion of what constitutes the political in cinema—a veritable Copernican revolution summarized in their famous formulation that "every film is political": "Every film is political inasmuch as it is determined by the ideology which produces it."[8] This is because a film registers the ideological conditions of existence of the mode of production that creates it, namely capitalism. But if it is true that from the standpoint of ideology every film is political, it does not automatically follow that all films are political in the same way—or, to put it differently, that the dimension of the political that emerges in cinema is the same for every film. To be sure, Comolli and Narboni are fully cognizant of this aspect. They posit a fundamental difference between films that acknowledge and expose cinema as a branch of ideology, and films that merely propagate ideological discourses, including the "eminently reactionary" idea that cinema objectively registers reality in its neutral existence: "'Reality' is nothing but the expression of the prevailing ideology," they note.[9] This "vital distinction" spawns yet more distinctions that assume the form of a taxonomy of the possible relationships between cinema and ideology.[10] Because the primary militant concern here is demystification, the essay largely focuses on the different ways films do or do not recognize and make visible their nature as ideological artifacts according to various degrees of thematic and/or formal departure from dominant forms of filmmaking.

Comolli and Narboni's argument postulates the omnipresence of politics in the fabric of cultural production (every film is political); it has a clear prescriptive aim in defining what true political cinema should be, as well as in discerning that which is political cinema from that which is not; and finally, it provides a taxonomy that establishes the fundamental features of their object. At the cost of oversimplification, in this tripartite framework may be glimpsed a mapping of the much vaster field of the historical debates about politics and cinema, organized along three main axes, as follows. First is a militant preoccupation with criteria to assess the degree of revolutionary consciousness attained by individual films or filmmakers in form, content, or both. Here political cinema assumes the form of a quasi-Platonic idea, the horizon toward which films should bend. Second is the attention to the disseminated presence of politics as symptoms or traces in the texture of culture at large. In this scenario, every film is political because every film, being part of culture, bears the mark of ideology.[11] Third and last is the understanding of political cinema through the taxonomic lens of genre as a grouping of films that share certain formal and thematic features, with the common denominator of a conscious or unconscious concern with politics.

This is precisely from where the ideological critique of cinema derives its keen analytical power. The concept of ideology ties together these varied strands into one coherent method, de facto offering itself as the culmination of—and possible solution to—the theoretical debate around the relation between cinema and politics. Furthermore, ideology critique reinforces the thesis that a relation between cinema and politics does in fact exist: this relationship hinges precisely on ideology, which neatly functions as the missing link between the two domains. No more aporia: the problem of the link between cinema and politics seems to have been solved in (film) theory as much as in (militant) practice.

Yet Comolli and Narboni's taxonomy, however exhaustive, produces a remainder—what we might call a residual category of films that do not quite fit in the other typologies. We can briefly summarize their taxonomy as follows: (1) films that are imbued with the dominant ideology and show no signs of being aware of it; (2) films that deal with a directly political subject and combat their ideological substratum at the level of form or content; (3) films that have no explicit political content but become political by virtue of the formal treatment of their subject; (4) films with an explicit political content that fail to criticize the ideological system the informs them; (5) films of live cinema (*cinéma direct*), prey to the illusion that their avowed realism is in itself not ideological; and (6) films of other kinds of live cinema, where the films question their own modality of depiction of reality. The seventh category, the ill-fitting one, is defined by Comolli and Narboni in negative terms: the films that belong to this typology are characterized by "a noticeable gap, a dislocation" in their representation of ideology.[12] This gap is made visible by the films, whose textual functioning is split in two: a moment of acknowledgment, in which ideology is assumed as a limit of representation; and a moment of transgression in which limits are trespassed, and as an effect, ideology's normative essence is made visible. The presence of ideology in these films is therefore ambiguous. At first, it seems to pervade every aspect of the filmic text, but then the films confront us with the unexpected emergence of a critical gesture. Consider the following passage, in which Comolli and Narboni attempt to describe the category in question, to which they assign works by the likes of Ford, Dreyer, and Rossellini: "An internal criticism is taking place, which cracks the films apart at the seams. If one reads the film obliquely, looking for symptoms; if one looks beyond its apparent formal coherence, one can see that it is riddled with cracks: it is splitting under an internal tension which is simply not there in an ideologically innocuous film."[13] The gap is here qualified in terms of "cracks" or splits caused by an "internal tension" to which the films succumb. This tension is between the ideology that these films seem to mindlessly embrace and the same films' critical gesture of making this ideology visible. Ideology here does not emerge as a positive entity conjured by the films but rather as subject to an operation of "dislocation." For this reason, although the authors go to great lengths to accommodate this category in their taxonomy as just one cinematic genus among others, one should find in it a particular symptomatic significance. It is clear the films in this category pose a conceptual problem for the *Cahiers* editors, to the point where they literally do not know what to do with them. The authors refuse to join the "witch-hunt against them," but they also don't see them as the main subject of the journal's militant project. These films "criticize themselves ... and it is irrelevant and impertinent to do so for them." In other words, it is better to just leave them be: the *Cahiers* will simply engage in revealing "how they work."[14] It is not surprising that feigned indifference could be the most suitable response to these films' unresolved relationship to ideology, uneasily located as it is between complicity and resistance.

For us, this residual category reveals something about the logic of ideology critique itself—something qualitatively different from the spectrum of ideological self-consciousness covered by Comolli and Narboni's other categories. The formalization of a relationship between politics and cinema by way of ideology leaves behind a remainder that must be read as itself symptomatic of a limit of formalization. The films situated in this residual category are characterized by a paradoxical relationship to ideology (they are both inside and outside it), thus contradicting Comolli and Narboni's fundamental thesis, noted above, that films are "ideology presenting itself to itself, talking about itself, learning about itself." These films in which ideology does not relate to itself prove that ideology cannot function in all cases as the ultimate relational ground for the interaction between cinema and politics.

The improperness of these films (they do not belong with the rest) undoes the militant mirage of a "proper" political cinema. Any idea of political purity is done away with by the utter impurity of the films that belong to this category, compromised as they are with the capitalist-industrial mode of production and the seeming adherence to the bourgeois idea of art, as is the case of several of the films to be analyzed in the following chapters. At the same time, belief in the omnipresence of ideology is contradicted by the fact that these films need a specific category to account for their irreducibly singular way—internal and external to ideology—of bringing together politics and cinema. When met with this irreducible singularity, the taxonomic drive that underpins Comolli and Narboni's argument becomes the reason the taxonomy itself unravels: a desire for completeness prompts the emergence of a residual category, the very existence of which threatens to undo the taxonomy as a whole. Certainly I do not mean to argue that all films by Ford, Dreyer, and Rossellini are to be regarded as political cinema; nor, for that matter, that an auteurist approach is the best to adopt in this case. I want to highlight that a certain logic is at work here. Regardless of the auteurs' names and films associated with them, this logic points to a problem in the definition of political cinema articulated by ideology critique.

Here, where Comolli and Narboni's line of reasoning unwittingly falters, we glimpse the outline of a different paradigm through which to think political cinema. This slip in their argument has a double valence, negative and positive—negative insofar as the residual category is the symptom of a limitation in the taxonomy proposed by the authors, but also, and more importantly, positive because this fundamental inconsistency in the ideological critique of cinema points to a way to think political cinema in terms of an aporia. Instead of thinking cinema and politics together by starting from their nonrelation, ideology critique does the reverse. The relation between cinema and politics is secured by ideology as the object of mirroring, self-conscious problematization, or outright criticism on the part of the films. However, the residual category described by Comolli and Narboni speaks to the insistence of a nonrelation that their theoretical system cannot account for: a little Hegelian bone stuck in the throat of ideology critique. The transitivity between cinema and politics that was all but guaranteed by the deployment of the concept of ideology finds here its own limitation: these films pose a problem for Comolli and Narboni because the axiom of a relation between cinema and politics via ideology does not seem quite capable of explaining what it is that they do. The "noticeable gap" that characterizes the work of the Fords, the Dreyers, and the Rossellinis names precisely the nonrelation between cinema and politics that the *Cahiers* editors registered and then hastily repressed, for it was the one gap that the concept of ideology could not bridge.

The Figure

After registering the limitations of ideology critique, we must ask what kind of critical reading of political cinema can follow from the constitutive nonrelation between cinema and politics. How is this linkage between the two terms concretely invented by individual films, and what is this tie supposed to look like on the screen? The answer proposed in this book hinges on the concept of the figure, and more specifically on an argument for a recentering of its significance in the conceptualization of political cinema.

In the tradition of art history, the figure has been largely understood as a distinguishable aspect of the image that detaches itself from the background and that refers to a real, recognizable object (the Panofskyian concept of motif). This definition bestows a certain trait of exactness onto the figure, both in the visual sense of a clear shape with definite contours and in the semiotic sense of its iconicity—that is, with Peirce, its resemblance to the object it wishes to represent. In this sense, the figure, as well as figuration as the act of generating figures, fulfills a function of identification. As the centerpiece of the picture, the figure constitutes its signifying anchor, guiding the reader through the maelstrom of ambiguities naturally built into the image toward the safe shore of a stable, legible meaning. To be sure, nothing in the etymology or historical usage of "figure" contradicts this reading in the slightest; if anything, "copy," "simulacrum," and the like are among the primary meanings attributed to the term. In a way, this is precisely the issue. Given the vastness of the semantic galaxy attached to the term, no simplistic criterion of "correctness" of such-and-such a meaning can solve the unique conceptual and aesthetic problem the figure poses.

A proper historicotheoretical account of the concept lies beyond the scope of the present work, and one wonders whether such a feat is even achievable. Thus, relinquishing any claim to encyclopedic exhaustiveness, I wish to navigate our own route here—our own *poros*—across this immense semantic territory, with the fundamental question of this book, the question of political cinema, as our makeshift compass. (Perhaps it is not too self-serving to surmise that the field of the various theorizations of the figure is so vast that it does not just encourage a decision on what route to take to traverse it, but actually sanctions and even imposes it.)

In his landmark essay "Figura," Erich Auerbach embraces the essential complexity of the concept of the figure and paints a vivid picture of its etymological spectrum, which, at its most elementary level, references the plasticity of form (from the Latin *fingere, fictor, effigies*), but in a way that emphasizes aspects of change and becoming ("something living and dynamic, incomplete and playful")—a plastic form subject to endless transformation.[15] Auerbach identifies this dynamism as the function of a certain duality, an idea that has strong echoes in the work of later commentators such as Nicole Brenez and Georges Didi-Huberman.[16] "The figure," Brenez explains in her discussion of Auerbach, "is not primarily an entity, but the establishing of a relation: the movement of a thing toward its other."[17] "The movement" points to the dynamicity of a figure that is, in its very essence, always a figure of the Two: order and chaos, form and formless, figuration and disfiguration. The relation between the two terms, however, is not of inoperative externality but of dialectical coimplication: "not simply disorder," the figure stands "within a logic of identity" as its "intimate contestation."[18] The figure does not give up on form altogether; rather, it comes into existence as a disturbance of identity, an operation of disruption of self-sameness whereby the other emerges from within the same. There is a durative, labor-like dimension to the action of the figure. It carves into figuration, molds it, shapes it from within, to the point where figuration is barely recognizable yet not irretrievably lost.[19] Running counter to the traditional art-historic idea of the figure as illustrative support for the meaning of an artwork, the figure is thus best described as an aesthetic operation in which a relation is established between figuration and disfiguration wherein the two are not in a reciprocal position of externality, but one participates in and presupposes the other and vice versa.

It is important to bear in mind that for us, the figure is neither a transitory stage in a teleological movement of becoming nor a simple pastiche of two heterogeneous elements. Rather, it determines the point of articulation of a dialectic whose defining operation is neither that of illustration nor of mere signification but, I wish to suggest, of thought. In the words of Jacques Aumont, "The image can transmit ideas, and original ideas at that."[20] The passage of these ideas is made possible by the figure as a principle of formal organization of this thought: "the image thinks by way of figures" (*l'image pense par figures*).[21] Can we not recognize in this figural thought of the cinematic image precisely a form of *metis* in action? The "original ideas" that films think "by way of figures" are the passageways across the nonrelation between cinema and politics that are improvised anew with each political film. The figure thus indexes both the insistence of the nonrelation in any given political film and the invention of a way to cross it. On the one hand, it registers the nonrelation because the figure rejects the transitivity of simple representation (politics is not a reified content that can simply be illustrated). On the other, it invents a way to cross it in the dialectical unfolding of the figure as thought.[22] It is therefore in the form of the figure itself—the figure as the aesthetic support of a dynamic dialectical articulation—that the insistence of the nonrelation appears as the productive condition of negativity described by Kofman in her discussion of the aporia: the recognition of the unavoidability of the nonrelation and the inception of a desire to experiment with a singular way to bridge it. The concept of the figure thus offers first a general principle of formalization of the way in which the nonrelation and its traversal inscribe themselves in the films, and second the possibility to analyze the concrete iterations of the linkage between cinema and politics in the form of a multiplicity of figures, with each film inventing its own singular way of being political.

The refusal to let representation dictate the terms of artistic creation and the dramatization of the dialectical movement of thought constitute the figure's fundamental gesture. Referencing Giotto's frescoes in the Basilica of Saint Francis of Assisi, Brenez and Deleuze seize on this detachment from the realism of representation in favor of what they call, respectively, a "realism of figures" and "a liberation of Figures" that are equally oblivious to any sense of proportion and verisimilitude.[23] In the realm of political cinema, consider for instance the figure of the worker, discussed in chapter 2. If we were to suggest a possible genealogy of the representations of the worker in cinema, we would probably be looking at two different lineages. One aims for accuracy in its depiction of the existent, with authenticity as its ultimate horizon. Broadly, this lineage follows the traditional equation between social realism and militant engagement, which, at best, has produced poignant, if at times nostalgic or moralistic, portrayals of the *condition ouvrière*. The other lineage, whose instances are somewhat more sporadic, follows what Deleuze calls "the way of the Figure": the patient, meticulous rejection of the temptation of a purely realistic representation.[24] In this case, the figure of the worker remains unconcerned with verisimilitude and instead explores the limits of figuration in an attempt to dramatize the dialectics of openings and deadlocks of a given historical sequence. It would register, for instance, the disfiguring pressure that the demands for productivity put on the factory worker, bending his body and psyche out of shape and yet opening up the possibility of radical militant engagement, as is the case in Petri's *The Working Class Goes to Heaven;* or it would signal a blockage of that dialectics, evoking the claustrophobic condition of the migrant worker, exploited not only at the assembly line but also in a society that increasingly resembles an immense factory, as in Scola's *Trevico-Turin.*

The figure in political cinema, then, does not aim to approximate reality but to dramatize the subjective possibilities of a historical situation. The actual verification of these possibilities exceeds the purview of cinema, of course; only politics can confirm the existence and viability of collective political subjects. But what cinema can offer to politics is precisely this distance—namely, the nonrelation inscribed in the figure that allows films to stage their own autonomous historical diagnosis as the performance of a multiplicity of moving figures. This figural experimentation is proper to cinema and does not translate directly to politics, for a figure cannot be reduced to any one political subject; nor does the figure prescribe strategies for the creation of one. Instead, it is precisely by virtue of the nonrelation that cinema can think by way of figures the historicity of a sequence—its events, crises, and transitions—as a con-figuration in the fictional dimension of "as if."

The Holes and Hollow Spaces of History

In medieval Christian theology, the figure was interpreted as a link between two events in which the first prefigures the second, and the second fulfills the promise of the first. The transcendental guarantee of this teleological movement is divine providence itself, which resides in a timeless time, one without history. By keeping the historicity of an event intact, the medieval figure stands as a historically rooted index of this ahistorical time. While the past and the future are linked to one another in the figure, they evoke a time that transcends them both. As Kaja Silverman notes, "A figural view of history usually implies a redemptive eschatology," one that finds its guarantee in a transcendent principle.[25]

In secular modernity, the guarantee of an ultimate synthesis of historical time can be found in all ideologies of progress. But the modern situation of a history without God also opens up another possibility: that of a historicity devoid of the transcendent guarantee of a harmonic resolution. Instead, this historicity is animated by a totally immanent tension that generates a deadlock. As witness to this dialectic without synthesis, the figure here comes into existence as the form of a tension—Ernst Bloch calls it a "tension-figure"—that permits mediation between experience and historical time, making the latter legible.[26]

Bloch distinguishes two forms of such mediation. One is the "broad-calm" mediation, which is possible only when the world is perceived as a meaningful totality, as the (prehistorical) world that was or the (socialist) world to come. It is a world without conflict or divisions, identical to itself, that produces harmonious and static figures. The other, "abrupt" mediation, only emerges in times of crisis and transition, when history reveals its fundamental inconsistency: "An essential relationship behaves in an abruptly mediated way above all in those times when as a consequence of unsecured conditions *holes and hollow spaces open up in the previously smooth context;* about this and about that which appears in them the—one might say—irregular artists give information in their own way."[27] Neither the anticipation for Kingdom Come nor the rational unfolding of interconnected occurrences of progressivist mythologies of history, these "holes and hollow spaces" designate an alternative idea of history characterized by divisions and discontinuities that art seizes by way of tension-figures—that is, indexes of a historical "time of crisis."[28]

For Bloch, these figures are not beholden to an invariant, eternal form but are instead defined by a certain precariousness, subjected as they are to the contrasting forces that always animate times of transition: "Shapes in history exist only as figures of tension, as tendency-shapes, as experiments of the unknown life-shape, which so little exists that precisely for this reason shapes crack again and again and history continues."[29] Figures are tentative experiments of legibility of a given historical sequence. Because no overarching meaning or orientation is guaranteed by a transcendent principle, the figure must open itself up to the holes and hollow spaces that make up history in times of crisis. At the same time, figures provide a legible image of this disjointed historical time. Their distinctive dialectic of figuration and disfiguration is the aesthetic result of this fundamental disaggregation of historical reality. By registering the gaps in the historical continuum, tension-figures give shape to the fundamental fault lines that run under its visible surface.

We are now in a position to further specify the dialectic of the figure in political cinema by advancing the following hypothesis: the fault lines of a given historical sequence as a time of crisis can be mapped along two fundamental and dialectically intertwined coordinates. On one coordinate is an irruption of a force into an existing structural situation—a force that is born out of the structure itself and that aims at the structure's wholesale destruction. On the other coordinate, and in response to the intervention of the force, the ravaged structure recomposes into a new consistency.[30] These two coordinates—the action of an antagonistic force onto the structure, and the structure's response as crisis and recomposition—delimit the field of historical possibilities (and impossibilities) to which the dialectics of the figure gives body.

Because the cracks and crevices of a time of crisis remain impervious to any realism of representation, the task of making them visible can solely be accomplished by the tension-figure as the cinematic thought that gives form to the crisis. It is in this sense that we should understand Didi-Huberman's claim that figure is always "critical," for it is "the introduction of a crisis in every semblance."[31] Precarious and fragmented, the figural form of historical crisis presents itself as a crisis of semblance, a tension-figure that thinks the many instantiations of the dialectic between force and structure.[32] By giving body to this dialectic, the figure does not indicate the presence or offer a representation of a political subject. It may, for instance, point to a possibility that never materialized, like a failed attempt, an opportunity that remained unseized, or a structural difficulty that proved insurmountable. For this reason, alongside more readily recognizable political figures of the long '68 (worker, housewife, youth), I discuss other figures (saint, specter) that do not belong to the collective imaginary of the long '68. As such, these figures make it clear that cinema thinks the historical crisis in ways that are not reducible to those of politics. The aporia between cinema and politics means that the films think political subjectivity at a distance only by way of their own reconnoitering of the conditions, possibilities, and pitfalls of a given historical situation.[33]

It is only in this sense that these figures are realistic, for "reality in time of crisis is itself a largely split one."[34] The figure dramatizes the possibilities of a historical situation organized around a split or an impasse. In this sense, each figure I discuss here refers to some fundamental division that traversed the historical sequence of the long '68. The figure of the worker gives body to the impasse between the proletariat and the bourgeoisie—the impasse of class—that reveals the radical antagonism of capitalist social relations, indicating the militant thesis of the refusal of work as both the possibility of a condition beyond exploitation and an impossibility dictated by the authoritarian nature of capital. The figure of the housewife identifies an impasse internal to labor itself: the gendered division of labor between production and reproduction that the socialist feminist movements of the 1970s indicated as a point of leverage for anticapitalist struggle, to which capital responds by making the boundaries of reproductive labor ever more elusive. The figure of youth is anchored in the split between the liberation of one's own singular desires and the universalistic claims of radical politics. In the films, the impasse between these two projects provides the impetus for spectacular acts of rebellion while opening up the possibility of the violent subsumption of that same rebellion by the structure. The figure of the saint can be understood as a radicalization of the same impasse, whereby the uncompromising autonomy of the saint's desire threatens the consistency of the status quo, prompting the structure's adoption of extreme measures to neutralize and absorb this recalcitrant desire. The figure of the specter, for its part, reveals an impasse internal to the structure itself. As the remnant that haunts any conception of totality, the specter highlights the illusion of the self-identity of the sovereign power of the state, revealing it as inevitably split between excess (authoritarianism) and lack (powerlessness). This impasse of sovereign power is further dramatized by the figures of the tyrant, the intriguer, and the martyr as figures of the collapse of the postwar bourgeoisie, torn between its historical role as the ruling class and its own incipient obsolescence.

These impasses identify the fault lines that traverse the historical sequence of the Italian long '68. As a series of possible shapes of the tension between force and structure, the figures discussed in this book are attempts to name and map these fault lines. A figural reading of political cinema, then, is not a chronicle of the many political subjects that have been consigned to the archive of history but a choreography of some of the potentialities that could—and could not—have existed in the impasses of a time of crisis and transition. From the standpoint of politics, the historical sequence that is the focus of this book no doubt qualifies as such a time. Between the mid-1960s and the early 1980s, a series of interconnected occurrences (the rise of new forms of antagonism, a shift in the forms of labor, a drastic restructuring of capital and a renewing of its alliance with the state, a variety of momentous cultural and social shifts, and so forth) waved off the revolutionary politics of modernity and ushered in the beginning of a new era characterized by a certain disenchantment with radical political engagement.[35]

To better understand how politics have thought this time of crisis, consider the trajectory of what is arguably the dominant political subject of the twentieth century: the industrial proletariat. The transformations in the organization of labor that took place in Italy after the economic miracle (1958–63) jump-started a process of radical recomposition of the working class that changed its role and reach in the dynamics of struggle—a process that began in earnest in the early 1960s and reached its conclusion by the beginning of the following decade. Hard-pressed by worsening economic stagnation, the rise of forms of immaterial labor, and the repressive measures adopted by capital and the state, the factory worker lost political centrality.[36] The political thought of the time tried to diagnose and respond to this momentous vanishing. Radical theorists and militants tried to fill that subjective void, either by redefining the ontology of the worker (consider

Antonio Negri's theory of the *operaio sociale,* "social worker") or by looking for new political subjectivities elsewhere altogether (consider the Autonomia archipelago, with the centrality it afforded to figures left at the fringes of the productive process: students, the unemployed, sex workers, prisoners, the mentally ill).[37] This is what Paolo Virno calls the "carnival of subjectivities" of the long '68, marching through the streets and squares of the country from the late 1960s to the end of the 1970s.[38]

Cinema, for its part, engaged with the same historical moment of crisis and transition but gave it body in its own way. While politics thought the crisis by theorizing new political subjects and forms of militant organization, cinema did so by inventing new figures as experiments of historical legibility. These figures never posit the existence of a political subjectivity; nor do they advocate for it from a militant standpoint, as politics did. Rather, they dramatize a situation of crisis and transition in which possibilities and impossibilities alike coalesce around impasses—a "dance of figures."[39] In this sense, the image of the long '68 projected by cinema's figural choreography is different from the one that emerges from the political thought of the time, as the former made visible aspects of the historical sequence that the latter did not register, and vice versa. This difference, this gap between cinema and politics, today appears all the more essential for understanding the complexity of the long '68. While the resonances between the two remain evident, it is perhaps in the distance that separates a "dance of figures" from a "carnival of subjectivities" that we can find a more revelatory conception of this time of crisis.

2 The Worker

Subjectivity within and against Capital

> The working class does what it *is*. But it is, at one and the same time, the *articulation* of capital, and its *dissolution*.
> —Mario Tronti, "The Strategy of Refusal"

> The monsters were coming, the horrible workers.
> —Nanni Balestrini, *We Want Everything*

Two Workers

If we were to attempt a rough periodization of the figural manifestations of the worker, the fundamental watershed would be located in the 1960s, with two distinct figures on either side of the divide.[1] The first evokes the worker born with the socialist movement, who came of age in the fire of the October Revolution and went on to dominate the political scene from the 1920s to the beginning of World War II. In Italy, it is the figure that towered over the Biennio Rosso (Two red years, 1919–20), organizing strikes and factory occupations and leading factory councils modeled on the soviets.[2] Celebrated by Mario Monicelli in *The Organizer*, such workers took pride in their craft and saw the amelioration of their condition through union activism as inextricable from the collective advancement of the country as a whole, the responsibility of which rested on their shoulders. His hyperbolic version (parodied by Ugo Gregoretti in his quirky 1963 sci-fi comedy *Omicron*) would be the Stakhanovite, whose superhuman strength and dedication to the cause of rapid industrialization and rising productivity were offered by Stalinism as the ultimate aspirational model for the Soviet Union's workforce in the 1930s.

On the other side of the divide, rushed onto history's stage by a tidal wave of protests and strikes that traversed the 1960s and culminated with the massive workers' mobilization of the *Autunno caldo* (Hot autumn) of 1969, we find a different figure: a radical collectivity of workers who rejected capitalist exploitation and looked to dismantle the productive system altogether. The rise of this new figure brought with it a new politics: precarious and deskilled, the so-called mass-worker (generally identified as a poor Southern migrant looking for work in the industrialized North) took no pride in his craft and was exclusively animated by a desire to satisfy his primary material needs. This multitude of young, male, semiliterate workers was the *rude razza pagana* (rude pagan race) so vividly described by the Italian *operaisti* in the 1960s, immune from ideological capture into dreams of national progress and refractory to any co-optation into union-led negotiations.[3]

No film has better seized the moment of transition between these two figures than Elio Petri's *The Working Class Goes to Heaven*, a film that contends with the historicopolitical consequences of this shift as a veritable "time of crisis": an abrupt caesura in the historical continuum that, in Ernst Bloch's formulation, only tension-figures can capture and make visible.[4] Released in 1971, Petri's eighth feature film was poorly received by newspaper critics and altogether disparaged by militant film journals, radical unions, and the extraparliamentary leftist groups, who saw in it the unwarranted individualization of a revolutionary consciousness reduced to a mere psychological or existential matter. At the film premiere at the Porretta Terme film festival, radical filmmaker Jean-Marie Straub famously grabbed the microphone after the screening to call for the film to be burned, deeming it to be outright reactionary.[5] Such strong reactions might imply a clarity on the part of the film as to what its political message was, or wished to be. This, as we will see, is hardly the case. While the film undoubtedly displays at the level of representation elements that are easily legible as references to a specific historical context (the portrayal of the working class, the factory, the strikes), there is another, less apparent dimension to the way the film grapples with history. This dimension unfolds through the figure of the worker.

This figure thinks the historical situation along two fundamental coordinates: force and structure, intertwined in a dialectical relation. On the one hand, a force born within and against the existing structural situation aims at the interruption of the status quo's self-perpetuation and the structure's wholesale destruction; on the other, and in response to the intervention of force, is a recomposition of the ravaged structure into a new consistency. Alain Badiou calls these two temporalities "subjectivization" and "subjective process," respectively. Subjectivization splits into "anxiety" (the moment of interruption) and "courage" (the moment of destruction); the subjective process into "superego" (a recomposition of the structure as oppressive surplus of order) and "justice" (the establishing of a new situation based on new rules).[6]

Badiou's formalization of the logic of the subject—which he himself partially derived from Jacques Lacan—sheds light on the way *The Working Class Goes to Heaven,* one of the major examples of Italian political cinema of the 1970s, thinks the historical crisis of the period through a dialectic of force and structure. This dimension is not determined by the film's choice of content or representational elements, but by its invention of the figure of the worker as a way to give body to the crisis—and, in particular, to the impasse between labor and capital, with its attendant spectrum of historical openings, obstacles, and dead ends.

The singular significance of *The Working Class Goes to Heaven* shapes the structure of the chapter. In this reading, the film provides the matrix through which this figure of the worker in a time of crisis becomes legible across other films. After outlining the fundamental functioning of the figural matrix in Petri's film, the discussion will turn to the same paradigm's different permutations in other films: Lina Wertmüller's *The Seduction of Mimì* and Ettore Scola's *Trevico-Turin: Voyage in the Fiat-Nam.* Moving across these three films, the figure traces the many possible destinies of the worker in the historical sequence of the long '68.

"The Worker Does Not Exist": The Working Class Goes to Heaven

The Accident: Anxiety and Courage

The Working Class Goes to Heaven revolves around Ludovico "Lulù" Massa (Gian Maria Volonté), a factory worker in Northern Italy who only cares about his piecework rates and refuses to meddle in politics. His output, the highest of any worker on the shop floor, is used by the foremen as a measuring stick to set general standards of productivity, and Lulù's peers resent him for it. He, however, is only concerned with earning enough money to pay alimony and child support to his ex-wife and son, Armando, and to support his new girlfriend, Lidia (Mariangela Melato), and her son, Arturo. One day, Lulù's index finger is cut off by a machine in an accident. The event changes his outlook, and when he returns to work, he becomes increasingly involved with political struggles inside and outside the factory. Lulù finds himself torn between the reformist tactics of the unions (who wish to attain better piecework rates through negotiation with management) and the more radical demands of the student-worker alliance, who want less work at more pay, as well as the wholesale abolition of the piecework system. Caught in this situation, Lulù shows signs of increasing mental instability, especially in his private life with Lidia and his longtime friend, Militina (Salvo Randone), an older coworker confined to a mental hospital after assaulting an engineer at the factory. Fired by the company after he took part in a protest turned violent, and left by Lidia (who does not share his recent interest in politics), Lulù contemplates a move to Switzerland, until, thanks to the unions' intervention, he is reinstated. As a punishment, he finds himself reassigned to the assembly line.

The first part of the film pictures a remarkable dissonance between the figure of the worker and its background. Lulù is clearly introduced as a Stakhanovite, but the situation around him is, just as obviously, not that of a Stalinist factory. Regarded as a scab and despised by his colleagues, this worker from the 1930s teleported to the early 1970s hardly possesses any heroic halo. To try to mediate and reconcile this conflict between figure and background, Lulù has no choice but to give himself over completely to the company and fully submit to its abstract authority. In doing so, Lulù assumes the position of the pervert: he knows what capital—as the Other—wants (more production), and he turns himself into a mere tool in its hands. In psychoanalysis, perversions result from the subjective disavowal of lack (such as castration) in the Other; the subject identifies with the imaginary object of the Other's desire and makes the Other whole by becoming the tool of its enjoyment. The recurrent motif of the superimposition between labor and sexuality in the film speaks precisely to this entanglement of disavowed lack and to enjoyment by proxy. When Lidia laments the tendency of the rate of Lulù's libido to fall, as it were, he admits that he is only turned on while he's working. It is not by chance that the only sexual intercourse he has in the film (with his coworker, Adalgisa) takes place in an abandoned factory. As a pervert, Lulù can only experience enjoyment in the moment of his fullest submission to the Other. Furthermore, the Stakhanovite's perverted enjoyment is inextricably tied to repetition. Petri emphasizes the repetitiveness of factory labor with an obsessive visual focus on machinery at work and a soundtrack (by Ennio Morricone) that echoes its rigid rhythmical patterns. When Lulù is operating a machine, the camera lingers on Volonté's face with extreme close-ups that tend to deform his facial features (Figure 1).

In one scene, Lulù stares into space, angry and sweaty, talking to no one in particular: "I'm already focused, I'm already in another world. Think only about the piece! Even if it's no use. Every piece is a hole, every hole is a piece. Just don't fall in the hole! If you don't want to fall in the hole, think about Adalgisa's ass . . . a piece, an ass, a piece, an ass." Lulù's grotesque disfiguration shows the overwhelming intensity of enjoyment—a senseless, passionate attachment that goes beyond the limits of the rational and the useful ("Think only about the piece! Even if it's no use"). This enjoyment is solipsistic and essentially antisocial: "I'm already in another world." (While Lulù works, the camera wanders over the shop floor to show the small acts of sabotage perpetrated by a group of militant workers—acts to which the protagonist remains utterly oblivious.) For Petri, stakhanovism has the same structure as any other perversion. Lulù can only find his own enjoyment in, quite literally, working for the Other's enjoyment. His is an

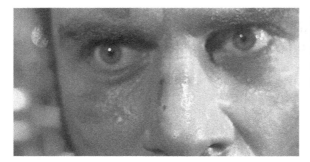
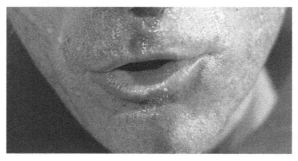

Figure 1. Lulù at work in *The Working Class Goes to Heaven* (1971).

enjoyment freed from the enigma of desire: Lulù does not experience the thorny uncertainty of guessing what the Other wants; he knows it. Perversion is, in fact, nothing but a way to keep the machine running smoothly by avoiding all the problems that inevitably arise for the subject when the lack in the Other and the consequent subjective indecision about what it wants come into the picture.

Eventually, lack does indeed appear to make Lulù's disavowal vacillate. All that is required to imperil the Stakhanovite's perverse relation to the Other is a little piece of metal jammed in the machine, which Lulù ill-advisedly tries to scoop out with his finger. The fundamental caesura in the film—the accident in which Lulù's index finger is mutilated—is therefore determined by a blockage, a small obstacle that obstructs the normal flow of production, interrupting the functioning of capitalist machinery. This undoing of the structure of perversion thwarts repetition while revealing the impasse that constitutes the very cause of that repetition: it reveals that there is a fundamental lack at the heart of the productive structure, and this lack determines the repetitive pattern on which the structure sustains itself. This lack around which the structure is organized suddenly presents itself as a positive materiality, an object whose presence appears as an obstacle to the normal pattern of the status quo: "Every piece is a hole, every hole is a piece," says Lulù. When it gets stuck between the gears, one of the countless perforated cylinders that he produces becomes exactly that: a hole *and* a piece, a void and its material appearance, a lack of being and the being of a lack. This is the object of the Other's enjoyment. It now confronts Lulù as, in Lacan's formulation, the object-cause of desire, which plunges him into the dialectic of lack and desire that defines the neurotic, as opposed to the pervert. The lack that the Stakhanovite pervert stubbornly disavowed returns here with a vengeance. What is the mutilation of Lulù's index finger if not the traumatic inscription of lack (castration) onto the body of a worker who for the first time has to question the desire of the Other—and, as a consequence, his own?

Lulù tries half-heartedly to downplay what happened, but the situation has changed. The guarantee of subjective consistency offered by his perversion has now revealed its precariousness. This sudden appearance of lack marks the subjective moment of anxiety. If anxiety, as Lacan says, is the only affect "that does not deceive,"[7] then it is because its onset always signals the subjective encounter with a truth, a confrontation with the lack that stands at the center of the structure and constitutes its hidden cause. The name of this point of anxiety in the figure of the worker invented by the film is labor power. Labor power is the elusive element at the heart of the capitalist relation of production that is at once disavowed and exploited by the process itself, and that furthermore constitutes its fundamental condition of existence. The reason for its elusiveness resides in the paradoxical nature of labor power itself as a commodity that is unlike all other commodities. This became apparent to Marx when he too was confronted with an enigma: how does the capitalist produce nonequivalence (that is, surplus value) within a regime governed by market laws, and therefore by the exchange of equivalents? The answer for Marx lies in the peculiar nature of labor power as a special commodity whose use value is to congeal value in commodities. The paradox is evident: the power to make commodities is itself a commodity that can be bought and sold. Labor power, therefore, is not a substance but rather the name of a coincidence between two qualities: being a commodity and having the power to make commodities.

Alenka Zupančič has argued that labor power, as a sort of impossible Möbius strip in which two terms are implied in each other while remaining separate, "is the point that marks the constitutive negativity, gap, of [the capitalist] system: the point where one thing immediately falls into another (use value into source of value)."[8] Sitting at this point we find none other than the worker himself, who alone possesses and sells this unique commodity. But if this is the case, Zupančič concludes in a remarkable turn of phrase, then "the Worker does not exist." What exists is the person selling his own capacity for work, never himself as such, for that would make him a slave.[9] This formula, reminiscent of Lacan's famous claim about the Woman ("the Woman does not exist"), is to be understood as both prescriptive and analytical. Prescriptively, it corresponds to Marx's admonition that the worker should not exist (the person selling his work "must constantly treat his labor-power as his own property, his own commodity," or he would end up converting "from an owner of a commodity into a commodity"[10]). Analytically, with Zupančič, it names labor power as the gap between use value and source of value, the structural point of negativity that capital exploits for profit.

Zupančič's point is convincing—so much so that it leaves us to ponder what implications it might have for our discussion of *The Working Class Goes to Heaven*. To put it bluntly, if "the Worker doesn't exist," then what is it we see in Petri's film? The answer resides in the film's ability to articulate a third way of understanding the formula. The statement "the Worker does not exist" should not only be read prescriptively and analytically but also figurally. The Worker as such does not exist. What exists instead is not only the person selling his labor power, or the gap at the heart of labor power, but also a figure of the tension between the two. The same element in the process of capitalist production—labor power—presents itself as internally divided. For the proletarian, it has no use value but only exchange value, so it constitutes a commodity to sell for money in order to survive. For the capitalist, it is a commodity available on the market whose use value is that of being a source of value. Initially, Lulù only sees labor power from the side of the proletarian. He trades his labor power for the capitalist's money, and it is precisely the equitability of this exchange that grounds his identity as a Stakhanovite, living proof (to himself) that the Worker does indeed exist. This perception is unsettled by the accident, which marks Lulù's traumatic encounter with the other side of labor power as the structural gap (use value as creation of value) that the capitalist exploits to his own advantage. This point of anxiety where Lulù's entire worldview vacillates is precisely where the worker becomes a figure. In the attempt to think the tension internal to labor power, the figure sheds any claim to a stable identity (the Worker) and instead stages the worker's confrontation with his own contradictory condition of freedom and exploitation.

The anxiety caused by the accident and mutilation marks the subjective moment of the vanishing of the Worker as a coherent, self-identical entity. "The Worker does not exist," then, means not only that the worker *should not* logically exist (or else he would be a slave) and the worker *cannot* structurally exist (or else capitalism would not have any negativity to exploit), but also, figurally, that the worker *does non-exist,* in the sense that the film gives this nonexistence a concrete figural form. After the accident, *The Working Class Goes to Heaven* becomes the drama of a worker grappling with his own nonexistence. This figure alone, with its irreducibility to representation, can account for this nonexistence and use it as the starting point of the worker's subjective destiny.

Once this lack at the heart of the structure is revealed, Lulù finds a way to turn this impasse against the structure itself, converting the lack of class relation into class struggle. This is the moment of subjective torsion that Badiou calls courage, and it corresponds in the film to the wager Lulù makes on the radicality of the student-worker movement's demands for less work and more pay. In the film, the gap that separates the student-worker movement and the union measures, respectively, the distance between a subjectivity based on lack (the lack *of* the structure and the torsion of this lack *against* the structure) and one based on a disavowal of lack. For the student-worker movement there is indeed no class relation and no fetishistic conception of the Worker. The union's position, instead, is defined by the conviction that a relation exists, and furthermore that it constitutes the foundation of any process of negotiation between workers and management. Once the truth of the absence of class relations becomes apparent, the figure of the worker morphs from a Stakhanovite to an agent of antagonism capable of transforming the anxiety-producing lack into a spur to action. This in turn translates into the worker's rejection of the assigned position within the system of production.

Lulù's courage materializes first in his defiance against management demands. Pushed to return to his preaccident output rate, he declines: "It's not that I can't, it's that I don't feel like it." When the foreman notices his deliberately slow working pace and warns him that he will be fined, Lulù mocks him in his thick Lombardian accent ("Ah yes, the fine! The fine! I was forgetting about the fine! Why don't you just fine me, then? Come on, fine me!"), then stops working altogether. He approaches the engineer's booth, yelling, "You have to give back everything that you've stolen from me when I was a Stakhanovite! You have to shit everything out! Even the finger!" This moment of courage expands into Lulù's incendiary monologue at the union assembly, where he openly sides with the student-worker movement and gives voice to their radical demands against the reformist tactics of the union leaders, and then reaches its culmination with the insurrection at the factory gates.[11] In these two moments, the figure of the worker makes visible the truth of capitalist society after Marx: "There are no such thing as class relations."[12] There is no relation, properly speaking, between the proletariat and the bourgeoisie, only an impasse and a fundamental antagonism, so that any notion of collaboration or harmony between classes, including the perverse fantasy of the Stakhanovite, is nothing but ideology at work.

Commodities: Superego (and a Glimpse of Justice)

The dialectic of anxiety and courage accounts only partially for the general dialectical logic at work in the figure of the worker in *The Working Class Goes to Heaven*. In Badiou's formulation, subjectivization names the point where the interruption of structural repetition (anxiety) meets the attempt at the destruction of the structure itself (courage). Anxiety and courage appeal to two other moments, superego and justice, that belong to a different temporality (subjective process) whereby new structural consistencies are explored and established. Specifically, anxiety appeals to the superego and courage appeals to justice. In the former pairing, the interruption of the structure's self-perpetuation (anxiety) invokes a surplus of the law (superego), a despotic order that is nothing but the obverse supplement of the structural lack. In the latter pairing, the attempted destruction of the existing order (courage) rests in principle on the idea of a new order grounded in new rules (justice).

Precisely because of this divided temporality, *The Working Class Goes to Heaven* can scarcely be read as the uplifting chronicle of a burgeoning class consciousness tending toward its glorious revolutionary fulfilment. Anxious interruption and courageous destruction of the structure do not exist in a vacuum. Both dialectically imply a certain reorganization of the structure they intervene within and against. For this reason, our analysis of the temporality of subjectivation prompts us to go back to the film and look for traces of the two moments that make up the subjective process.

Let us begin with the superego. Consider the opening scene, in which Lulù wakes up in his apartment and begins his daily routine. While Lulù feigns a blasé attitude toward a condition he seems accustomed to, the formal organization of the sequence tells a different story, one of underlying disquiet. The mise-en-scène, for one, is claustrophobic: the space of Lulù's apartment is dark and crammed with souvenirs, toys, and knickknacks. Some of these objects sit in the background, crowding the frame; others are brought to the foreground, as the camera lingers on them and places them in a series of shot/reverse shots with Lulù, as though engaged in a silent conversation (Figure 2). One is reminded here of Theodor Adorno's description of the predicament of the occultist, who disavows the man-made character of commodities in the name of a modern animism. The commodity form forces Lulù into the position of the occultist "who draws the ultimate conclusion from the fetish-character of commodities: menacingly objectified labour assails him on all sides from demonically grimacing objects."[13]

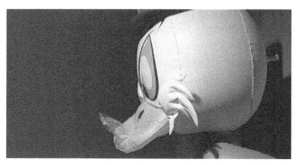

Figure 2. The menacing presence of objects in Lulù's apartment in *The Working Class Goes to Heaven* (1971).

This sense of enclosure in *The Working Class Goes to Heaven* is emphasized even within the frame. Petri relies heavily on close-ups of characters and objects, fragmenting the space and denying any sort of organic relation between it and the characters. As we have seen, the magnification of Lulù's face imparts a certain deformation, grotesquely exaggerating some features. Furthermore, close-ups of Lulù and Lidia are always occupied by foreign bodies (the interlocutor's head, a coffeepot) that tend to obstruct the frame and partially block vision. This pervasiveness of occluded vision is not limited to the opening scene; it constitutes a motif throughout the film. Home appliances, souvenirs, factory machines, walls and fences, and of course the omnipresent fog all conjure an image of the worker as a figure under siege, perpetually in danger of being swallowed by an encroaching background. In this invasive surplus of presence of Lulù's environment may be located the moment of the superego as an excessive affirmation of an order bent on crushing the worker.

However, the setting assumes a menacing quality only insofar as the figure itself throws the background into relief and reveals its oppressive character. The thick materialities of machines, bodies, and objects become the overbearing reminders of the regime of oppression and exploitation to which the worker's life is subjected. Employed by the machine (and not the other way around), massified into an anonymous and atomized collectivity, and surrounded by the worthless fruits of his labor, the worker sees the reality around him gain a surplus of tyrannical consistency even before witnessing its collapse in a moment of anxiety (the accident). The order of things, whose value the moment of anxious interruption reveals to be grounded in lack, returns here with a vengeance. The excessive reaffirmation of the existing order by what may be termed a foregrounding of the background clarifies that if there is a gap in the structure, it is capital's prerogative to exploit it.

Yet, however pervasive, the film does not permit this despotic excess of the world of commodities to turn into an eternal reign of terror. If anxiety conjures the superego, courage unceremoniously beheads it. Let us consider Lulù's final act of courage in the film. Laid off and abandoned by Lidia, Lulù contemplates as a last resort the possibility of leaving everything behind and migrating to nearby Switzerland ("There is no other definition of courage: exile without return, loss of one's name"[14]). Lulù, with Lidia gone, gathers all the knickknacks cramming the apartment, intending to resell them and start a new life across the Alps. But as he itemizes them and their value in terms of hours of labor, he realizes that there is no profit to be made. While he wonders about what compelled him to buy these commodities in the first place, Lulù is left to meditate on what Marx calls the "phantom-like objectivity" of the "homogeneous human labor" congealed in them.[15] Remarkably, in this final moment of courage, the superegoical, oppressive valence of the commodities that saturate the filmic space is somehow suspended. Lulù names these commodities, talks to them, even assaults them (he taunts and deflates Scrooge McDuck with a cigarette burn). However, precisely in the act of lamenting the uselessness of these commodities *and* rattling off their prices in the form of hours of labor, Lulù reveals the persistence of a nonrelation—namely, that between the commodity as use value and exchange value.

Once the form of the commodity itself is divided by Lulù's courage, it loses its terror. Lulù is no longer an occultist; the menacing surplus of ghostly life that the object possessed earlier in the film ("the demonically grimacing objects") has now dissolved. Knickknacks, appliances, and souvenirs become lifeless waste. Lulù's compulsive purchase of useless commodities with the wage earned from the sale of labor power to the capitalist is precisely an attempt to regain and enjoy the surplus that was subtracted from him in the first place. What these commodities do instead is function as reminders of the original exploitation of Lulù's labor power as well as of the asymmetrical relation that that the worker and the capitalist have to the world of commodities. While commodities for the worker only have use value (they are consumed for subsistence), they have exchange value for the capitalist alone, who realizes a profit by monetizing the value (including the surplus value) of the commodities produced by workers. Faced with the ineluctability of this situation, Lulù desists. From this moment on, Volonté mostly plays him with a sense of detached disorientation that vividly contrasts with the energetic portrayal he provided up to this point.

What of justice, then, in such a bleak portrayal of the political horizon of the working class? One can perhaps discern in the student-worker alliance's demand for the abolition of the piecework system a glimpse into a possible advent of justice as the fourth and final moment of the figure. It would be easy to argue that Petri's sympathies lie with this radical position and not with the union. The student-worker movement advocates for an end to exploitation by way of a separation of wage from productivity, the project of a new order conjured to replace the existing one. The union, however, simply aims to adjust the rate of exploitation to a more acceptable level, thus refusing to call into question the system as such. Perhaps the film's implicit championing of the student-worker alliance is enough to contend that justice is indeed present in the film, however fleetingly or virtually. However, it is also important to emphasize that after the insurrection, a spiraling down of the figure of the worker begins, as though courage exhausted its upward thrust and the possibility of storming heaven became increasingly unlikely. The result is Lulù's disorientation, which intensifies when he learns the news of his reinstatement, brought by the film's own version of the deus ex machina—the union—which signals Lulù's return to factory work, but this time in the brutal regime of the assembly line.

The Assembly Line: Lapsing

The final sequence is an extensive ensemble piece that sees Lulù and his coworkers frantically performing repetitive tasks, trying to talk to each other over the deafening machinery noise. Screaming at the top of his lungs, Lulù recounts a dream he had: he is dead, trapped in a sort of purgatory separated from heaven by a wall, and along comes Militina, who incites Lulù to break through the wall. When the wall finally comes down, the workers are ready to storm heaven. Beyond the wall, however, Lulù only finds a thick fog from which all the characters in the film start emerging, including a doppelganger of Lulù himself. The account of the dream is interspersed with remarks and questions from Lulù's coworkers who, because of the noise, mishear most of what he says. Formally, the scene is characterized by extreme fragmentation, fast-paced

50 The Worker

Figure 3. Confusion at the assembly line in *The Working Class Goes to Heaven* (1971).

editing, and a wide variety of shots and angles that depict the thwarted conversation among the characters (Figure 3).

On the surface, the scene can be read as an allegory of the defeat of revolutionary aspirations brought about by capital's authoritarian suppression of working-class struggle. In its basic structure, what the scene offers is the materiality of brutal exploitation on one side, a confused dream of revolution on the other, and only noise and fog in between. Where previously the condition of the worker provided the opening for a radical politics of refusal, now that condition finds itself unmoored from any collective political project. Incommunicability, isolation, disorientation—these are the affective dominants not only in the scene's depiction of assembly line work but also, and perhaps more tellingly, in Lulù's dream itself. The thick fog enshrouding seemingly everything in the film makes one last appearance here, as Lulù's description links it directly to the illegibility of a political situation in which the stakes of class struggle have become elusive.

The motif of occluded vision recurs throughout the film, but the saturation of space that previously marked the onset of the superego assumes here a new valence. The fog becomes the perfect metaphor of a condition of disorientation—a "fog of class war," as Evan Calder Williams called it, that symbolizes the worker's inability to make sense of his own position within the capitalist relation of production, and from which the illegibility, atomization, and entrapment of the figure of the worker derive.[16] The fog, in this sense, evokes the obfuscation of the fundamental impasse of the capitalist relation of production: class antagonism.

After all, what is Petri's working class going to heaven to do, exactly? To storm it? Or to die and rest in peace, its antagonistic potential neutralized once and for all? The ambiguity of the expression "going to heaven" easily accommodates both options. But the working class in Petri's film is not simply dead; it is still living labor exploited by capital. Nor is it glorified in the apotheosis of revolutionary violence. The final scene dramatizes the tension inherent in this ambiguity. On the one hand, the dream actualizes a sense of collective yet impotent rage; on the other, the shots of the characters at the assembly line portray a peace that is only the result of capitalist disciplinary repression. This working class on its way to heaven finds itself in limbo: the undoing of the coordinates of class struggle in the historical sequence of 1968 leaves the working class disoriented, lost. Historically, the loss of the hegemonic position of the worker registered by the film is due to the onset of a stagnation of the global economy and the consequent process of capitalist restructuring that began at the end of the 1960s. One of the effects of this restructuring was the marginalization of the antagonistic role of the factory worker within the process of production. Already by the mid-1970s, the factory begins to lose its status as the paradigmatic site of class struggle, as we witness the rise of a new proletariat whose labor power is not necessarily exploited within the walls of the factory. Antonio Negri famously named this emerging political subject *operaio sociale* (social worker), signaling a new process of capitalist exploitation—and its correspondent form of antagonism—that takes place in society at large.[17] With the fragmentation and recomposition of the working class that occurs under the pressure of capitalist restructuring, the factory worker finds himself unable to map his own position within this transformed landscape of production.

The final scene evokes this disorientation by exceeding the immediate semantic halo of repetitiveness, exploitation, and dehumanization (with its attendant corollary of social critique of working conditions) that is usually associated with the assembly line in the cinema of '68.[18] The assembly line dominates the film's final scene, yet nothing of the fluid, horizontal movement that defines it is retained in the scene's formal organization—quite the opposite. What the appearance of the assembly line comes to signify instead is the reactive restructuring of capital that undoes existing forms of working-class subjective consistency, with the extreme aesthetic fragmentation of the scene as the formal correlate of this undoing. This line of reading also offers a possible interpretation of the enigmatic last shot of the film, where the camera assumes the point of view of the piece of machinery built by Lulù and his coworkers as it is unloaded from the assembly line and carted away, all in one long take. The contrast with the rest of the scene is stark. When the film looks at the situation from the point of view of the worker, all it sees is isolation, interruption, and a disjointed frenzy. However, as soon as it assumes the point of view of capital in the form of the machine, fluidity and continuity take over as signs of a new consistency acquired by the structure.

As Chaplin showed in *Modern Times*, the inexorable flow of production embodied by the assembly line is fundamentally dehumanizing—not, however, because of some generic socio-ethical preoccupation about the harshness of labor conditions, but, more literally, because industrial capitalism is predicated on a forced adaptation of the human to the machine. The mode of production needs to deform the human in order to make it fit the standards of efficiency dictated by machinery. *The Working Class Goes to Heaven* refines Chaplin's (and Marx's) point and pushes it further. The incessant process of assemblage in the final scene is less about dehumanization than about political desubjectification.

This is where our analysis must part ways with the Badiouian formalization of the logic of the subject. In the position where Badiou's matrix conceptually locates the advent of justice, we must recognize in the film the consolidation of a new order that has little to do with justice. Instead, to borrow an apt term from Sylvain Lazarus, we would identify in the appearance of the assembly line the moment of "lapsing" of working-class subjectivity. In Lazarus, lapsing takes the form of a cessation of subjective categories that determine the end of a given historicopolitical sequence, which he calls "saturation." This cessation, however, does not simply name a political failure to be disavowed. Rather, it is an opening onto a certain possibility whose termination at the end of the sequence must not erase the fact that that possibility did once exist: "When tackling a political body of work that once mattered, the alternative is between disavowal and saturation. In effect, declaring, for instance, the lapsing of the Leninist problematic of the Party, based on the simple observation of his historical discredit, without indicating in any way what this lapsing opens onto or leads to, amounts to a de facto disavowal."[19]

Lazarus calls "intellectuality" that which a lapsing "opens onto or leads to" and that lives on after the political subjectivities of a given sequence disappear. If one were to read *The Working Class Goes to Heaven* from a purely historical standpoint, the film would be nothing but a snapshot of the evaporation that occurred between the late 1960s and the early 1970s of the factory worker as the hegemonic subject of anticapitalist struggle. However, would this not be tantamount to a disavowal of the intellectuality generated by the figure of the worker in the film after its subjective lapsing? It is undeniable that there is a certain irrevocable objectivity to the defeat of the workers' movement captured by Petri in the final scene, especially if examined from the vantage of an almost half century of hindsight. But a figure does not merely represent what is available to perception—in this case, the being there of a historicopolitical situation. As we have seen, lapsing is but one moment in the larger matrix of a logic of subjectivity, and in no way does it retain primacy over the other moments. It is precisely in the articulation, and not hierarchization, of anxiety, courage, superego, justice, and lapsing that the figure of the worker in the film thinks one of the enduring intellectualities produced by the historical sequence of 1968: a working-class antagonism impervious to the reformist rhetoric of the unions, driven by desires and not rights, and adopting a revolutionary stance against both capital and the state. It is not a legacy, monumentalized and thus inert, but rather the singular thought of a historical moment of crisis and transition.

Figural Variations

With Lulù, we have seen what happens when the worker traverses the moments of anxiety, courage, superego, justice, and lapsing. The other two films analyzed in this chapter articulate two possible permutations of the logic established in Petri's film: courage without anxiety (*The Seduction of Mimì*) and anxiety without courage (*Trevico-Turin*). These shifts prompt a recombination of the original dialectic, which in turn generates different variations—and different destinies—of the figure of the worker.

Courage without Anxiety: The Seduction of Mimì and the Logic of Debt

Carmelo "Mimì" Mardocheo (Giancarlo Giannini), a Sicilian worker, loses his job at a sulfur quarry in Catania after he refuses—more out of spite than political conviction—to vote for the candidate supported by the Mafia in the local elections. Unemployed, he is forced to leave behind his young wife, Rosalia (Agostina Belli), and migrate to Turin, in Northern Italy. There, after a few run-ins with the local Mafia chapter, he becomes a metalworker at FIAT and falls in love with Fiore (Mariangela Melato), a young leftist activist, with whom he has a child. Transferred by the company back to Sicily, Mimì finds out that his wife has cheated on him with a *carabiniere*, Amilcare (Gianfranco Barra). Because he now thinks of himself as an emancipated metalworker, Mimì does not give in to the patriarchal imperative to punish her with death. Instead, he devises a plan to get revenge and settle the score: seducing Rosalia's lover's wife, Amalia (Elena Fiore). Once Amalia discovers that Rosalia is pregnant with Amilcare's child, although she is offended by Mimì's ploy, she reluctantly agrees to play along and becomes pregnant of a bastard child of her own to spite her adulterous husband. The plan succeeds, but before vengeance is served, one last showdown must take place. At Sunday Mass, where the entire town is gathered, Mimì openly taunts Amilcare, who threatens to kill him, unaware that Amalia had unloaded his gun. At the height of tension, a Mafia *sicario* swoops in, kills Amilcare, and pins the crime on a stunned Mimì, who goes to jail for a crime he did not commit. Once he has served his sentence, Mimì is forced to work for the Mafia to provide for Fiore, Rosalia, Amalia, and their respective children. In a circular ending, he starts running a campaign of intimidation for the upcoming local elections. Fiore, disappointed in Mimì, breaks up with him and leaves with their baby.

The film is organized in three acts by place: first Sicily, where Mimì opposes the Mafia rule; then Turin, where he finds a sort of utopian situation in which a new love and a new politics become suddenly possible; and finally, the return to Sicily, where a chauvinistic and violent way of life demands its pound of flesh. The film opens with an act of courage against this rule. Armed solely with a feeble guarantee that his defiance will not come back to haunt him (his friends in the local PCI assure him that the vote is secret—until it isn't), Mimì decides to oppose what he perceives as an inherently Sicilian—and thus local—form of oppression and goes into exile in Turin, because, he says, "there's no Mafia and mafiosi up there." Similar to Lulù, Mimì envisions the possibility of refusal and exile as liberation, but, unlike his counterpart in *The Working Class Goes to Heaven*, Mimì's act of courage is not predicated on the torsion of a lack of the structure against the structure itself, for there is no lack to speak of in the first place. The subjective moment of confrontation with structural lack is utterly absent in *The Seduction of Mimì*, which therefore begins with courage, but without anxiety. Mimì's rebellion is presented as voluntaristic—that is, it is not only autonomous from the dictates of the structure (every act of courage is) but also utterly independent from it, to the point where this antagonism configures itself as simply oppositional, giving the impression of a sort of sovereign decision that repudiates any dialectic between force and structure. We will see later how Wertmüller denounces this idea as a mere fantasy and plays it for comic effect against her protagonist's longing for a pure emancipation. For now, let us note how this absence of anxiety gives rise to a logic of subjectivation that constitutes an inversion of the one articulated in *The Working Class Goes to Heaven*. Lulù had to first confront the impasse and experience anxiety as the collapse of his Stakhanovite self in order to mount a properly courageous offensive that would be a match for the reactionary power of the structure. Wertmüller instead has Mimì outright ignoring that moment of disorientation, which results in a courage that is completely blind to the impasse of the structure it wishes to subvert.

By way of Mimì's act of courage without anxiety, the film's first act establishes a situation of imbalance, which is then resolved by a compensation: Mimì owes something to his community (a vote for the candidate backed by the Mafia), but he refuses to make good on his due, and because of this refusal to abide by an unwritten code of rules, he has to pay a price and loses his job. This is, in its most elementary terms, an example of the logic that sanctions the relationship between creditor and debtor: someone deserves harm or loss for something that he owes and is not able or willing to provide. The punishment, however, needs to be commensurate to the harm done. An equivalence is therefore established between what is owed to the creditor and the punishment that must befall the insolvent debtor. In a somewhat Nietzschean fashion, *The Seduction of Mimì* establishes from its beginning the logic of credit and debt as the paradigm of social relations, a transactional logic of equivalences based on trade that precedes the properly capitalistic relation between production and wage labor.

Within this general framework, the original situation of imbalance seems to have been compensated. Mimì has paid his dues by losing his job and is now seemingly free of debt, so he can now embark on a journey away from Sicily and its backward, oppressive way of life, because "in Turin, they pay workers, and even Agnelli [FIAT's principal shareholder] tips his hat to them! In Turin, labor is free and respected!" Turin, FIAT, and the condition of the factory worker that these names evoke in early 1970s Italy are cast by Mimì as a utopia of fairness, freedom, and progress where the Sicilian logic of always already being in debt has no purchase. The film, however, wastes no time in denouncing the fantasmatic nature of these beliefs. The passage between the first and second act is an abrupt cut that juxtaposes the sunny streets of Catania with the smog and fog of Turin, with Mimì stranded on a traffic island, an urban castaway unable to wade through the raging waves of cars (Figure 4). With her customary humor, Wertmüller has an aria from Giuseppe Verdi's *Il trovatore* accompanying the scene: "We've arrived; there's the tower where the State's prisoners languish. / Ah, the hapless man was brought here!"

The prophetic halo of the scene couldn't be more transparent, as the clutches of mafioso oppression seize Mimì immediately after he arrives in Turin, again in the form of a logic of creditor/debtor. The Sicilian Brotherhood Association is happy to help out fellow Sicilians by providing jobs at a construction site, but only if the workers are willing to obey and keep their mouth shut. Mimì's encounter with a supposedly Sicilian logic outside of Sicily is marked by a flash of uncanniness. The manager of the association, Tricarico, is played by Turi Ferro, the same actor who impersonated the mafioso boss in Catania. Mimì is stunned to notice that Tricarico bears the same identification mark as the boss: three moles on the right cheek.[20] This is one of the running jokes

Figure 4. Mimì leaves Sicily for Turin in *The Seduction of Mimì* (1972).

in the film. The antagonists and figures of authority (the mafioso bosses in Sicily and Turin, a cardinal, a spy disguised as a communist activist, a police chief) are all played by Ferro, sporting the same three moles. Always presented with the same shot/reverse shot dyad that registers Mimì's repeated astonishment, the three moles are the distinctive mark of power. They are the master signifier that intervenes when Mimì strays a bit too far, reminding him of his condition of debtor and immediately resuturing him into the structure.

Confronted with the pervasiveness of debt as a paradigm of social relations embodied by the omnipresent mafioso network, Mimì romanticizes the condition of the Torinese working class as a possible way out of this circuitous logic. Mimì's job at FIAT, the burgeoning relationship with Fiore, and the novel political commitment with the PCI seem to confirm the possibility of a new beginning under the auspices of a progressive working-class subjectivity. Again, there is no trace in *The Seduction of Mimì* of the impasse that was at the heart of the figure of the worker in *The Working Class Goes to Heaven*. As the monolithic torchbearer of progress, the worker functions for Wertmüller as an entity external to the debt-centered mafioso network, thus remaining oblivious to the fundamental impasse of the capitalist mode of production that Petri's film throws into relief.

Mimì's faith in the worker as an inherently progressive figure betrays an idea of progress that has some content (a relinquishing of the logic of debt) but no form. It is hardly a progress based on struggle, of which the worker would be the agent. Instead, "worker" is for Mimì the name of progress as such, a figure that is fantasized as intrinsically emancipated and modern. Halfway through the second act, this idealization of the worker starts to break down. Mimì is pressured by the sudden appearances of Ferro's characters, who invariably manifest themselves at turning points in Mimì's new life—the arrival in Turin, the local PCI meeting, his son's baptism. But Mimì's self-fashioned progressive identity also starts to crack from within. Once Fiore becomes pregnant, for instance, Mimì's political commitment starts to wane, as he abandons the union meetings to focus on petty bourgeois concerns. When Fiore asks him about recent developments in the struggle, he dismisses the question and shifts the conversation to her pregnancy. To his coworkers who accuse him of having defected to the "side of the *padroni*," he replies, "Yessir, I have a job and I'm trying to be better at it. I have to think about my son."

For Wertmüller, however, it is not simply a matter of morally chastising the character's hypocrisy and the cynical opportunism of his commitment to the cause of the working class. Rather, we should read Mimì's vacillation as the index of a certain tension inscribed in the film between the opposite poles of reaction and progress, oppression and emancipation, tradition and modernity. The worker is the site where this tension becomes visible, and the illusion of a clear-cut separation between the two poles is revealed to be just that: an illusion. The Italian title of the film, *Mimì metallurgico ferito nell'onore* (Mimì the metalworker wounded in his honor), captures precisely this split, juxtaposing progress (the factory worker as the hegemonic revolutionary subject of modernity) and reaction (honor as the primary currency in the archaic system of values). But the title also points to a contradiction. If Mimì is a "metalworker"—that is, a progressive, emancipated individual— how can he be also "wounded in his honor"? If the world of progress and that of reaction are strictly separated, as Mimì believes, how is the retrograde concept of honor still an operative category in the modern world? The two domains, it turns out, cannot be separated once and for all. The impasse of being "a metalworker wounded in his honor" is what the film thinks through the figure of the worker, but remains unthought to Mimì himself.

To be sure, this problematic copresence of the archaic and the modern and the maladjustment of the individual to new customs is at the core of one of the most influential and long-lived subgenres in Italian cinema history: the Italian-style comedy. With its stereotypical characters and its penchant for cynical, grotesque humor, Italian-style comedy undoubtedly inspired Wertmüller.[21] While the golden age of the subgenre was long gone by the early 1970s, she revitalized it by combining its features with not only the grandiosity of operatic arias, but also the spectacle of suffering of Hollywood melodrama, with its insistence on close-ups that highlight the violence of pathos.

This conjunction between Italian-style comedy tropes and

melodramatic aesthetics is most evident in the third act. On his return to Catania, Mimì learns of his wife Rosalia's adultery, and this brings his newly minted working-class identity to the breaking point. Again, Wertmüller shows, the Worker (in this case an emblem of pure emancipation) does not exist. To a friend who observes that a communist would never murder his wife and lover to regain his honor, Mimì curtly responds, "Fuck you and your communism—I'm a cuckold!" A fight between Mimì and Rosalia ensues, with overwrought screaming, cursing, crying, and wrestling turning melodrama into a grotesque farce. Wertmüller captures the parodic intensity of the acting through a series of close-ups (Figure 5).

While the grotesque is captured formally, its origin remains structural. What the deforming close-ups and twisted physiognomies point to is the deadlock Mimì finds himself in. His honor is wounded, and the patriarchal code demands blood to wash away the offense; but he is a metalworker, and there is no place for this kind of backward thinking in his newly acquired political perspective. He is thus caught between two logics, but without the possibility of giving into the structural imperative of the former or autonomously affirming the subjective emancipation of the latter. The choice offered by the two logics would be between swift revenge and forgetfulness. In *A Genealogy of Morals,* Nietzsche identifies these two as the options of the aristocrat of heroic cultures, who either takes immediate action and retaliates without a thought, or simply lets the offense fall into oblivion out of a sheer sense of superiority. In either case, the ressentiment brought about by the offense does not linger to poison the nobleman's psyche. Mimì is, however, more akin to the other protagonist of Nietzsche's mythical dramatization of the origins of morality: the slave. Lacking the means to enforce any code of honor, the slave is doomed to experience the full brunt of ressentiment. In the impotence that his condition of weakness prescribes, the slave broods and lets ressentiment fester. However, this ressentiment is always addressed to someone, so revenge becomes first and foremost a gruesome fantasy in which all the enjoyment that the nobleman has stolen from the slave is taken back—and then some. This is the paradox of the slave's condition: his revenge is oblique, calculated;

Figure 5. Mimì confronts Rosalia about her infidelity in *The Seduction of Mimì* (1972).

yet his calculations fail to establish proper equivalences because the envy of the Other's enjoyment makes it so that the original balance can never be fully restored. Can we not see in Nietzsche's description of the slave's ressentiment the predicament in which Mimì finds himself, forced to devise a plan of action that excludes either a swift reaction or forgetfulness? The result is, of course, a perverse and absurd mixture of the two, fueled by the misleading illusion that scores can in fact be settled.

The sexual encounters between Mimì and Amalia capture precisely this grotesque dynamic of ressentiment. The supposedly heroic customs of vengeance are turned into a parody in which doing what needs to be done is as inevitable as it is absurd. Amalia's exaggerated physical features, magnified by Dario di Palma's cinematography, together with Mimì's stoic resignation, speak to the conundrum of a world that has gone off-kilter precisely by following a logic of pursuit of balance to its extreme.[22] "The figures don't add up . . . but I swear to God, I'll make them!" guarantees Mimì. Little does he know that this brand of bookkeeping only works for masters, never for slaves (or workers).

The encounter between Mimì and the managing director of the refinery (Ferro again) on a terrace overlooking Catania offers the ideal crystallization of this disparity. A cousin of Tricarico's, the director reveals that it was he who had orchestrated Mimì's transfer from Turin, and that Mimì should expect a successful career at the refinery, for he must now consider himself "one of us." (In accordance with the mafioso code of *omertà,* Mimì refused to press charges against Tricarico and his henchmen after a botched attempt at his life in Turin, so he is now regarded as a man of honor.) As the inexorable logic of debt continues to exercise its authority, Mimì tries to resist: "I don't want anything to do with you lot. I'm not like that. I believe in decent people, workers." When Mimì, pointing to the rampant real estate speculation in the area, accuses the director and people like him of being "lackeys of the *padroni,*" the director warns him that he should relinquish all his "dreams of communism," then reminds him that they "need *padroni*" in Sicily to maintain the status quo and continue reaping profits.[23] The director, who sees right through Mimì's hesitant political commitment, rhetorically asks why he never named

Tricarico to the police or the unions, concluding, "I know what you're made of. . . . You're on our side." After exposing Mimì's essential impasse, the director lays out his conspiratorial plan: "Two or three months of bag-snatching, robberies, kidnappings, a few bombings pinned on the anarchists, some propaganda against our enemies in Rome, and we're set. People are clamoring en masse for protection and order. And we give it to them. . . . It's politics." The director's plan—evidently reminiscent of the strategy of tension (discussed in depth in chapter 6)—clarifies that the Mafia is but a stand-in for a more rapacious, and thoroughly modern, form of exploitation and control. The revelation of the scope of this conspiracy that melds together the capitalist drive to accumulation and the rise of the surveillance state can be read as the moment of emergence of the superego in our logic of subjectivity. Pressured by the remnants of Mimì's courage, the network of archaic social relations that constitutes the fantasmatic support of the Mafia reveals its excessive face—one that is all too modern: financial interests, real estate speculation, political lobbying, state violence, and so forth. Sicily is then elevated from local pocket of backwardness to synecdoche of the networks of oppression and corruption that envelop Italy as a whole.[24]

The scene ends with a climactic moment that seals Mimì's fate. The director takes a coin out of his pocket and casually throws it on the ground, then asks Mimì to pick it up for him. Mimì, hesitant at first, gives in to the director's insistence and picks it up, inadvertently kneeling before him. What Nietzsche calls the "very material concept of debt" could not have received a more transparent representation.[25] This is not a simple debt, however; if it was, it would be based on a system of equivalences, and as such it would imply, at least in principle, the possibility for it to be extinguished. But this debt that Mimì contracts with the director and his organization cannot be repaid, and his being in debt translates into an unconditional submission to the sovereignty of the creditor. The reason why this debt cannot be paid is that there is surplus enjoyment that the master derives from his being creditor and that will always escape the transactional logic of debt and repayment; in the scene the presence of this surplus enjoyment is indicated in the director's malevolent laughter at Mimì's kneeling. The disparity between creditor and debtor, with their respective mirroring relations to enjoyment (surplus versus envy), asks whether the relation between credit and debt as a zero-sum game is even conceivable. Be it through the ressentiment of the slave or the surplus enjoyment of the master, one is left to wonder whether such a thing as a simple debt, entirely comprised within a logic of trade, may actually exist.

Mimì will never escape this logic of debt. Instead, his debt will only increase, as the horde of kids (Fiore's, Rosalia's, and Amalia's sons and daughters) that overwhelm him outside the prison ironically alludes to. The circular ending of the film signals precisely this inescapability: Mimì is now part of the same mafioso crew that was running a campaign of intimidation among the quarry workers for the elections. In his study of the logic of debt, post-*operaista* thinker Maurizio Lazzarato writes: "The principal explanation for the strange sensation of living in a society without time, without possibility, without foreseeable rupture, is debt."[26] This is the form that subjective lapsing takes in *The Seduction of Mimì*: time becomes objectified—that is, entirely determined by the structure of debt—thus suffocating any space for subjective antagonism. Debt, writes Lazzarato, neutralizes the risks inherent in time by anticipating "every potential deviation in the behavior of the debtor the future might hold.... Objectivizing time, possessing it in advance, means subordinating all possibility of choice and decision which the future holds to the reproduction of capitalist power relations."[27] The ending of *The Seduction of Mimì* stages precisely this predictability of the indebted man, as well as the defeat of the progressive utopia previously embodied by the worker. The final shot/reverse shots between Mimì, Fiore, her kids, and Peppino (a leftist friend of Mimì) are characterized by a surprising level of affectlessness—no rage, anxiety, or desperation, only an enigmatic hesitation, tinged with disappointment and resignation, as though the characters were taking stock of this seemingly irreversible objectification of time (Figure 6).

But there is still room for one last comical moment. "They are all cousins!" Mimì screams in the last shot, referring to Ferro's omnipresent doppelgangers, as he runs after Fiore to protest his innocence. It is curious that in order to be made sense of, a countrywide

Figure 6. The last good-bye between Mimì and his family in *The Seduction of Mimì* (1972).

network of relations of violence and exploitation needs to be reduced back to the known, and utterly inadequate, form of the family. Even more remarkable is that Mimì, as it were, still does not get *it*. Mimì is a fool because he is unable to understand his role in the scripted theatrical performance that unfolds in the film.[28] His initial rebellion—courage without anxiety—created the illusion that a break from debt bondage was possible, that he could somehow write himself out of the performance. The comic effect in the film is generated precisely by Mimì's unwillingness to acknowledge the structural determinations of his existence. Courage without anxiety means lunging to assault the structure without having seen its impasse, the point of vacillation. But what would anxiety without courage look like?

Anxiety without Courage: The Absent Factory in Trevico-Turin: Voyage in the Fiat-Nam

Trevico-Turin occupies a peculiar position within Ettore Scola's filmography. For a director and screenwriter mostly known for his star-studded and widely popular comedies, the film constitutes a remarkable creative detour: no professional actors (except for Paolo Turco in the leading role), small budget, and bare-bones screenplay—but, most notably, also refusal to release the film in the commercial movie theater circuit.[29]

The film is a sort of docufiction *ante litteram* in which an aesthetics akin to cinema verité meshes with a dramatized account of the condition of Southern migrants looking for work in Turin in the early 1970s. The title refers to the voyage undertaken by young migrant Fortunato Santospirito from Trevico, his (and Scola's) native rural town in Campania, to Turin, in hopes of finding a job at FIAT. This "Voyage in the Fiat-nam" has Fortunato wander across the city as Scola guides the spectator through derelict apartments, overcrowded dormitories, and soup kitchens, but also places like a train station at night, where the marginalized gather; or Porta Palazzo square, where the Southern immigrant community meets every weekend.

Fortunato's voyage comprises a series of encounters: with the nameless real-life people that inhabit the urban landscape, and to whom the protagonist cedes the stage, receding into the background as an improvised off-screen interviewer; but also with four characters that are thrown into relief: a young barman, Beppe, who helps Fortunato in his search for an accommodation; a priest who illustrates the hardships that Southerners face in Turin; an older worker and PCI militant; and, most importantly, Vicky, a student associated with the radical left (she is part of Lotta Continua) who becomes Fortunato's love interest.

In radical circles, the film was dismissed as a clumsy exercise, a children's story whose sole merit was to have shown in an educational fashion the awakening of the protagonist's class consciousness.[30] Others, like Lino Miccichè, lauded Scola's political intentions and the sociological accuracy of the portrayal of the working class in Turin in the early 1970s.[31] Surely such critical verdicts are predicated on an analysis of what, so to speak, is *there*, either in the film (Fortunato's narrative trajectory) or in its immediate vicinities (the sociohistorical context). This is, after all, what the film shows: the didactic political discussions, the familiar iconology of immiseration, the humanism of the migrants' faces captured in prolonged close-ups, the sentimentalism of Fortunato's letters to his mother. In general, *Trevico-Turin* betrays an evident concern with a representation of the working class that would respond to criteria of accuracy and authenticity while at the same time offering a political statement consonant with Scola's and the PCI's reformist agenda. The film, in this sense, has a fairly clear political thesis, epitomized in the final scene with Fortunato's letter to his brothers in Trevico: a doleful *j'accuse* against capital and the state which turns into a demand for more jobs in the South ("It's important that you know what awaits you if you come here or go abroad. They have to give us jobs where we are born"). But the political crux of the film lies less with what it shows—or intends to show—than with what it thinks. To unearth this aspect, we need to look past *Trevico-Turin*'s obvious sociologizing implications. This would be, in a way, the ultimate testing ground for a figural reading of political cinema: how does one see a figure where only sociological stereotypes are visible? The beginning of an answer lies in the hypothesis that what is not there—the absences and ellipses—might be more significant that what is.

The most conspicuous absence in *Trevico-Turin* is, of course, that of the factory itself. Scola had planned to shoot inside the infamous FIAT Mirafiori plant—one of the major sites of the workers' struggles in Italy in the 1960s and 1970s—to which the management opposed a categorical refusal. He therefore had to settle for the rudimentary solution of title cards, which nonetheless makes for an eerie estranging effect, with static and repetitive snapshots abruptly interrupting the flow of moving images (Figure 7).

By way of this enabling constraint, *Trevico-Turin* asks: what happens to the worker when the factory disappears? What kind of figure is tied to the void left by a factory that is hiding in plain sight? As we begin to discuss how the film might offer an answer to these questions, it would perhaps be useful to retrace our steps and observe the ways the worker and the factory—the figure and its background—are linked in the films we have already discussed. In *The Working Class Goes to Heaven,* the factory incarnates what Badiou might call an "event site,"[32] which is the space where the

Figure 7. Intertitle for *Trevico-Turin: Voyage in the Fiat-Nam* (1973).

clash between force and structure occurs, and where a new political commitment suddenly manifests itself as actually being possible. It is on the factory floor that Lulù confronts the disorientation of anxiety caused by the accident, just as it is there, again, that he turns this anxiety against the structure in the moments of courage marked by the workers' assembly and the insurrection at the factory gates. In the film, the figure of the worker hinges on the centrality of the factory, which must be grasped dialectically: the factory as "House of Terror" for paupers,[33] where the worker is subjected to the unchecked exploitation of piecework labor; and, at one and the same time, the factory as event site from which a new emancipatory politics and a new subject may arise.

In *The Seduction of Mimì*, the protagonist fantasizes about the factory as a utopia of fairness and freedom without being able to see and recognize the system of capitalist exploitation that subsumes not just the factory but the country as a whole. Whereas Mimì only sees an imagined event site, the real house of terror ravages the country and manages to force him into submission. The result, as we have seen, can only be the birth of the Nietzschean man of ressentiment, a figure whose defining impotence is precisely determined by an inability to properly recognize situations of real antagonism.

In *Trevico-Turin*, as the factory disappears from sight, it hardly dissolves into nothingness. On the contrary; its ghostly presence towers over the film, haunting all the various places depicted in it. In fact, *Trevico-Turin* seems to suggest that the condition of being a worker—and specifically a migrant worker—cannot be confined to the factory and the process of exploitation that occurs therein. It requires mapping on a much larger scale. The film can therefore be read as a diagram of the urban space as an extension of the factory. By vanishing, the factory exists everywhere. To Petri's designation of the factory as event site and Wertmüller's deployment of the factory as deceptive utopia, Scola adds the factory as a structuring absence capable of refashioning the urban space in its own image.

Taken individually, the spaces of *Trevico-Turin* can be considered nonplaces, according to Marc Augé's famous definition. They are all places of transience that structurally preclude any form of inhabiting or stable dwelling, thus dooming Fortunato and the other immigrants to a fate of endless errancy. But *Trevico-Turin* does more than simply provide a generic catalog of sites of alienation; it also traces back these individual snapshots to the unitary colonizing logic of the (absent) factory. The film casts the factory as the absent structural cause of the totality of urban space, manifesting itself only in the singularity of its tangible effects. "Turin is all FIAT," declares Vicky. The process of exploitation of the working class is no longer confined within the walls of the physical factory. Now it takes place in the social fabric itself. As Vicky tells Fortunato, "They exploit you in the factory, at school, when you sleep, when you breathe." Can we not read in the grain of this violent factorization of society the presence of a certain surplus of the structure that aims to extend its rule beyond its typical territories and subjugate all aspects of the individual's life?

Trevico-Turin depicts a situation in which anxiety escapes from the Pandora's box of the factory and saturates the social. Neither concentrated into an uncanny flash of revelation (as in Petri) nor simply absent (as in Wertmüller), anxiety turns into a soft, all-pervasive condition of constant uneasiness that cannot be assigned to a specific place or moment but envelops the film as a whole. Fortunato's anxiety is born out of a repetitive encounter with the various aspects of exploitation within the social fabric as the capitalist logic of production spills into the urban space, and starts dictating the terms of the process of reproduction of labor power too. This surplus of authoritarian presence of capital is how the correlate of anxiety—the superego—appears in the film. Capital reorganizes the worker's life in such a way that Fortunato, unlike Lulù, is prevented from recognizing the void at the heart of the structure. Instead of marking the impasse as the point of revelation of the precariousness of the system, the anxiety of the worker in *Trevico-Turin* turns inward and becomes the symptom of Fortunato's own precariousness within a system that conversely appears invincible in its omnipresence.

Most of the spaces that Fortunato and the other characters populate are monuments to this sense of precariousness. With their emphasis on transience, anonymity, and disjointedness, the various snapshots of the urban landscape that make up *Trevico-*

Turin reflect the subjective situation of the figure of the worker. Places like the train station, the dormitory, the lumpenproletarian ghetto, and the abandoned monorail are all reminders of a precariousness marked specifically by the condition of not being at home. The Southern migrant roaming these places precisely embodies this situation; as Paolo Virno suggests in his reading of Heidegger, once the individual is deprived of community, she falls prey to an anxiety that is ubiquitous and constant.[34] The spaces in *Trevico-Turin* thus oscillate between the poles of objectivity and subjectivity. Their physical consistency is always in some way overdetermined by the subjective situation of precariousness experienced by the characters inhabiting it.

This indiscernibility between the objective and the subjective points to an interesting parallel between the spaces in *Trevico-Turin* and the "any-spaces-whatever" that Deleuze indicates as one of the hallmarks of the modern cinema born after World War II with Italian neorealism. Deleuze describes the "any-space-whatever" as a "disconnected . . . emptied" space in which a point of indiscernibility is reached between objective and subjective, or real and imaginary.[35] These "any-spaces-whatever" give rise to "pure optical and sound situations" in which characters are no longer subjected to the dictates of stimulus/response or action/reaction (the "sensory-motor schema") that define the mode of classical Hollywood cinema. Instead, according to Deleuze, beginning with neorealism, we see a "slackening" of these connections, which translates into the rise of a new breed of characters who privilege a passive demeanor over action and an exploration of space through aimless wandering over the strictures of narrative motivation. It is, in Deleuze's words, "a cinema of the seer and no longer of the agent," where the protagonist "records rather than reacts."[36]

In this sense, Fortunato is undoubtedly one of the epigones of De Sica's and Rossellini's characters. He is, first and foremost, a witness who sees and records. He roams an urban space that reflects his and his fellow migrants' precariousness and alienation, while his presence on screen and off gives voice to the plight of the poor and disenfranchised. It is no secret that Scola held the neorealist tradition and its ethicopolitical project in the highest regard—indeed, he explicitly celebrated its legacy and lamented its demise in *We All Loved Each Other So Much* (1974). It is thus not difficult to see how a film like *Trevico-Turin* would for Scola be a homage to that filmic lineage, trying its best to reclaim some of the neorealist aesthetic features so perceptively captured by Deleuze.

Among them is also the significance of the encounter. Quoting Cesare Zavattini, Deleuze writes that neorealism is "an art of encounter—fragmentary, ephemeral, piecemeal, missed encounters,"[37] and what is *Trevico-Turin* if not a chronicle of encounters? The friendly barman, the priest, the PCI militant, and Vicky—not to mention the myriad nameless people Fortunato meets along the way—all conjure some idea of solidarity for Fortunato. Yet all these encounters are somehow missed. After Beppe helps him out, Fortunato looks for him, but he is told that he does not work at the bar anymore; the priest and the PCI militant are both mentors to the protagonist, but then disappear from the film; and finally, with Vicky, the distance between the immigrant worker and the rebellious student from a well-to-do family proves unbridgeable, and a burgeoning love affair ends abruptly.

It is in these missed encounters that we ought to look for clues regarding the fate of courage in the film. We know what happens to courage when it is disjointed from anxiety, as in *The Seduction of Mimì;* it becomes blind voluntarism, a show of force that remains oblivious to the determinations imposed by the structure. As glimpses of solidarity, the encounters in *Trevico-Turin* constitute an opening onto the possibility of courage as a collective forcing of the structure. At its most elementary, this solidarity takes on the form of friendship, which offsets the worker's isolation (Beppe). With each encounter, however, this solidarity becomes more properly political, envisioning the prospect of collective forms of resistance against the structure—forms based on the humanistic unity of the exploited (the priest), the organized unity of the party (the PCI militant), and finally the unity specifically thought by the event of 1968, that of workers and students (Vicky). But all these encounters, as we have seen, are missed, for they do not coalesce into a proper collective forcing of the structure.

To be sure, the impact of these encounters on Fortunato's budding class consciousness is hardly negligible. Fortunato openly confronts the gloomy reality of exploitation in Turin that another migrant proletarian, Mimì, desperately wanted to disavow. While Mimì holes up in Fiore's apartment, forbidding her to join the workers' protests raging in the streets, Fortunato constantly navigates the city and does not shy away from struggle; he participates in strikes at FIAT and stands up for himself against a foreman at the assembly line. But the film maintains a certain distance even from these displays of courage, making them too, in a way, missed. The strike is only evoked by Fortunato's voice-over reading a letter to his mother, and the incident with the foreman is briefly alluded to in one of the title cards. And when Vicky, the true source of courage in the film, exhorts the dwellers of a public housing to organize and demand better living conditions, she does so by evoking other struggles and other places, to which the interlocutor replies: "They had the courage to do it, and they were united. But here it's one, two, three, four people at most. The others won't do it." Even the final moment of refusal—Fortunato kneeling in the deserted street screaming "Enough!"—is tinged with impotence and desperation, amplified by the muted soundtrack that elides Fortunato's cry. In a film in which what is absent is just as important as what is shown, these missed moments of courage—evoked, invisible, silenced—become the correlate of diffused anxiety. Anxiety and courage are reduced to precariousness and frustration, purely reactive stances that already carry within themselves the seed of political defeat, for they remain entirely determined by the monstrous surplus of control of the capitalist structure. It is not by chance that the last image has Fortunato trudging toward the ironworks in depth of field, like a young working-class Monsieur Verdoux walking to the gallows (Figure 8). We can very well imagine that he might not leave that plant again.

It is here that *Trevico-Turin*'s avowed neorealist afflatus meets its breaking point. However closely they might resemble each other, a fundamental difference separates Deleuze's any-space-whatever from the landscapes in the film, and it has to do with their evental potential. This is what Deleuze had to say about the "potentialization" of the any-space-whatever in his 1982 seminar on cinema:

> The any-space-whatever is inseparable from a simple potentialization. This is why it is not an actualized space: it is a pure

Figure 8. Fortunato walks to the factory gates in *Trevico-Turin: Voyage in the Fiat-Nam* (1973).

> potentialization of space. What does it mean, a potentialization of space? It means that it is a space which, because it is empty . . . anything can happen in it: but what? Something [*quelque chose*], any event [*un événement quelconque*] can occur, at the same time from without and within.[38]

"Any event can occur." To the nondescriptiveness of the space corresponds the potential for something—an event—to take place. For Deleuze, any-spaces-whatever are event sites in the sense that they open up the possibility for "anything" to happen—something that cannot be entirely foreseen because it is not determined by the "sensory-motor schema" that makes space a function of narrative and action. Yet the spaces in *Trevico-Turin* do possess a degree of determination. They may be physically empty, but they are not anonymous spaces of pure potentiality. The indeterminacy of these spaces, and thus their potentialization, is always already limited by the invisible presence of the factory. The long sequence of Fortunato and Vicky wandering through the monumental ruins of the so-called Italia '61 area, named after the exposition celebrating the centennial of the unification of the country, exemplifies this relationality between these nonplaces and the elsewhere of the factory. Something may occur in them, but not anything. The abandoned monorail, the massive Palazzo del Lavoro, and the Palazzo a Vela in the distance are spaces that seem to open up the possibility of an event—love between Fortunato and Vicky, of course, but also a political alliance between workers' and students' struggles. At the same time, however, they are signifiers of the absent factory, as Vicky explains to Fortunato: because the Italia '61 exposition area was conceived as a publicity initiative for FIAT, it can be compared to "a soap salesman who dresses up to sell more soap. Turin is dressed up so it can sell more cars" (Figure 9).

Aesthetically, the film presents the spaces as any-spaces-whatever with a degree of evental potentiality. However, from the standpoint of the structuring absence of the factory, these spaces are far from indeterminate, inextricable as they are from the history of Italian capitalism and the many forms of its rule over society.[39] In the case of Scola's film, the ruins of Italia '61 do not simply express potentiality in themselves; their potentiality (for love and class struggle) is also affirmed only in the relation between these abandoned spaces and what constitutes their hidden cause: industrial capital, as personified by FIAT.

This primacy of the absent factory in *Trevico-Turin* makes visible a different facet of the figure of the worker in Italian political cinema. As opposed to Lulù in *The Working Class Goes to Heaven*, who starts off as a parody of the Stakhanovite worker from the 1930s, Fortunato is fully a worker of his time. A young, unskilled Southerner migrating to the industrialized North in search of a job, he embodies the mass worker described by the *operaisti* in the 1960s. The figure of the worker and that of the migrant become indiscernible; indeed, as Scola himself quipped, "Fortunato is not a hero, a revolutionary, or a unionist—he is a Southerner."[40] Fortunato undertakes the same trip as Mimì, but while in Wertmüller the experience of the migrant is largely reduced to clichés of mutual incomprehension between different cultures, *Trevico-Turin* focuses more attentively on the structural role played by Southern workforce within the Italian capitalist system. This role, to

Figure 9. The Italia '61 exposition area in Turin in *Trevico-Turin: Voyage in the Fiat-Nam* (1973).

borrow Marx's term, is that of a surplus population that is readily available to offset phases of contraction and expansion of the capitalist labor market.

In Scola's film, the city becomes an immense storage facility for this surplus population, which includes not only the employed but also the unemployed and the unemployable. *Trevico-Turin* thus signals a dissipation of the figure of the worker into the more capacious figure of the proletarian, which includes young workers like Fortunato, the unemployed still looking for jobs, and ex-workers considered too old to be rehired. But this figure stretches even further out to the margins of the process of production to touch the territories of what Marx calls pauperdom, exemplified in the film by the lumpenproletarian who turn to stealing to survive and the mentally ill person whose desperation foreshadows Fortunato's final cry. In a way, the irreducibility of the figure of the worker to any one character discussed in chapter 1 is nowhere more explicit than in *Trevico-Turin*. Every face and every voice in the film become part of a larger mosaic that extends well beyond the contours of the factory worker.

In the film, this surplus migrant population is presented as the by-product of the omnipresent rule of the absent factory, which mobilizes it as a necessary part of the process of production, what Marx (who himself borrowed the expression from Engels) calls the industrial reserve army. Commenting on the significance of this concept in *Capital,* Fredric Jameson describes it as

> a stage of "subsumption" in which the extra-economic or social no longer lies outside capital and economics but has been absorbed into it: so that being unemployed or without economic function is no longer to be expelled from capital but to remain within it. Where everything has been subsumed under capitalism, there is no longer anything outside it; and the unemployed ... are as it were employed by capital to be unemployed; they fulfill an economic function by way of their very non-functioning.[41]

"Where everything has been subsumed under capitalism, there is no longer anything outside it." What better way to capture the surplus of the rule of the structure over the city than the idea of a place that has no outside? With its depiction of the rule of the absent factory over the urban social space, *Trevico-Turin* gives body precisely to a situation in which "the extra-economic or social no longer lies outside capital and economics but has been absorbed into it."

We should not, however, make the mistake of assuming that all *Trevico-Turin* does is document an objective state of things—namely the process of capitalist subsumption of the surplus population as a buffer against structural cycles of expansion and contraction. What political cinema thinks is not just the status quo of things as they are but also includes the unforeseen subjective forcings and antagonisms that occur in the situation, with the figure as the point where this dialectical relationship between structure and force is made visible. Although a certain pedagogical intent is undoubtedly present in *Trevico-Turin,* the film can be read as less concerned with an authentic representation of the working class than with thinking the impasse that marks the field of subjective possibilites of the worker when the factory disappears and exploitation comes to colonize every aspect of human life.

As the factory worker in *Trevico-Turin* dissipates into the Fiatnam and becomes indiscernible from the unemployed and the unemployable, he is reunited under the more capacious banner of a new proletariat, of which the social worker is the emblem. The consequences of the rise of this new worker in the 1970s will be enormous. On the one hand is an expansion of the field of class struggle beyond the walls of the factory; on the other is a certain difficulty in pinpointing this elusive form of political subjectivity and channeling its force along a revolutionary trajectory. A dissipation of energy always causes entropy. The Italian radical left in the 1970s will go on to learn from the figure of the mass worker and its courageous struggle, just as it will have to endure the challenges posed by its dissipation.

Ressentiment and Victimhood

In this chapter, I have provided an account of the ways the worker becomes con-figured across different films, with *The Seduction of Mimì* and *Trevico-Turin* offering two possible permutations of the figural paradigm established with *The Working Class Goes to Heaven*. Despite their differences, what all these iterations of the figure of the worker have in common is that they ultimately register a defeat. Lulù finds himself isolated by the noise of the assembly line, having nightmares about the revolution; Mimì becomes what he despised, a mafioso thug; Fortunato is broken by the pressure imposed by his condition as an immigrant worker at FIAT. If we were to read the films from a purely historical standpoint, this kind of political pessimism would do nothing but point to the evaporation during the late 1960s and early 1970s of what the *operaisti* had called the "workers' centrality" (*centralità operaia*)— that is, the theoretical and political primacy of the factory worker as the hegemonic antagonistic subject in the struggle against capital.[42]

While *The Working Class Goes to Heaven* follows Lulù through all the moments of his subjective coming into being, the other two films explore the effects of a shift from a dialectic between anxiety, courage, superego, and justice to the pitfalls of a courage without anxiety (*The Seduction of Mimì*) and an anxiety without courage (*Trevico-Turin*). These recombinations of the original dialectic trace different possible destinies of the figure of the worker. In the case of *The Seduction of Mimì*, it is the man of ressentiment, oblivious to the structural constraints that determine the individual's actions and therefore seething with misdirected anger toward a fantasized Other out to steal his enjoyment; in *Trevico-Turin*, it is the victim, largely impotent in the face of a power too vast and pervasive to be fought.

We might be tempted to ask what it means to retrace the genealogy of the man of ressentiment and the victim, whose presence appears so ubiquitous in our times, to the thwarted dialectic of figure of the worker—and, more specifically, the figure of the worker of the 1960s and 1970s. What would this genealogy tell us about the ascent of the man of ressentiment as one of the most dominant reactionary figures of our times? What about the specular rise of the victim, whose fundamental traits (the privation of agency and the exclusive claim to a transcendent truth guaranteed by suffering) go hand in hand with the contemporary withdrawal from politics as a practice of conflict?[43] In fact, one might go so far as to suggest that the two constitute sides of the same coin. Does not the man of ressentiment always think of himself as a victim, ready to disavow his own contradictions and project them onto the most readily available Other? Does not the victim always harbor some form of moralizing, inward-turned ressentiment? The figural centrality of the worker in Italian political cinema may provide a starting point to articulate such questions.

3 The Housewife
Figuring Reproductive Labor

> The female houseworker is capital's greatest technological invention.
> —Leopoldina Fortunati, *The Arcane of Reproduction*

> Without a break, when can I breathe?
> —Paola Masino, *Birth and Death of the Housewife*

Figure or Figurant?

From the outset, the housewife presents herself as a paradox that challenges the traditional definition of what a figure is: what stands in relief against a background. In the Italian cinema of the long '68, the housewife is everywhere but rarely stands out, relegated as she is to ancillary roles that put her into the backdrop of any given scene. More than a figure, in fact, the housewife resembles a figurant: the underpaid, nonspeaking extra on a film set, often tellingly referred to in filmmaking parlance as "atmosphere" or "background." It is hardly surprising, then, that the type of labor associated with this figure would follow a similar fate of obscurity, left for the most part out of the frame. Yet the fruits of this labor are visible throughout: clean, tidy apartments, children dressed and ready for school, sexual comfort for the weary worker, food on the table, a coffee always ready to be had. Even if one looks solely at the films discussed in the previous chapter, this pattern becomes apparent. Consider Lidia, Lulù's partner in *The Working Class Goes to Heaven,* or Fiore and Rosalia, Mimì's lover and wife, respectively, in *The Seduction of Mimì:* secondary characters framed as domestic fixtures and love interests whose labor remains largely unseen by the spectator and unthought by the films, centered as they are on the wage labor of the factory worker. In cinema as much as in the social sphere, reproductive labor is as necessary as it is often invisible.

The question of the marginalization of reproductive labor in the analysis of capitalism is nothing new. The published feminist debate on housework and the gendered division of labor began as early as 1825, with the publication of *Appeal of One Half of the Human Race, Women, against the Pretensions of the Other, Men,* a socialist pamphlet by Anna Wheeler and William Thompson.[1] The authors sought to shift the focus from the oppressiveness of the gendered division of labor to an understanding of unpaid—and thus invisible—domestic work as an integral part of the process of production. Within the socialist tradition, intellectuals and revolutionaries like Friedrich Engels, August Bebel, Alexandra Kollontai, and Clara Zetkin helped carry over the analytical focus on the nexus between productive and reproductive labor from the nineteenth to the twentieth century. After the pioneering attempt by onetime Communist Party USA member Mary Inman in her 1940 book *In Woman's Defense* to directly link housework to the production of labor power, the discussion culminated in the 1970s with the so-called domestic labor debate, a multiyear international conversation involving such iconic thinkers as Margaret Benston, Peggy Morton, Pat Mainardi, Sheila Rowbotham, and the theorists of the Wages for Housework movement, most notably Mariarosa Dalla Costa, Selma James, Silvia Federici, and Leopoldina Fortunati. In close vicinity to the debate was a vast constellation of polemical interventions. Drawing mainly from the work of Communist Party USA member and activist Claudia Jones in the late 1940s, Black thinkers like Angela Davis and the members of the Combahee River Collective unearthed the racialized components of reproductive labor while still affirming the political necessity of a socialist analysis of the relations of production. Radical feminists like Shulamith Firestone and Kate Millett who were considerably more suspicious of the Marxist tradition posited patriarchy and capitalism to be parallel systems, but they identified the former as the primary cause of women's oppression.[2]

When the intellectual momentum waned toward the end of the decade, the question of the relationship between housework and capitalism had been posed and probed in the most forceful of ways. Among the positions staked in the debate, the one articulated by Wages for Housework most thoroughly addressed the question of the invisibility of housework from a Marxist analytical perspective while also theorizing, from a militant standpoint, the rise of the housewife as a possible revolutionary subject. Largely indebted to the *operaista* tradition of the 1960s, and in many ways anticipating some of the intuitions of the Autonomia, Wages for Housework was from the beginning a resolutely internationalist political project, but with strong Italian roots.[3]

"Capital," Federici writes in 1975, "has been very successful in hiding our work."[4] The goal, then, was to tear away this veil of invisibility. In rejecting the idea of the housewife as a figurant in the capitalist mode of production, the movement proposed to use the demand for a wage as the fundamental leverage to make housework visible, and consequently to open it up as a terrain of struggle:

> To demand wages for housework does not mean to say that if we are paid we will continue to do it. It means precisely the opposite. To say that we want money for housework is the first step towards refusing to do it, because the demand for a wage makes our work visible, which is the most indispensable condition to begin to struggle against it, both in its immediate aspect as housework and its more insidious character as femininity.[5]

A wage, Federici admonishes, should not be understood as a thing. Rather, "wage" names a relation that opens up the possibility for the articulation of the housewife into a new feminist militant subject, but with an important caveat: struggles in reproduction are different than struggles in the workplace, for in the former, no direct confrontation obtains between capital and labor. In the struggle between labor and capital, wagelessness amounts to political nonexistence.[6]

If capital did well in hiding domestic labor and films, with some notable exceptions, conformed themselves to this obfuscation, then what is needed is a method of analysis adequate to the obstinate marginalization of the figure in question. In a figural reading of the housewife's presence in Italian political cinema, then, we will have to look for her in the interstices of the action, less in what the image declares than in what it represses. Inevitably, the portrayal of this figure will be partial, in the sense of both incomplete and partisan. Like the specter (discussed in chapter 6), the figure of the housewife invents its own form of appearance: omnipresent yet largely unseen, the housewife retreats from the magnifying lens of systematic inquiry and appears always on the brink of vanishing altogether. She is what we might call a receding figure. A certain forcing, then, must take place. In order to wrest the housewife from oblivion's ever-threatening clutches, one needs to take her side, resolutely. In practical terms, this means that one should not be afraid to read the films tendentiously and adopt the partial perspective of this receding figure and of the unseen labor she performs.

Reflecting back on her experience in the Wages for Housework movement, Federici writes in 2000: "Discovering the centrality of reproductive work for capital accumulation also raised the question of what a history of capitalist development would be like if seen not from the viewpoint of the formation of the waged proletariat but from the viewpoint of the kitchens and bedrooms in which labour-power is daily and generationally produced."[7] Indeed, what would that history be like? For its modest part, this chapter looks at cinema from "the viewpoint of the kitchens and bedrooms in which labour-power is daily and generationally produced," and it explores the ways in which the receding figure of the housewife might point to an emergent political subjectivity.

In the attempt to discover the housewife behind the worker, much in the way the Wages for Housework theorists "discovered the home beside the factory,"[8] we will return to *The Working Class Goes to Heaven* (analyzed in chapter 2) and look at it from the perspective of Lidia, Lulù's partner. Before that, however, we will direct our attention to Marco Ferreri's *The Ape Woman* (*La donna scimmia*, 1964). Seemingly removed from the long '68 for chronological and thematic reasons, the film offers a formalization of the relationship between housework and capitalism as well as of the mediating role played by the wage, which implicitly draws from earlier, more celebrated representations of housework in Italian cinema. In this sense, *The Ape Woman* departs from its setting in the immediate aftermath of the Italian economic miracle to establish some coordinates useful in the cinematic thinking of historical crisis via the figure of the housewife that other films will articulate in the 1970s.

The development of this figural thought will be traced across two films: *The Working Class Goes to Heaven*, where the historical possibilities (and limitations) of the housewife coalesce around an act of demanding; and Ettore Scola's neorealist melodrama *A Special Day* (*Una giornata particolare*, 1977), in which the housewife is presented as the agent of a reappropriation of time against the gendered division of labor imposed by capital and enforced by fascism. The chapter concludes with a discussion of the way in which two films have given body to the separation between the housewife and housework: on the one hand, a housewife without housework in Michelangelo Antonioni's *Red Desert* (*Deserto rosso*, 1964); on the other, housework without a housewife in Ferreri's *Dillinger Is Dead* (*Dillinger è morto*, 1969). These two films posit an enigmatic situation in which the condition for a piercing diagnosis of the malaise of contemporary capitalism is the displacement and disintegration, respectively, of the housewife herself.

The Archaic of Reproduction: *The Ape Woman*

The Ape Woman opens with a public event held at a convent in Naples. A missionary priest shows a crowd of paupers a series of slides documenting a recent Catholic apostolate in Africa. Manning the projector is Antonio (Ugo Tognazzi), a small-time wheeler-dealer always on the lookout for opportunities to make money. Perusing the convent's kitchen in search of some free food, Antonio notices a young woman (Annie Girardot) working next to the older cooks, but he can't make out her face. He teases her ("I'll take you to the dance hall"), and when another cook tells him that she's completely covered with hair, he approaches to see her face. After initial resistance, Maria complies with Antonio's request, the camera zooming forward to a close-up of her hairy face. To avoid upsetting her, Antonio feigns indifference ("Here I was thinking I would see something extraordinary [*chissà che cosa*]. . . . Just a little beard, that's all") and sits back at the table to finish his lunch. When one of the cooks further reiterates the peculiarity of Maria's appearance ("She looks like an ape"), Ferreri captures the instant when Antonio realizes that there might a profit to be made from Maria's bizarre appearance. While eating, Tognazzi mimics the facial expression of an ape, the conceit of an ape woman to be exhibited to the public presumably forming in his head.

The sequence hinges on two shots: Maria's first appearance and Antonio's attempts to turn the situation to his favor. In its structuring themes and formal organization, the opening of *The Ape Woman* evokes that of Luchino Visconti's *Ossessione* (1943). Similar to *Ossessione,* Ferreri's film begins by foregrounding domestic labor. In both films, the site of the fateful encounter between the two protagonists is the kitchen. Like Giovanna in *Ossessione* (Clara Calamai), Maria is cooking when she first appears on screen; and like Gino (Massimo Girotti), Antonio happens on the scene of domestic labor only fortuitously, looking for something to eat. Furthermore, money is at the center of both scenes. Before leaving, Gino pays for his meal, but Giovanna pretends with her husband that he did not, which in turn leads to Gino's staying at the roadside tavern and beginning his affair with her. Cesare Casarino has observed that the centrality of money and the money–exchange relation in the scene is conveyed by a close-up of Gino as he flips a coin, his face (which we first see a long four minutes into the film) "split and scarred by money."[9] In Ferreri, money does not attain the same level of visibility, yet it is conjured in the close-up of the scheming Antonio. The two sequences mirror each other. The deferred revelation of Maria's and Gino's faces occurs with the same zoom forward; Antonio's calculating stare evokes Giovanna's triumphant countenance when her plan to keep Gino at the tavern proves successful, while their respective protagonists remain unaware of their scheming (Figure 10).

Figure 10. First encounters in the kitchen, with Maria and Antonio from *The Ape Woman* (1964) and Gino and Giovanna from *Ossessione* (1943).

These chiastic pairings, however, signal an inversion of gendered roles. In *Ossessione*, it is the housewife who is looking to exploit any opportunity to abandon the unbearable drudgery of domestic life, including seducing the handsome newcomer. In *The Ape Woman*, however, it is Antonio who involves the domestic laborer in his devious scheme. In this inversion, the male protagonists find themselves in opposite positions, highlighting their own internal contradictions: in Visconti, a thief and trespasser willing to abide by the social rules of money exchange ("I can pay," he assures Giovanna); in Ferreri, a self-styled entrepreneur talking his way into stealing a meal.

Although the encounter between the protagonists occurs in the same space (the kitchen), the sites where the kitchens are located differ markedly. The encounter between Gino and Giovanna in *Ossessione* takes place at the roadside tavern, where, as Giuliana Minghelli has argued, the intricate web of relations that define capitalism under fascism (money exchange, private property, patriarchal discipline) is put on display.[10] In *The Ape Woman*, the convent's kitchen constitutes an archaic, precapitalist enclave in the immediate aftermath of the economic boom. As such, the convent functions according to different principles than the tavern. Unlike Giovanna's domestic labor, Maria's is detached from any logic of monetary compensation. This difference measures the distance between the two houseworkers. Giovanna longs to relinquish the role of housewife but finds herself chained to it, as she cannot bring herself to let go of the tavern once her husband is out of the picture. Maria performs domestic labor in the convent but is not, strictly speaking, a housewife. In fact, she exists completely outside the capitalist relation of production (and reproduction: she serves meals to the paupers and unemployed) and is only interpellated as a subject of that system by Antonio.

In Antonio's interpellation, emancipation and subjection find themselves intertwined. He promises normality as emancipation ("Wouldn't you like to go out, to be like everybody else?"), but this emancipation takes the form of the ruthless exploitation and commodification of Maria's body. Formally, the film frames the moment with a certain irony. When Antonio seems to have persuaded Maria to leave the convent and follow him into the outside world, the circus music–like theme that will accompany Maria's performances until her death (and beyond) can be heard, providing an implicitly scathing commentary on the duplicitousness of Antonio's intentions.

In opposition to Giovanna in *Ossessione,* Maria's struggle is, in fact, to *become* a housewife—that is, to attain a defined social position, however marginal. While Ferreri is more interested in the grotesque lengths Antonio goes to in order to exploit Maria's unusual appearance, the film is also punctuated by brief vignettes of housework that delineate Maria's almost clandestine attempt at domestic normalcy. While Antonio waxes visionary on the financial opportunities of her exploitation, Maria is busy cooking, making coffee, and cleaning the apartment. She demands that conjugal roles be respected in the bedroom as well. Ultimately, she seems to find her own realization at the prospect of becoming a mother, thus fulfilling the set of requirements for the role she thinks she has been called on to assume.

This social desire to become a housewife, coming on the heels of an economic boom, has specific historical coordinates. While in the early and mid-1960s domestic labor had not yet been identified as a possible terrain of emancipatory struggle (in this sense, *Ossessione* is ahead of its time), one finds in *The Ape Woman* the statement, at the very least, that not only does housework exist, but it also assigns the domestic laborer a certain socially determined position whose name is "housewife." The housewife position, Ferreri suggests, may be associated with a certain antagonistic impulse, however rudimentary its form. As in *Ossessione,* in *The Ape Woman* the housewife emerges as a figure of conflict against the status quo—of fascist society in the former and postboom Italy in the latter. In Ferreri, the figure of the housewife emerges in intaglio in the tension between the slave-like commodification of the female body imposed by Antonio and the semblance of domesticity Maria strives to create. This tension traverses the film, reaching a breaking point in the wedding scene, where Antonio makes a publicity stunt of the ceremony by having a reluctant Maria sing a song as an amused crowd cheers them along.

The absence of money exchange in the form of the wage relation forces Maria into a quandary that straddles questions of political economy and subjective ontology. Drawing from Marx, Federici highlights the role of the wage relation in separating laborers from their labor power as a commodity that can be bought and sold:

> To have a wage means to be part of a social contract, and there is no doubt concerning its meaning: you work, not because you like it, or because it comes naturally to you, but because it is the only condition under which you are allowed to live. But exploited as you might be, you are not that work. Today you are a postman, tomorrow a cabdriver. All that matters is how much of that work you have to do and how much of that money you can get.[11]

In the first part of the film, Maria *is* her work. She is not selling her labor power as a commodity she owns; rather, she herself is sold as a commodity. Her place in the social contract is entirely determined by her appearance and the possibility it offers to be capitalized on as a circus attraction and object of sexual trafficking. As a consequence, her deformity comes to define her absolutely—a verdict that she fights through her dedication to domestic labor. Ferreri, however, is careful not to pin the moral blame of Maria's predicament exclusively on Antonio's supposedly innate deviousness. Rather, the film frames Maria's position as the effect of the capitalist logic at work, of which Antonio is but a bearer, to borrow Marx's famous formulation. In fact, Ferreri depicts Antonio's relation to Maria and her deformity in ambiguous terms. Even in their first encounter, his reaction to Maria's shame is to reassure her by downplaying her appearance. He then grows to love her and is obviously pained by her and their child's untimely demise. In any event, any attempt at a psychologization of the character is quickly rebuffed by Ferreri. In the film's ending, the capitalist drive to accumulate through exploitation reasserts itself in no uncertain terms, superseding any moral considerations.

It is in this context that the multiple references to Italy's colonialist past in Africa disseminated throughout the film should be situated. Already suggested in the opening by the images of the Catholic apostolate, the idea of colonialism permeates the film.

The very conceit of an ape woman captured in the heart of the African continent stems from the overtly racist fantasy of the colonized as an uncivilized, subhuman species. Antonio uses it to exoticize Maria's medical condition (Maria's mysterious origins are, of course, a ruse; abandoned by her mother, she grew up in the convent). While Maria engages in housework to provide a semblance of domesticity to her condition, Antonio embraces the stage role of the intrepid explorer roaming perilous uncharted territory. These are opposite and equally mystifying fantasies. They serve as disguises, one grounded in the normalcy of the domestic space and the other in the exceptionality of the exotic adventure, concealing the relationship of ruthless exploitation that exists between the two protagonists.[12]

The terms of this colonialist fantasy are altered in the second part of the film, after Antonio and Maria sign a contract to perform at a nightclub in Paris. The two reprise their roles as explorer and ape woman, but their new act stages a reversal. After killing Maria's father (a stuffed chimpanzee), Antonio is sexually teased by her. Reluctant at first, Antonio lets himself be seduced by his supposed prey, who ultimately steals his gun and kills him with a shot to the head. In this performance, Maria's body is exceedingly sexualized. She wears only a see-through organza dress, and her facial hair is covered in glitter. Her seductive dancing and coquetry prove too much for the explorer to resist. Yet her deformity is equally exaggerated, absorbed into the fictionality of the stage setting as one prop among others.

Her performance, in this sense, assumes the traits of a masquerade. As Mary Ann Doane argues in a landmark essay on feminist film theory, the masquerade may function as a distancing device for the feminine subject. By overemphasizing womanliness, the masquerade reifies it into a facade "which can be worn and removed," thus opening up the possibility of breaking down ossified patterns of gendered identification.[13] In this sense, the mask separates Maria from herself. If in Antonio's circus act her being was reduced to her commodified deformity, now the glamorized flaunting of that same deformity allows her to find some distance from it. This is also reflected in the schematic narrative of the striptease. Once a trophy animal to be exhibited, Maria now plays a role more akin to femme fatale, with agency shifting from colonialist explorer to exotic temptress.

This reversal of the colonialist plot is more than a simple revenge fantasy. It is grounded in the changed material conditions defining Maria's relation to her labor. Maria's nightclub performance implicitly introduces the mediation of wage between the worker and labor power—here in the form of the contract signed with the impresario. It is not, however, the content of the show that somehow expresses the wage relation but rather its form. Maria's masquerade—the performative separation between herself and her identity as a curiosity—is made possible by the mediation of wage, for now she is paid to don the mask of the ape woman without having to be one.

Even in this changed situation, Maria holds on to her housewife role. Right before relocating to Paris, Maria tells Antonio that she is "a little sad, leaving the apartment like that, now that it's all renovated (*sistemata*)." In Maria's fantasy, the home is glorified as a private space of authenticity, separate from the public sphere where her deformity is exhibited. With the pregnancy, the contradictions of this fantasy are laid bare. Maria has prepared lunch, and as they sit at the table to eat, Antonio first complains that he doesn't like what she cooked, then makes a nonchalant remark about the child's being a great investment ("You, the kid . . . we'll make a lot of money"). In a stark illustration of a housewife's rebellion, an infuriated Maria throws a plate of spaghetti at him. The untenability of the idea of a neat separation between public and private life becomes evident. Maria's dream of a normal family life is shattered by Antonio's call to put that very familial domesticity on public display. One is reminded of Juliet Mitchell's forceful critique of the family as a sanctuary of intimacy: "The belief that the family provides an impregnable enclave of intimacy and security in an atomized and chaotic cosmos assumes the absurd—that the family can be isolated from the community, and that its internal relationships will not reproduce in their own terms the external relationships which dominate the society. The family as a refuge from society in fact becomes a reflection of it."[14] The absurdity described by Mitchell of a clear-cut separation between family and society comes to the fore in the film's ending. The death of Maria and the unborn child allows Antonio to finally realize his vision. Embalmed together, the mother and son are featured in a touring freak show, the extraction of value from their deformity continuing unabated even after their untimely demise. Again, this should not be taken solely as Ferreri's moral indictment of Antonio's deviousness. Rather, it is a perfect demonstration of capitalist logic at work. Antonio's resigned demeanor at the opening of the performance highlights the inevitability of this conclusion. The dictates of capitalist accumulation, evident here in the abject form of the desecration of corpses, pierce through any fantasy of separation of the familial from the social, or the private from the public.

A "Practice of Demand:" *The Working Class Goes to Heaven*

The reverberation of the capitalist relation in the private sphere of the family is also at the center of the relationship between Lidia and Lulù in *The Working Class Goes to Heaven*. The character of Lidia in Petri's film maintains an intermittent presence throughout, always appearing in an ancillary position to Lulù's existential crisis. She complains about their sex life but then briefly provides affective care for him when he laments the tense situation with his colleagues at the factory. She also complains about housework: she repeatedly suggests that Lulù not use the living room because then she would have to clean it up. Yet the exchanges between the two always appear out of synch, as though they were engaged in two separate conversations. This disconnect culminates in a gesture of unexpected domestic violence: Lulù's threatening to stab Lidia with a fork at the dinner table.

At one point in the film, Lidia comes home after work to find Lulù with a group of students who need a hideout after the riot at the factory gates. Visibly flustered by the invasion, Lidia is greeted with a request for food; the guests have immediately identified her as a housewife. The exchange between Lidia and the unwelcomed guests quickly turns political, with Lidia harshly addressing the students and reclaiming her role of waged worker: "What would you be without the *padroni,* a deadbeat [*morto di fame*]. . . . I'll never be a communist! Never! I am for freedom! . . . And I like mink, and one day I'll have it because I deserve it, you understand? Because

I work! I've worked since I was twelve and I deserve it because I'm good [brava]."

The students launch into a pedestrian ideological analysis of Lidia's position, accusing her of wanting to emulate her own exploiters by adhering to models propagandized by television. What is remarkable, however, is the sense that Petri is siding with Lidia in this particular instance. This reading is articulated on two levels. First, Petri thematizes the pervasiveness of ideology, then implicitly derides the students' illusion of being able to exist outside of it. The supposed source of indoctrination—the TV screen—is prominently displayed across the entire scene, casting its bluish light indiscriminately on Lulù, Lidia, and the young Arturo, as well as on the students themselves. This suggests that all the characters (worker, housewife, youth) participate in the same totality and are equally—if in different guises—affected by this totality's ideological formations.[15] The students correctly detect the role played by media propaganda in the reproduction of the existing structure, but they fail to understand the implications of its pervasiveness. In this sense, the home cannot be completely separated from the factory or the university. Again, we see an artificial distinction between the public and the private collapse.

However, on another level, beyond the smoke screen of her false consciousness, Lidia expresses something else: she wants a mink coat. This is not a need, but a desire. The superfluousness of the object (the mink coat as the epitome of aspirational luxury for the working-class housewife), coupled with the clarity of her demand, inform a further dimension of the character while implicitly denouncing the dead ends of left-wing asceticism. The students' mockery of Lidia illustrates in a nutshell what Dalla Costa calls "the 'political' attack against women." Isolated and invisible, the housewife, argues Dalla Costa, often compensates for her exclusion from socially organized labor by purchasing things—a behavior that prompts accusations from her male counterparts of fomenting divisions within the working class. Of course, "the idea that frugal consumption is in any way a liberation is as old as capitalism, and comes from the capitalists who always blame the worker's situation on the worker."[16] Thus, when observed from the viewpoint of the housewife, the scene in *The Working Class Goes to Heaven* reverses: the students, who accuse Lidia of wanting to emulate her exploiters, are in fact the ones parroting the capitalist with their moralistic call for asceticism. Lidia is identified as the bearer of a desire—one that all but loses its political significance if simplistically reduced to its object.

To better understand the import of this affirmation of desire in the film, it is useful to look at what Kathi Weeks terms a "practice of demand," a political perspective whose genealogy she traces back to Wages for Housework. For Weeks, the practice of demand functions as a subjectivizing moment. It entails a request—wages for domestic labor—whose legitimacy cannot be recovered from any objectively existing situation but originates purely from a subjective "statement of desire."[17] This statement introduces a cut in the existing symbolic order in that it interrupts the logic governing the status quo that adjudicates which desires are trivial and which are not. It is around this cut, this fissure introduced by the demand, that a new political subjectivity may come into being.

In the context of Wages for Housework, this subjectivation has two intertwined aspects: an ideological one, in which a critical understanding of one's own position within the capitalist relation of production is gained,[18] and a militant one, with the formation of radical collectivities capable of meeting the level of class struggle imposed by capital. The demand of Wages for Housework as a perspective "functioned to produce the feminist knowledge and consciousness that it appears to presuppose; as a provocation, it served also to elicit the subversive commitments, collective formations, and political hopes that it appears only to reflect."[19] So in a way, subjectivity comes into being as the attempt to catch up with the radicality of a founding gesture of demand. It is important to emphasize that it is a mere attempt, meaning that there is nothing in the existing state of things that guarantees a successful revolutionary outcome of the process of subjectivation. In this sense, the practice of demand always presents itself as "a risk, a gamble, the success of which depends on the power that the struggle for it can generate."[20]

The collective demand for wages for domestic labor and the individual expression of a desire for a mink coat have, of course, vastly different political scopes and imports. The motives underpinning

Lidia's stance remain trapped within a logic of meritocracy and recognition (she deserves the mink coat because she was "good") that tempers the autonomy of her demand. The Wages for Housework theorists recognized early on the limitations of such a logic. In the groundbreaking essay "Counterplanning from the Kitchen" (1975), Silvia Federici and Nicole Cox argue that the demands of the housewife were never about the recognition of their efforts and sacrifices: "Our power does not come from anyone's recognition of our place in the cycle of production, but from our capacity to struggle against it."[21] Lidia presents her demand as justified on the basis of external recognition (of the *padroni,* of capitalist society), while her anticommunist vitriol and ideological investment in freedom further obfuscate the subversive potential of her statement of desire.

What should not be ignored, however, is the fact that such a statement exists at all. If, as I have argued, the housewife in Italian political cinema (and cinema in general) is by and large a receding figure, then the limits of one's own reading practice must be pushed in order not only to account for the marginal and fragmentary nature of the housewife's manifestations, but also to detect the potentialities to which this figure gestures, however obliquely. Lidia's outburst in *The Working Class Goes to Heaven* is one such manifestation. It occupies a decentered position with respect to the main story arc, and it could easily be dismissed as a pure ventriloquizing of the dominant ideology. Yet one can recover in Lidia's peroration the presence, however feeble, of an affirmation of autonomy, for her statement of desire explicitly exists without any recognition from Lulù. It is telling, in this sense, that the scene ends with Lidia abandoning the apartment with Arturo while Lulù tries to calm her down by promising that he would grant her wish ("I'll get you the mink"). Lulù misses the point, of course. Lidia is not asking him for permission to make the purchase; nor is she angling for a gift. Her decision to leave the apartment can be read in a similar light: a refusal to participate in a domestic sphere in which her desires and aspirations, however petty bourgeois they might be, are repeatedly stifled. Indeed, Lidia's misguided defense of the *padroni* may be read as the perverse effect of the modicum of freedom afforded to the housewife by waged labor as, quite simply, time away from the prison of housework.

Centering precisely on the question of time, *A Special Day* explores on a considerably larger scale some of the potentialities and deadlocks alluded to in *The Working Class Goes to Heaven*.

The Houseworking Day: *A Special Day*

On May 6, 1938, Hitler is received in Rome by Mussolini for a state visit that culminates in a military parade. Antonietta (Sophia Loren), a housewife and mother of six, is left home alone when her husband Emanuele (John Vernon), a vulgar man and fervent fascist, takes the children to the parade. The large residential complex empties out, except for a nosy building manager (Françoise Berd) and Gabriele (Marcello Mastroianni), a recently fired radio announcer awaiting deportation to Sardinia as a result of his homosexuality. Antonietta and Gabriele meet fortuitously when her pet myna escapes from its cage and lands near his apartment window, just as he is contemplating suicide to avoid being deported. After some initial diffidence, the two grow closer. Unaware of Gabriele's sexual orientation, Antonietta flirts with him as he teaches her to dance a rumba. However, when he reveals first his antifascist sentiments and then, in a tense confrontation, his homosexuality, Antonietta is taken aback, her foundational beliefs in the virtuousness of the fascist regime shaken. After a moment of reconciliation and just before Antonietta's family returns home, the two have sex. At nightfall, taking a rare moment for herself, she begins reading a copy of *The Three Musketeers* that Gabriele gave her, then looks on from her window as he is taken away by fascist officials. She is then called to bed by Emanuele, who wants to have a seventh child to qualify for the regime's financial aid for large families. The child's name, he announces, will be Adolfo.

A Special Day is the story of an encounter unfolding in accordance to a peculiar, even contradictory, temporality. For a housewife, a "special day" starts just like any other day. Antonietta is already up when we first meet her, ironing clothes and making coffee before waking up her children and husband, directing access to the bathroom, and washing the youngest in the kitchen sink in a series of automatic gestures impressed in her mind and body by endless repetition. Scola captures this routine with an elaborate long take that begins with a pan showing the tenants in the residential complex starting their day. The camera enters Antonietta's apartment from the window, following her through the various rooms. Thus, from the very beginning, the time of the housewife is presented as a time of repetition without cut or interruption. The various actions that make up Antonietta's daily drudgery bleed into one another, with domestic labor becoming one long, sweeping, endless gesture.

Yet this *is* a special day, not just because of Hitler's historic visit presaging the signing of the Pact of Steel a year later, but because of the radical break that the encounter with Gabriele will introduce in Antonietta's life. Scola foreshadows this break in two seemingly irrelevant occurrences, which are almost hidden in the opening scene. Antonietta inadvertently bumps her head on the kitchen lamp, twice, which causes a minor interruption in her tedious activity. Then, on her way to the master bedroom, she furtively sips her husband's coffee, and, when he complains, she lies to him ("I made you a *ristretto*"). The lamp and the coffee will return later as markers of the proximity between the two protagonists (Gabriele will fix the sliding lamp for her and offer to grind the coffee). In the context of the long take, they signal, respectively, an unexpected obstacle that hinders her housework routine, giving her pause, if only for a moment; and a nascent desire for emancipation in the form of reappropriation: she is the one who woke up early to make the coffee, so she deserves to drink it first. These two seemingly contradictory temporalities—the repetition of the same as the eternal law of housework and the singular, contingent occurrences that trouble that repetition—are put by the film in a dialectical tension with the figure of the housewife at its center.

Right after Emanuele and the children leave, Antonietta stares at the empty complex from her window, and, as she resumes her domestic routine, pokes fun at the syrupy Italian motto, *"Di mamma ce n'è una sola"* (There's only one mom), with a properly materialist retort: "Here we would need at least three. One cleans the rooms, the other takes care of the kitchen, and the third, which would be me, goes to bed and sleeps." After cleaning up the kitchen table with methodical, efficient gestures, her gaze inadvertently rests on a comic magazine lying on the floor. As she absent-mindedly starts to read about fascist action hero Dick Fulmine's exploits in the Land of the Pigmies, she falls asleep, only to be awakened by the myna calling her name. Scola's explicit referent here is *Ossessione*, specifically the scene in which Giovanna, exhausted after a day of hard work at the tavern, falls asleep while reading a newspaper, surrounded by piles of dirty dishes (Figure 11).

Cesare Casarino has noted that "Giovanna is not tired. She is exhausted. This whole sequence expresses exhaustion," and reads her predicament, with Deleuze, as that "of someone who has exhausted all of the possible, of someone who can no longer even imagine any possibility."[22] We can perhaps also recognize Antonietta in this description. As with Giovanna, the dirty dishes that

Figure 11. Exhausted housewives Antonietta and Giovanna in *A Special Day* (1977) and *Ossessione* (1943).

surround her are "veritable monuments to housework past and housework to come," the tangible expression of the endless temporality of repetition associated with domestic labor.[23] Casarino goes on to compare the depiction of housework in *Ossessione* to that of a film at the opposite chronological end of neorealism: the celebrated scene of Maria's morning routine in Vittorio De Sica's *Umberto D.* (1952). Casarino argues that although Maria, like Giovanna, may have "exhausted all of the possible," she is the bearer of a different philosophical lesson than Visconti's heroine. Maria's gesture of stretching out her foot to close the kitchen door is read by Casarino as an affirmation of potential itself in the face of the exhaustion of possibility: "*Can she do it?* . . . Somehow, over and beyond all, possibility, she still has it in her to seek and express sheer potential, with no external goal or signification."[24]

Both *Ossessione* and *Umberto D.* are evident points of reference for *A Special Day*. Scola's film claims its own kinship to them not only by way of a series of affectionate homages but also through an attempt at replicating the peculiar temporality of housework that these films first made visible in cinema. With a particularly felicitous expression, the film has been called the "untimely offshoot of Neorealism."[25] While Scola's profound admiration for neorealism is on full display in *A Special Day*, it is this untimeliness that must be interrogated. What does it mean to make a neorealist film in 1977? What kind of contemporary political fault lines can be made visible by resurrecting and simultaneously displacing an idea of cinema that belonged to a different historical sequence? What exactly does this afterlife of neorealism make possible at the level of thought in the long '68?

Casarino hints at these questions by looking at them from the angle of historical causality. In his reading, the occurrence of neorealism in the postwar period is partly responsible for making possible the rise of a new political thought later on: "I am suggesting . . . that neorealist cinema and its preoccupation with domestic labor constitutes an integral part of the cultural and historical conditions of possibility of Marxist-feminist understandings of housework—and, in particular, of the Wages for Housework movement—in Italy in the 1970s."[26] Casarino does not further elaborate his position, but from a cultural and historical standpoint, one would be hard pressed to disprove its accuracy. Yet the avowed untimeliness of *A Special Day* compels us to adopt a different perspective. The "conditions of possibility" established by neorealism come to fruition not only with Wages for Housework but also with Scola's film—that is, within cinema itself, and with the way in which cinema thinks the time of crisis of the 1970s by way of the figure of the housewife.

As theorists in the Wages for Housework movement have repeatedly pointed out, at the center of this question of housework and subjectivity stands time. Indeed, one of their most striking conceptual gambits was that of subordinating the question of time to the question of subjectivity. Drawing in part from Marx's analysis of labor-time in *Capital,* the theorists of the movement understood time as a fundamental terrain of political struggle onto which a process of subjectivation could be articulated, specifically around the question of the working day. In the most substantial critique of the Marxian concept of reproduction articulated within the movement, Leopoldina Fortunati links the rise of a "new working figure" with a change in the way capital organizes time. She argues that capital has progressively shifted from "a houseworking day posited as an extension of the factory working day, to a houseworking day characterized by the fact that it has no limit other than the duration of the day itself. Thus a new working figure is born, the housewife."[27] The rise of this "new working figure," then, is inseparable from a specific, materially determined appearance of time as a working day without limits if not those of the day itself, over which capital has no power.

What we are given to see in Scola's "untimely offshoot of Neorealism," then—the very substance of its untimeliness—is the housewife as a new working figure whose primary terrain of struggle is time. As closely related to her forebears as she is, Antonietta undergoes a process denied to Giovanna and Maria. Where domestic labor in *Ossessione* and *Umberto D.* gave rise to an exhaustion of possibility that, at least in the latter, still affirmed the pure potentiality of time, in *A Special Day,* time assumes the specifically capitalist form of the houseworking day, but redoubled into a special day. On the one hand is the drudgery of a routine that repeats itself day in and day out; on the other is the absolute singularity and contingency of an encounter that, in a dialectical turn, reveals the point where a subjectivation of the housewife can take place. Mediating the two temporalities is the state, with a national holiday that pretends to interrupt the daily routine of labor, but manages to interrupt nothing at all, especially for those left at home.

For Antonietta, exhaustion marks the point of a specific impasse in the capitalist relation of production. No longer a closure of the horizon of possibility, as it was in Visconti and De Sica, in *A Special Day,* exhaustion indicates a point of impossibility. It constitutes the material effect of an irreducible split inherent to capital—namely, that of the gendered division of labor. As we have seen in chapter 2, the exhaustion of the male factory worker derives from the split at the heart of labor power that the capitalist exploits to the limit. The exhaustion of the housewife derives instead from the gendered division between productive and reproductive labor. This gendered division presents itself as follows: on the side of productive labor, there is wage labor performed within the fixed temporal limits of the working day by a male laborer at the workplace; on the side of unproductive labor, there is unpaid domestic labor performed without fixed temporal limits by a female houseworker at home.[28]

This split is also exploited by capital. In order to keep housework unpaid, capital engages in an operation of mystification by projecting an opposition between two kinds of labor: productive labor performed by the male worker at the factory as abstract, socially necessary, and simple; and reproductive labor performed by the housewife as concrete, individually necessary, and complex. However, as Fortunati observes in an illuminating passage, "Capital can only posit housework as abstract, . . . socially necessary and simple labor to the degree that it represents itself as concrete, individually necessary, and complex."[29] In other words, the condition for capital to be able to control and exploit labor power in the home as if it were in a factory is to make that labor appear as its opposite—that is, totally heterogeneous, even antithetical—to the labor that occurs in the sphere of production.

This contradiction points us directly toward the question of political subjectivity, for casting the housewife outside of the capitalist relation of production drastically limits her space for struggle. The creation of a space seemingly outside of the capitalist relation mystifies reproductive labor as an act of love and familial care. Indeed, the antidote concocted by capital to the dehumanizing exploitation of the worker on the shop floor is the humanist ideology that celebrates "the family as a 'private world,' the last frontier where men and women 'keep [their] souls alive,'" which in turn conceals the equally brutal exploitation that occurs behind the closed doors of the home.[30]

Antonietta's exhaustion in *A Special Day* marks the manifestation of this contradiction as a limit point of impossibility, whereby housework finally appears as two opposite and incompatible types of labor at once: concrete, individually necessary, and motivated by a dedication to the family, but also abstract, socially necessary, and exploited. The housewife's exhaustion is caused by the former (no one punches a time clock for performing acts of love), but it is revealing of the latter (exhaustion is a function of her exploitation). This is the housewife's impasse. She is situated at the intersection of the material conditions that determine the form and temporality of her labor, and the ideological structure that reproduces these conditions by concealing them.

The little fascist scrapbook that Antonietta puts together, which Gabriele amusedly peruses, captures this impasse. On the one hand, there is the mystification of the gendered division of labor as a natural fact, with the enshrinement of Mussolinian clichés like "fascist women, you must be the angels in the house" and "man is not man if he is not husband, father, soldier." On the other hand, there is a subtle hint at the socioeconomic structure underpinning this division of labor; consider the picture of Mussolini shaking hands with FIAT founder and senator Giovanni Agnelli, which symbolizes the alliance between fascism and industrial capital. The contradiction between this partnership and the populism of some of the fascist slogans collected in the scrapbook is lost on Antonietta, but even as she cannot quite conceptualize yet the source of her discontent, she is forced to confront the impossibility of her position, first inchoately, through exhaustion, and then, more poignantly, through her encounter with Gabriele.

With his quiet charm and gentle irony, the queer presence of Gabriele functions as an agent of disturbance that scrambles the frequencies of fascist propaganda—both metaphorically and literally, as he often talks over the omnipresent radio announcer's voice chronicling the military parade. When Antonietta invites him to sit at the dining table, because "the kitchen is not a man's place," he replies that he's used to it because he is a bachelor; and when they are folding the laundry on the rooftop, he declares that he "always helped at home." But one particular exchange crystallizes Gabriele's subversive effect on Antonietta. It is worth looking at in detail. Gabriele reads aloud from the scrapbook: "Incompatible with the physiology and psychology of the female, genius is strictly masculine." Then he asks her, point-blank, "Do you agree?" Antonietta mechanically feigns certainty ("Of course I agree. Why?"), but Loren's acting reveals an infinitesimal crack in her character's fascist facade. She immediately stops smiling, taken aback by Gabriele's question as though nobody has ever asked her, in her entire life, what she thought. Even when she answers, her eyes turn inquisitive, seemingly looking for confirmation that that is indeed the correct answer. Even her retort ("It is always men who fill up the history books, no?") is made to seem less motivated by true conviction than a desire to assuage a certain anxiety. Gabriele's reply ("Yes, maybe even too much, so that here's no room for anyone else. Least of all women") gives her pause as she stares into the void, thinking. Her troubled demeanor is further accentuated after Gabriele talks to her about his mother, who defied many of the gender roles of the era by becoming the head of the family after her husband left. A subtle formal choice by Scola highlights the significance of the moment (Figure 12). The close-up of Antonietta that concludes the scene is visibly closer than any other in the conversation. It magnifies her anxiety as she stares into space with her hands clasped, clearly pondering with alarm the sudden manifestation of a fracture in her perception of the world.

Troubled by Gabriele's queerness, the "natural" nonrelation between production and reproduction now finds itself denaturalized and exposed as a fundamental contradiction. Suddenly the unthinkable destruction of the gendered division of labor is "placed in the position of possibility."[31]

As mentioned above, the construction of the figure of the housewife in *A Special Day* has time as its pivot. Early in the film,

Figure 12. Antonietta thinks about her own condition of oppression and exploitation in *A Special Day* (1977).

there never seems to be enough of it. During their first encounter in Gabriele's apartment, Antonietta is reluctant to stay for coffee because she has to get back to her routine. When she does, she sets her alarm to go off every hour so she can get a more accurate measure of the time she has left for domestic labor. Gabriele, for his part, repeatedly glances at his wristwatch, counting the hours that separate him from deportation; and when he repeatedly offers Antonietta a copy of *The Three Musketeers* as a gift, she replies that as much as she would love to read it, she surely won't have the time.

But then something changes. Antonietta reappropriates time from her domestic duties to be with Gabriele. On the rooftop, her domestic labor is again interrupted by Gabriele's presence, until she stops folding laundry altogether and declares her infatuation to him. This is a first, misguided attempt to respond to the impossibility with which Gabriele confronts her, a clumsy gesture of refusal of her own condition. The inadequacy of this response derives not only from her inability (and unwillingness) to see Gabriele's homosexuality, but also, and more importantly, from the fundamental acceptance and perpetuation of the status quo that it implies. This is the meaning of Gabriele's harsh dismissal of her, delivered as they hastily descend the stairs to Antonietta's apartment: "What were you hoping for? Kisses? Love bites? My hands up your dress? . . . Is that what a man does when he's alone with a woman? . . . You're just an ignorant little housewife in heat, but oh so very proper! One of those who say 'It was a moment of weakness, what must you think of me?' Prepared to be fucked on the rooftop, but ready to judge and condemn." With his invective, Gabriele exposes Antonietta's desire as a mere fantasy of transgression—a "moment of weakness" that in no way challenges the dictates of fascist society and that in fact reaffirms them absolutely. The desire of the fascist subject, Gabriele indicates, is predicated on the interplay between fantasies of transgression and petty bourgeois ideals of respectability and decorum.

Transgression possesses its own temporality. It is that of the punctiform occurrence, the exception that leaves the rule untouched. As such, the scene on the rooftop hardly qualifies as a fundamental subjective turn for Antonietta, but it does mark the beginning of her tentative experimentation with the temporality of subjectivation. This process, whose seed had been planted in scrapbook scene discussed earlier, receives further articulation in Antonietta's last encounter with Gabriele. The scene's prelude is another interruption of housework where Antonietta, shaken by Gabriele's exacting words, reluctantly makes the bed and cleans off the table, only to then show up again at his doorstep to apologize. The two have lunch together, and she describes the profound misery of her life as a homemaker: "There are a lot of times when I feel humiliated too, treated like a nobody. My husband doesn't talk to me, he orders me around, day and night." After the two have sex, Gabriele somberly remarks, "It was nice, but doesn't change anything." What matters to him, he explains, is their encounter, the time they spent together on this special day. This is the temporality of a process made up of a succession of occurrences (departures and returns, misunderstandings and reconciliations) that, unlike the punctiform appearance of transgression, extends through time. The effects of this process are asymmetrical. For Gabriele, whose destiny is already decided, it provides temporary solace at a difficult time. For Antonietta, it opens the possibility of a different conception of time altogether: a time for herself. The remarkable redoubling of a previous shot during their last good-bye suggests as much (Figure 13). In the first iteration on the rooftop, the two uneasily embrace in depth of field, surrounded by hanging white sheets; in the second, the laundry has disappeared and with it, if only for a moment, the prison of domestic labor.

Immediately on her family's return, Emanuele scolds Antonietta for neglecting the housework, to which she finds the courage to retort, "Wasn't it national holiday for everybody today?" After Emanuele's crass reply ("But you stayed home, in bed"), Scola slowly zooms in on Antonietta, who reciprocates the gaze of the camera.[32] As the fourth wall breaks, she isolates herself from the babbling about fascism's radiant future that surrounds her at the dinner table, remaining faithful to her encounter with the impasse, the impossible turned possible of the recognition and refusal of her own oppressed condition.

The reappropriation of time that has so far characterized this encounter culminates in Antonietta's quiet defiance of Emanuele's request to immediately come to bed. Instead, after washing

Figure 13. Antonietta and Gabriele share a moment on the rooftop, then in his apartment, in *A Special Day* (1977).

the dishes, she sits by the kitchen window—with a view of Gabriele's apartment—and starts reading *The Three Musketeers* aloud. It is, of course, an effusively melodramatic moment of nostalgia for a love without a future. But it also signals a shift in the figure of the housewife. Antonietta carves out from her routine a time that did not exist before. This is a courageous gesture of revolt, a blind wager performed in the absence of any inkling of what it might bring about. Antonietta's nascent antagonism toward the established rules of gender inequality is suggested by the film's use of sound. As Gabriele is taken away to Sardinia, one of the fascist songs heard during the day resonates extradiegetically in the background. A simple piano tune initially follows the melody of the chant but then begins to drift away, all but drowning it out. The piano motif finally lands on a rudimentary rendition of *Aranci* by Daniele Serra—the rumba that Antonietta and Gabriele danced to earlier in the film, and that was itself made inaudible by the radio chronicle of the military parade. The auditory counterpoint between the two melodies and the final overpowering of the fascist song by the rumba formalize Antonietta's process of subjectivation: a dull acceptance of the status quo traverses a moment of discrepancy and as a result divides into two, giving rise to an antagonism between fascist oppression and exploitation on the one hand, and a tentative subjective thrust toward emancipation on the other.

The film, however, ends on an ambiguous note. A long take, mirroring the one we saw in the film's opening, follows Antonietta as she turns off the lights and goes to bed. The last shot of the film shows her bedside table, with the alarm clock—the one that partitioned her day in one-hour intervals—prominently displayed. Does this announce Antonietta's forthcoming return to her daily drudgery, as if nothing happened? Or is it simply a reminder that the objective conditions within which her subjectivity arose have not simply ceased to exist? The uncertainty remains. Perhaps a better question to ask about the conclusion of Antonietta's arc in *A Special Day* is the one Casarino formulated about Maria in *Umberto D.*: "Can she do it?"—not, however, in the sense of an affirmation of the pure potentiality of time, as it is for Casarino, but rather as a question about the subject's ability to sustain herself through her desire. Can she do it? Can Antonietta keep alive the subjective process opened up by her encounter with Gabriele, or will she be crushed by the status quo of gender inequality, of which Emanuele is but one enforcer?

"The real," writes Badiou, "is what the subject encounters, as its chance, its cause, and its consistency."[33] The figure of the housewife in *A Special Day* provides us with a way to think the relation between this real and the subject. Unannounced and enigmatic, the real irrupts in Antonietta's life precisely as a chance encounter that pierces through the repetitive temporality of housework. The real is also the cause of the rise of a new subject. It is in relation to this unsettling real that a form of subjective antagonism against one's own structural situation can emerge; after all, is not the myna calling Antonietta's name before instigating her encounter with Gabriele an apt metaphor for this interpellation of the real? Last is the issue of consistency. Can the real of this special day provide enough of an anchoring for the subject to sustain herself through her struggle? Can she do it? This is the question Scola leaves us with.

A Housewife without Housework: *Red Desert*

It seems significant that in order to pose the question of the housewife as a figure of struggle, Scola opted to return to the late 1930s. In this sense, *A Special Day* feels like a tactical retreat into a past that is perhaps best suited to clear-cut depictions of everyday oppression and exploitation, with the intertwined authoritarianisms of patriarchy and fascism as the obvious foils of Antonietta's nascent subjectivity. Yet Scola's choice ought not be mistaken as mere didacticism; we might read it as a symptom of the difficulties of imagining how the housewife's subjective trajectory may manifest itself with that same clarity in a present—the second half of the 1970s—where apparatuses of oppression and exploitation are at the same time less apparent and more pervasive.

Michelangelo Antonioni's *Red Desert* and Marco Ferreri's *Dillinger Is Dead* contend precisely with this conundrum. They do so by shifting the social background of the housewife away from the working-class environment of the films analyzed thus far, and toward a thoroughly recognizable bourgeois milieu. This class repositioning is made apparent in the narrative and the mise-en-scène—but also, and more crucially for our discussion, in the fact that in these films, housework is paid, as housemaids tend to children, cook dinner, and shadow the protagonists as they wander through the rooms of their luxurious modernist apartments. What happens, then, when wages for housework ceases to be a political battle cry for proletarian women and becomes the ordinary reality of bourgeois families? How does this semblance of freedom from the drudgery of domestic labor affect not only the housewife but also reproductive labor itself?

In *Red Desert,* bourgeois housewife Giuliana (Monica Vitti) engages in housework only sporadically. There is no sense that domestic labor in any way determines her everyday life and her relationship with time, the way it did for Antonietta. She is, we could say, a housewife without housework. She too is tired, but, she admits, "not always," just "sometimes." Domestic labor is performed by somebody else, so her tiredness is not a direct effect of the exploitation at home, as it was for Antonietta. Rather, it is a symptom of a more elusive malaise. We have seen how, for Antonietta, exhaustion marks the point of contradiction between housework as a labor of love and as unpaid labor necessary for the reproduction of the capitalist system. The position of the housewife in Scola thus emerges as an impossible one. Antonietta's encounter with Gabriele exposes this impasse, shaking the foundations of her perception of herself and the reality of fascist Italy, which in turn allows her to begin to articulate a conscious refusal, however tentative, of her own condition of oppression. Antonioni hardly affords the same opportunity to Giuliana. Her tiredness does not reveal housework as a point of inner contradiction of the structure. Instead, it is framed as a random aberration—a pathology—within a structural situation that is otherwise running all too smoothly.

This situation—evoked in the film's opening by the apocalyptic landscape of Ravenna's industrial district—is that of a rapidly modernizing Italy on the tail end of the economic miracle, a moment of radical socioeconomic transformation to which Giuliana seems unable to adapt. Her existential and psychological crisis is the film's focus. We learn that she was recently involved in a car crash, and she hasn't yet mentally recovered. It is then revealed that it may have been a failed suicide attempt, and that Giuliana spent time in a clinic to cure her psychological ailments. Not even a budding love affair with the industrialist Corrado (Richard Harris), a business associate of her husband's (Ugo, played by Carlo Chionetti), can alleviate her pain; her behavior becomes increasingly erratic as the film progresses.

The way the film presents the figure of the housewife is strikingly original. Not only does Antonioni separate her from her defining activity (housework); he also reverses her standard regime of appearance. No longer a figurant who appears everywhere but never prominently, the housewife is now assigned a preponderant position in the narrative while being simultaneously displaced on a formal level. For example, her narrative centrality is constantly offset by a series of formal decenterings. Her voice is often accompanied by a host of intruding mechanical sounds. Long shots, repeated *décadrages,* and the camera's deliberately pulling out of focus subordinate her presence to that of objects in the background. The editing (false eyeline matches, absent transitions) challenges the spectator's perception of the spatiotemporal coherence of her actions. One possible interpretation of the film may offer a solution to this paradox of a decentered centrality of the housewife: the deviations from classical cinematic syntax are to be read as the expression of Giuliana's troubled interiority, so that her fractured perception of the world acts as the matrix of the film's formal organization. From this perspective, the subjective bleeds into the objective. Reality is transfigured by Giuliana's *apprehension*—in the mutually codetermining meanings of perception and disquiet. As a consequence, this blurring of the distinction between subjectivity and objectivity would grant to the spectator access to Giuliana's psychology, now externalized into objective reality.[34]

Subjectivity and objectivity clearly constitute one of the fundamental oppositions that structure the film. But if we look at Giuliana as a figure—the figure of a housewife without housework—then this opposition cannot simply be resolved into an indiscernibility between the two terms. Instead, subjectivity and objectivity must be put in a dialectical relation. Far from being reducible to her psychological makeup, then, Giuliana's subjectivity exists in tension with the objective world that surrounds her. On the one hand, Giuliana's interiority constitutes the subjective effect of objective conditions; the transfixed world of the film should not be explained as a consequence of the existential predicament of the protagonist but rather as the form of appearance of objective forces that in turn determine the character's inner world. On the other hand, Giuliana's subjectivity exists in excess of the rule of the structure; she is marked by a certain maladjustment, an inability to fully comply to the interpellation of the objective forces that surround her. The question posed by the peculiar figure of a housewife without housework, then, is that of a subjectivity in crisis whose reach exceeds any psychologization of the character or projection of her inner world onto reality. But how exactly do these objective forces appear in the film?

The visual primacy gained by the objects that populate Giuliana's environment is perhaps the most conspicuous trait of the transfigured world of the film. Often the camera purposefully abandons human action to wander over industrial equipment (oil pipes, steel ducts), stacks of commodities (glass jars), and even the walls of a warehouse or domestic furniture. *Red Desert*'s painterly references have been amply discussed by critics, but the visual articulation of this upended relationship between individuals and things is strikingly reminiscent of the work of Italian visual artist Leonardo Cremonini, to whom Louis Althusser dedicated an illuminating 1966 essay.[35] In Cremonini's paintings and lithographs, Althusser argues, "normal connections between men and objects are inverted and dislocated" as we encounter "'men' fashioned from the material of their objects, circumscribed by it, caught and defined once and for all."[36] These formulations would seem to describe *Red Desert* just as accurately. In both Antonioni's film and Cremonini's images, objects assume visual predominance and seem to take on a life of their own, while human bodies seem constantly restrained, enclosed by windows, doorframes, and mirrors.

Althusser terms Cremonini a "painter of the real abstract," of "the real relations (as relations they are necessarily abstract) between 'men' and 'things,' or rather, between 'things' and their 'men.'"[37] Capitalism depends on abstractions (the commodity form, the value form, and private property, for instance) like no other mode of production before it; as Marx famously puts it in the *Grundrisse*, "Individuals are now ruled by abstractions, whereas earlier they depended on one another."[38] The very fact that abstractions can "rule" individuals under capitalism is proof of their concreteness. Real abstractions are not mere illusions or diversions that dissimulate the existence of some true, deep essence; nor are they mere figments of the individual's imagination.[39] They are, in a word, objective. They originate from the actions of individuals in society but then transcend those actions to achieve a seemingly autonomous existence, with the result that the eminently social origin of the abstraction remains unthought to the individual, who comes to perceive it as something akin to a law of nature. This, for Althusser, is the human being that appears in Cremonini's works. As a "profoundly anti-humanist and materialist" artist, Cremonini pictures his human beings not as the bearers of some recondite interiority, but as purely exterior structural effects of the abstract relations that govern them.[40]

Because these abstractions defy direct representation, they manifest themselves in the image as fragments of the "objective" background encroaching on the human figure. This is what the repeated *décadrages* in *Red Desert* highlight. The camera's deliberate insistence on objects and shapes in the background suggests the predominance of abstract yet objective constraints over human life. These abstractions can be evoked more or less explicitly. Ships, ducts, and commodities, for instance, conjure the intangible but very real movement of value in the global capitalist system. Linear shapes like the steel rails in Giuliana's home and Corrado's hotel room, or the blue stripe painted on a warehouse wall, stand as more enigmatic signifiers of a pervasive, controlling presence whose extension and logic remain largely unintelligible to the characters themselves, particularly to Giuliana ("There is something terrible in reality," she laments, "and I don't know what it is").

When Corrado asks her what she is afraid of, Giuliana cries out, "Streets, factories, colors, people, everything!" Giuliana feels the weight of abstractions. She instinctively grasps their pervasiveness but fails to understand their inner logic. This is most evident in the scene where she attempts to board a cargo ship docked in the Ravenna harbor and engages in a mutually unintelligible conversation with a Turkish seaman. The question she addresses to him ("Does this ship carry passengers too?") reveals a fundamental confusion, which illustrates the incommensurability between the abstract logic of movement of value in international trade and the concrete logic of movement of individuals as it is understood by Giuliana. The process of the circulation of value on a global scale (the ship carries commodities—that is, capital waiting to be realized) possesses its own objective rationality, and it exists independently from the desires, intentions, and aspirations of individual human beings.[41]

But what happens when one wants to bridge that incommensurability, turning a freighter into a ferry—or perhaps a lifeboat? It is precisely in Giuliana's misunderstanding about the cargo ship that lies a further dimension of her subjectivity. The film, as we have seen, presents Giuliana as a by-product of her environment. But her subjectivity cannot be reduced to a purely mechanical emanation of the structure. In fact, she is also the bearer of a certain subjective surplus, which in the film takes the form of a sort of inchoate resistance against her own environment. Recognizing the strangeness of a world in which relations among humans are mediated by relations among things, she finds herself unable to adapt to it. The terms of this inability are peculiar. As the behavior of individuals becomes exteriorized into objective social forms, Giuliana's struggle against reality undergoes an equal and opposite process of interiorization. It begins from the objective pressure of abstractions, then turns inward to become a pathology to be stigmatized—or, at best, pitied—by the other characters, who do not experience the same maladjustment. Ugo, for instance, seems to adapt to the rule of abstractions without many qualms. Even Corrado, tormented as he may appear, abides by that rule; he behaves in accordance with his social role as a capitalist, chasing after surplus value in observance to the law of competition and the imperative to cut costs in order to increase profitability. The only true figure of the film, in this sense, is the housewife. Giuliana alone indexes a proper tension between the dictates of the structure and the individual's inability to fully adjust to them.

Why is that so? What is it that makes the housewife uniquely situated to register this subjective tension between the objectivity of all-encompassing abstractions and the individual's failure to comply to their command? It has to do, at least in part, with the ideological work that the housewife is forced to perform. As we have seen, the position of the housewife within the capitalist mode of production is inextricable from the fantasy of the home as a private refuge from the oppressive and predatory practices of capital in the social sphere. The explicit humanism that underpins this ideological formation (domesticity as sanctuary of nonalienated labor and authentic human relations where the individual can flourish and simply be herself) makes the housewife into the guardian of a space where the abstractions that rule modern life should have no purchase. The decentered centrality of the housewife in *Red Desert,* then, depicts a limit situation in which it is precisely by registering the effects of real abstractions on a figure ideologically tasked with warding them off that the true reach of their rule can be measured.

The humanism that underpins the ideological position of the housewife also creeps into Giuliana's imagined solutions to her own crisis. Be it her simple attempt to board a cargo ship or her tortured love affair with Corrado, Giuliana is looking to escape from these haunting abstractions toward some haven of authentic human experience. The futility of such escapes is perhaps best captured in the conclusion of the long party scene that occurs halfway through the film. Terrified by the unexpected arrival of a cargo ship (seemingly with an undisclosed outbreak on board), Giuliana forces everyone to leave, even though none of her companions shares her concern. After a series of close-ups of the characters on the foggy pier, Antonioni returns to a close-up of Giuliana, who is now observing Ugo, his friend Max, Max's wife, and her friend, all grouped into a medium shot, staring back at her, while a ship's horn can be heard in the distance (Figure 14).

The fog suddenly thickens and swallows the motionless group, making them all but disappear from sight. Clearly distraught by

Figure 14. Ugo and his friends stare at Giuliana on the dock in *Red Desert* (1964).

the vision, Giuliana runs to the car and drives it to the end of the jetty—a further attempt to escape that is also, perhaps, a partial reenactment of her earlier suicide attempt.

Her attempt to escape from the ominous presence of the infected ship ends in a confrontation with an image that is perhaps even more unsettling. The thinglike fixity of the staring partygoers functions as a reminder that no true human essence is to be found behind the veil of abstractions, for the latter are constitutive of human relations as such, mediating not only professional bonds but also private and familial ones. Even the idyll of the famous scene set on the island of Budelli cannot be imagined without the intrusion of the nonhuman capitalist logic of global trade, embodied by a mysterious ship without a crew ("One of those ships that braved all the seas and the storms of this world, and, who knows . . . out of this world"). No place is immune from the rule of real abstractions. Every elsewhere evoked in the film, no matter how exotic, is also intimately connected to the dreary landscape of Ravenna, as illustrated by the scene where Corrado recruits workers to send to Argentina. The workers' situation of exploitation will be the same in the new continent because they will be ruled by the same abstractions, a point the film makes with a repeated raking focus blurring the faces of the workers to show the capital that surrounds them in the form of glass jars and the walls of the warehouse.

Yet even in a situation that is becoming increasingly disorienting as a result of incipient processes of globalization and delocalization, the workers in *Red Desert* can still identify a terrain of struggle. In fact, the film opens with a strike just outside the gates of the plant Ugo manages. The outcome or even the motivations of their action are not revealed, but at a minimum, the potential for forms of collective antagonism is assumed for the workers, who can still identify the factory as the possible event site of their subjectivation (see chapter 2). Giuliana, the housewife without housework, finds herself in a very different predicament. Housework is, we might say, the figurally specific way in which the capitalist relation appears to the housewife. It can become a terrain of struggle through the affirmation of a statement of desire that exceeds common notions of what a working-class housewife can or cannot want (Lidia in *The Working Class Goes to Heaven*) or a process of subjectivation driven by a reappropriation of time (Antonietta in *A Special Day*). Without housework, the housewife in *Red Desert* finds herself untethered from this terrain of struggle.

This is not to argue that the housewife should cling on to her own exploitation—quite the contrary. However, the separation between the housewife and domestic labor staged in *Red Desert* has consequences for the potential emergence of a subjectivity. The theoretical-political gambit of Wages for Housework, as we have seen, was that of redefining the role of domestic labor in the capitalist relation of production in order to reveal the home as a site of class struggle. From a purely sociological standpoint, Giuliana still identifies as a housewife, but figurally, she has no field of struggle to call her own, one she could use to articulate the beginning of a subjectivity. No event or encounter—certainly not the one with Corrado—can reveal to her the impossibility of her own position, and therefore point her toward the possibility of a subjective reckoning. Nor does the oppressiveness of her condition become apparent to her qua housewife—that is, in the form of the drudgery of domestic labor or patriarchal tyranny, like it did in *A Special Day*. As a consequence, while the cause of said oppression (the capitalist mode of production) remains the same as it was for

Antonietta, its manifestations become dispersed and inscrutable. Giuliana thus follows a different trajectory than Scola's protagonist. The proletarian housewife springs from monolithic conceptions of reality and of her own place in it that are inextricably tied to domestic labor, only to then radically question them. The bourgeois housewife is always already mired in a situation of generic maladjustment to reality; the causes of her malaise are interwoven into the very fabric of the social, making it impossible for her to pinpoint them, let alone revolt against them. In this sense, her interiority comes from without. The characters' subjectivity as crisis comes into existence as an effect of the modern conditions of real abstraction under capitalism.[42]

This is, in the last analysis, the tragic limitation of the housewife's subjective horizon in *Red Desert*. As the point of lack in the proper functioning of the structure, her maladjustment gestures toward a potential antagonism. In this sense, she stands for a sort of degree zero of subjectivity—the subject as the gap in the symbolic, the point of inner contradiction of the structure. However, this lack becomes interiorized and psychologized as a form of paralyzing anxiety not too dissimilar from the one we saw envelop Fortunato, the protagonist of *Trevico-Turin* discussed in chapter 2. The fate of the bourgeois housewife and the fate of the migrant factory worker are surprisingly similar. Once they lose their event site (the home and the factory), both are forced to surrender to the seeming omnipotence of the structure, with the political process of their subjectivation thwarted and reduced into a psychodrama of individuality.

Housework without a Housewife: *Dillinger Is Dead*

Any residue of this psychodrama, and the effect of interiority that it projects, disappears in *Dillinger Is Dead,* where the protagonist (an engineer who remains unnamed during the film but is identified as Glauco in the credits, played by Michel Piccoli) is deliberately presented as devoid of any psychological depth. One summer night, back home from the office, he engages in a series of disconnected and largely unmotivated actions, while his wife, Anita (Anita Pallenberg), lies in bed with a migraine and the maid,

Sabina (Annie Girardot), has taken the night off. Uninspired by the dinner Sabina left for him, he turns on the TV and sets out to cook a gourmet meal for himself. Thus begins a night of relentless reproductive labor. While looking for an ingredient, Glauco stumbles on a rusty gun wrapped in old newspapers from 1934 reporting on the death of John Dillinger. While cooking, he disassembles the gun and polishes it to bring it back to functionality. Meanwhile, the maid returns; after a brief encounter with Glauco in the kitchen, she retires to her room, where she dances to pop songs in front of the mirror while wearing lingerie. Glauco eats his meal with gusto, watches some Super 8 films of his and Anita's vacation in Spain projected on the living room wall, reassembles the gun and then paints it red with white polka dots, seduces Sabina, and finally returns to the bedroom to kill a sleeping Anita with three shots to the head. At daybreak, he leaves the city and takes a swim at Byron's Cave in Porto Venere, Liguria. He then boards a ship headed to Tahiti and insists on replacing the cook, who just died. As he makes a chocolate mousse ordered by the young female shipowner, the ship sails toward its destination bathed in an unnatural red light, as an immense sun burns on the horizon and the image turns to negative.

In *Dillinger*, the housewife disintegrates. The figure splinters into three characters: Anita, who does not perform domestic labor because she is indisposed (and, presumably, because she has hired somebody else to do it); Sabina, who is supposed to be performing that labor but is otherwise occupied; and Glauco, who actually performs it. As a consequence, the received structure of the gendered division of labor falters, and the figure itself ceases to provide the marker of a subjective position, be it around a kernel of presubjective antagonism (*The Ape Woman*), a statement of desire (*The Working Class Goes to Heaven*), or a reappropriation of time (*A Special Day*). Yet the shards of this exploded figure remain recognizable, especially in the extended sequences Ferreri devotes to Glauco as he cooks dinner while wrapped in a conspicuous red apron. But along such defamiliarizing depictions of housework, we notice in *Dillinger* a series of curious displacements. Glauco puts the disassembled gun in a bowl, drizzles it with olive oil, and mixes it as if it were a marinade; then, after painting it, he leaves it hanging on the terrace to dry like laundry. These acts point to a situation in which housework persists after the disappearance of the housewife. The form of the activity itself remains practically intact, but its ends become warped, so that polishing a gun and leaving it out to dry become indiscernible from, respectively, marinating a piece of meat and hanging up wet laundry.

The disintegration of the housewife and the correlated perversion of housework compel us to ask what kind of reproductive labor *Dillinger* represents. The picture of reproduction that we can glean from Marx's sporadic treatment of the topic is one defined by scarcity—a scarcity of time, resources, and means for the development of the individual that is imposed by the structural logic of capitalism. As a result, the wage laborer in the capitalist relation of production is always already reproduced, to borrow Tithi Bhattacharya's expression, as somewhat "lacking," always in want of more opportunities to develop himself.[43] Yet Glauco seems to be facing the opposite problem. Hardly animated by a frustrated desire to better himself, his relationship to reproduction is one marked by abundance. He has the entire night for himself, with plenty of opportunities to indulge his every recreative whim. His essential dimension, then, is not lack but rather surplus, expressed in the host of objects that surround him and in his relation to them, which is marked by a compulsive operosity. His inscrutable behavior assumes the form a totally depsychologized, automaton-like, repetitive activity oriented toward a multiplicity of partial objects.

In this sense, more than the logic of desire (grounded in lack), Glauco should be associated with the logic of the drive (defined by surplus). The significance of the drive in Ferreri's cinema has been emphasized by Gilles Deleuze. In *Cinema 1*, Deleuze identifies Ferreri as one of the foremost auteurs of the drive-image, which is directly connected to "naturalism."[44] Ferreri, writes Deleuze, is "one of the few recent directors to have inherited an authentic naturalistic inspiration and the art of evoking an originary world at the heart of realistic milieux."[45] Naturalism, it should be pointed out, has nothing to do with any ideological representation of reality as it is, but rather with the irruption of the drive onto the scene. The source of this drive is the "originary world," "a pure background, or rather a without-background, composed of unformed matter, sketches or fragments, crossed by non-formal functions, acts, or energy dynamisms which do not even refer to the constituted subjects."[46]

The emergence of this "originary world" of the drive within a "realistic" milieu is what distinguishes the drive-image from the other subsets of the movement image. Realism persists, but transfigured. The realistic milieu constitutes the medium through which the drive can emerge. Concretely, this means that the elements that compose the milieu (the behavior of its characters, the objects that populate it) become separated from themselves. Behaviors and objects are transfigured, respectively, into drives and fragments (or partial objects). Deleuze specifically locates this operation in Ferreri's *Bye Bye Monkey* (*Ciao maschio*, 1978), but one can see it at work in *Dillinger* as well, perhaps even more prominently.

Keeping in mind the framework offered by the concept of the drive-image, we can now return to the question of reproductive labor in the film, particularly the relation between Glauco's operosity and the mass of objects surrounding him. From the living room to the kitchen, the master bedroom to the maid's quarters, the study to the terrace, Glauco incessantly roams the spaces of his apartment, looking for something—anything—to occupy himself. Deleuze calls this type of roaming an "exploration" of the milieu in which the drive does not intentionally pick and choose its objects; rather, the drive "takes indiscriminately from what the milieu offers it."[47] The object of the exploration, then, is determined not by some intrinsic quality of the drive but externally, by the milieu itself.

Dillinger thus translates into the sphere of reproduction the dramatic dislocation of the relationship between individuals and objects that we first saw staged in *Red Desert*. Almost immediately on the protagonist's return home, the configuration of reproductive labor undergoes a reversal—not purposeful activity, but the endless distracted exploration of any object that "the milieu offers." As one critic observes, "The reason for using the object follows the encounter with its shape and not the other way around. Glauco's silent soliloquy composes the following dogma: I do not need the object, but given that it now finds itself in my hands, I will use it."[48] There is nothing purposeful in Glauco's consumption of his means of subsistence; the purpose, in fact, seems to be coming from the object themselves. *Dillinger* seems to swiftly refute Marx's claim that the worker belongs to himself in the sphere of individual, reproduction-oriented consumption. In the incipient stage of late capitalism at the end of the 1960s, the worker is, in fact, as separated from himself in the sphere of reproduction as he is in the sphere of production. If *The Working Class Goes to Heaven,* discussed in chapter 2, showed us a factory worker who "doesn't exist" because of the inner division at the core of labor power itself, then *Dillinger* depicts a managerial employee at home who never acts as himself but rather in conformity to a drive that remains unthought to him.

In Ferreri's drive-image, then, the relationship between man and the things that surround him undergoes a reversal. The latter cease to be inert matter and assert their autonomous command over the former. The real abstractions that presided over Giuliana's tormented existence in *Red Desert* return here to colonize the sphere of reproduction as well, domineering an automaton-like character who knows no anxiety. The antihumanism that tinged Antonioni's film is here explicitly avowed, with the protagonist reduced to an emanation of the commodities that surround him, an "appendix" of sorts, "without any lighting or shot angle reestablishing the hierarchy" between the human and the nonhuman.[49] Even more than Giuliana, Glauco is the cinematic epitome of the "hardly outlined" characters Althusser saw in Cremonini's paintings. He is an "anonymous being" whose enigmatic facade does not express anything other than the effect of the real abstractions that rule over him, and that determine even his "experience of freedom."[50] For Glauco, this experience of freedom is not at all free, as the ironic use of pop songs in the film makes clear. Two in particular are prominently featured: Patty Pravo's "Qui e là" (Here and there) and Jimmy Fontana's "Cielo rosso" (Red sky), both from 1968. They tell stories, respectively, of uncompromising affirmation of individual freedom and melancholic longing for a fantasized elsewhere. In the context of the film, however, the voices coming from the radio seem to mock Glauco's predicament while at the same time predicting his doom.

This illusion of the worker's freedom in the sphere of reproduction has deep historical roots; it rests on the assumption of a spatial and structural separation between workplace and home, whereby the former is associated with production under capital's direction and the latter is associated with unsupervised labor. The latter's freedom is the obverse of the former's strict social control, however. In capitalism, any instance of concrete, use value–oriented, seemingly nonalienated labor is always already overdetermined by alienated social relations that have their material basis in the wage relation—what Bhattacharya calls the "conditioning impulse of wage labor" on the unpaid labor of reproduction.[51] Marx frames the worker's "freedom" to reproduce himself on his own time and dime as a concession that capital all too happily grants, for it satisfies in the most cost-efficient way its need for the renewal of labor power. As such, the individual reproduction of the worker is to be considered "a mere aspect of the process of capital's reproduction," and therefore is totally overdetermined by it.[52]

The depiction of vacation in the film, in particular, offers an example of this dynamic. While perceived as essentially free time, vacation is in fact the ultimate emblem of the "conditioning impulse of wage labor" on reproduction. In *Dillinger*, a ghostly redoubling of reproduction takes place. Projected on the wall as a Super 8 home movie, vacation becomes commodified into an object "included in the system of production/consumption and abstract in its exchange-value," and therefore no different in nature from a cookbook, a gun, or the projector that generates its images.[53] Far from free time in which the worker can temporarily suture the split of his own alienation, vacation too partakes in the despotic command of things over their men in the sphere of reproduction.

In *Dillinger*, this slavery leads Glauco to the final illusion of freedom in the form of murder and the most banal of escape fantasies (is this ship the same one that haunted Giuliana's fable?)—a fantasy that the film invites us to see as a dead end, if not as an outright apocalyptic vision. This motif of the end of the world, which will be on Ferreri's mind well into the 1970s, is a constituent part of the drive-image: "The originary world is a beginning of the world, but also an end of the world, and the irresistible slope from one to the other."[54] For Deleuze, naturalism in cinema is therefore composed of two aspects. On the one hand is the extreme fragmentation of partial objects in the "originary world;" on the other is the inexorable clinamen that leads all fragments toward entropy and waste. Cremonini belongs fully in in the former condition, clinging to a certain suspended fragmentation; in contrast, Ferreri, illustrating the latter condition, rushes the heap of partial objects headlong down the slope, toward a destiny of death that appears as inevitable as the insistence of the drive. But if it is true, as Deleuze says, that naturalist directors provide diagnoses of civilization, then what social ailment has been discovered by *Dillinger*'s enigmatic relationship between reproductive labor and the destiny of demise to which the slope inevitably leads?

In her video essay *Philosophy in the Kitchen* (2014), Domietta Torlasco posits a direct link between housework and death—murder, in particular—in cinema. As the voice-over declares that "murder is the outcome, the aberrant offspring of domestic labor," scenes from several European films, including *Dillinger*, are juxtaposed in split screen: *Ossessione*, *Sabotage* (Alfred Hitchcock, 1934), *Elena* (Andrey Zvyagintsev, 2011), *Repulsion* (Roman Polanski, 1965), and *La Cérémonie* (Claude Chabrol, 1995). While Torlasco notes that in all these instances violence and death are associated with domestic labor, a crucial difference sets *Dillinger* apart. In the examples cited in the video essay, the occurrence of murder attains a particular level of narrative significance that distinguishes it from housework. It can be the dramatic climax of a mounting psychotic breakdown within the domestic space *(Repulsion)*, the end game of a housewife's plotting *(Ossessione)*, or the interruption of domestic labor *(Sabotage)*. In *Dillinger*, however, we find a different configuration whereby housework and murder become practically indistinguishable. In the context of Glauco's feverish activity, just as no hierarchy is established between human beings and things, no act or gesture is more or less important than any other. Ferreri does not put any particular narrative emphasis on the final uxoricide, opting instead for a pure record of facts that reads like a perverse homage to Cesare Zavattini's neorealist aesthetic of *pedinamento*. Murder and death in the film, then, are less the "aberrant offspring of domestic labor" than a mere moment in the naturalist world of the film, an activity like any other—like cooking, eating, drinking, fucking, and watching home movies.

Yet the film's universe, with its chaotic proliferation of partial objects and unmotivated gestures, bends toward some kind of apocalyptic ending. What if, *Dillinger* asks, there is no tomorrow? Glauco's activity resembles the customary representation of reproductive labor, yet it finds itself deprived of its structural aim in the capitalist mode of production because the proverbial next day at the factory, when Glauco will expend his regenerated labor power, never obtains. But this disjunction between reproduction and production, as we have seen, does not assume the form of a liberation of free time from the "conditioning impulse of wage labor." On the contrary, *Dillinger* paints the picture of a reproduction that finds itself fully colonized by the real abstraction of the capitalist relation. This is, in a nutshell, Ferreri's diagnosis of Western civilization at the dawn of late capitalism. The drive-image in *Dillinger* captures the real subsumption of domestic and reproductive labor under capital; purposeful labor is thus forced into the inherently perverse curvature of the drive, as means of subsistence are transfigured in an endless array of partial objects, and all hierarchy between human beings and things disintegrates. This in turn leads to an apocalyptic conclusion whereby a strange night of restlessness ends with the sphere of reproduction orbiting away from that of production, as Glauco sets sail to Tahiti. What *Dillinger* diagnoses is an impasse internal to late capitalism: the impasse of a social relation for which it is increasingly difficult to reproduce itself.

In a way, this diagnosis is made possible by the very disappearance of the figure of the housewife. The film calls on Glauco, Anita, and Sabina to relinquish their humanity and become objects among other objects. What remains, then, is reproductive labor without a subject—housework without a housewife. In a way, the film interrupts the precarious process of subjectivation of the housewife we have traced across *The Ape Woman, The Working Class Goes to Heaven,* and *A Special Day.* At the same time, *Dillinger* carries to the extreme consequences *Red Desert*'s intuition about the limitation of the housewife's political horizon. Indeed, if *Dillinger* points to a subjectivity, it does so exclusively to the extent that this subjectivity be understood in its strict Althusserian sense—that is, purely as an effect of the structure. All this subjectivity has to offer—and it is no trivial matter—is "a knowledge of the laws of [one's] slavery" to abstract relations.[55]

4 The Youth

The Dialectic of Enjoyment

> Sometimes... the unique situation arises that bourgeois conformists want to renew life. Here the air is not quite so heavy as before. But it does not blow yet, it just raises dust.
> —Ernst Bloch, "Unchecked"

> Every truth is marked by an indestructible *youthfulness.*
> —Alain Badiou, *Saint Paul: The Foundation of Universalism*

A Modern Invention

Of the figures examined in this book, the youth—*il giovane* in Italian—is perhaps the most elusive. In common parlance, "youth" indicates a state of transition between two identifiable stages in the biological and social life of the individual. Caught in a gray area between the child and the adult, the youth is no longer undergoing biological development but is not yet considered fully mature from a social standpoint. Furthermore, the historical emergence of this category has been fairly recent. In the nineteenth century, one would be hard pressed to find youths in the industrial proletariat, as young workers were to relinquish childhood as early as possible to immediately become part of the workforce employed in factories and subjected to the same hardships as their parents. Even in the upper classes, the youth was just an adult *in fieri,* preparing to succeed his father at the helm of the company, follow in his footsteps in the military, or assume the duties of his medical practice.

In this sense, the youth as a distinct actor on the social scene is by and large a twentieth-century invention. This is certainly the case in Italy, where the rise of the youth is inextricable from the economic miracle of the late 1950s and early 1960s. The sudden onset of economic growth brought about the emergence of a new middle class whose defining ambition was that sons and daughters would climb further up the social ladder than their parents. Education (high school, but also college) started to be perceived as essential for career advancement, and with the increase in the average number of years spent in school, a new demographic of young people who were no longer kids but not yet adults suddenly appeared on the national stage.

Before the rise of the youth, the dominant nonadult figure in Italian cinema was the child. One of the most iconic presences of Italian postwar cinema, the child was already prominently featured in one of the forerunners of neorealism (Vittorio De Sica's *The Children Are Watching Us* [*I bambini ci guardano*], 1944) and maintained its centrality in the later development of the movement. The contrast between the child and the youth in the context of Italian cinema is revealing. In neorealism, the ideological investment in the figure of the child is obvious; it embodies the possibility of building a new future on the ruins of the war—a possibility that is celebrated (*Rome Open City* [*Roma città aperta*, Rossellini, 1945]; *Bicycle Thieves* [*Ladri di biciclette*, De Sica, 1948]) as much as mourned (*Germany Year Zero* [*Germania anno zero*, Rossellini, 1948]; *Shoeshine* [*Sciuscià*, De Sica, 1946]). In either case, there is an innocence or purity that sets the child apart from a troubled and hostile environment. This innocence can be lost, but the basic presupposition remains that a childlike purity once existed and that it should constitute the moral basis for a new national beginning.

The youth is considerably less transparent. There is no fantasy of innocence to be celebrated here; the youth is too old not to have already been somewhat determined by his place in the social structure. But he is also too young to have a full grasp of what belonging to that structure entails, and therefore he is also too young to be held to the standards of accountability of an adult. The youth is not only suspended between two biological stages but also, as a figure, trapped in a no-man's-land between two fantasies: childhood as innocence and adulthood as duty. One could argue that these fantasies are actually two sides of the same coin, with one side the pure immaturity of enjoyment without guilt of the child, and the other the pure responsibility of guilt without enjoyment of the adult. In Italian postwar cinema, and especially from the beginning of the 1960s on, the youth insinuates himself in the middle of this fantasmatic distinction and breaks it apart. As we will see, the youth's pursuit of enjoyment is deliberate, as is his rejection of the set of values shaping the life of the older generation.

The social and political unrest of 1968 marks the youth's coming of age, his definitive affirmation on the national—and international—stage. But however prominent a role he may have played in this historical sequence, it is important to point out that the youth is not an immediately political figure. His generality (part biological, part sociological) prevents him from being easily captured by the confines of a political subjectivity. As opposed to the worker, the youth is not defined by the central position he occupies in the direct process of production. The *centralità operaia* (worker's centrality) discussed in chapter 2 situates the dialectics of the worker's subjectivity—his submission to capitalist exploitation and potential for radical antagonism—squarely at the point of the impasse between labor and capital. With the youth, this dialectic does not obtain with the same paradigmatic clarity. Also, unlike the worker, the youth has no single event site to call his own—not even the university, as the student remains at the margins of filmic representation in those years. Surprisingly, the university is evoked in the films I discuss as a distant place. It is more a device or reference for readily identifying a social type—the rebellious bourgeois—than a historically concrete site of contradiction and class struggle.[1]

In a way, what we might call the figural gap between the worker and the youth reflects the problematic history of alliance and enmity between these two dominant actors of the long '68, a history determined as much by the waning political centrality of the factory worker as it is by the elusiveness and precariousness of the youth as a political subject. It is telling that to describe the new subjectivities that arose from the changing political landscape of the 1970s, Nanni Balestrini and Primo Moroni resort to the definition of the youth as a "general generational class,"[2] a moniker that attaches to the youth a certain indistinction, superimposing as it does three levels: a lack of specificity (general), an age-related connotation (generational), and a socioeconomic grouping (class).

We can perhaps glimpse in this definition the idea of the youth as a figure without a specific event site to call his own. The logic of dialectical interplay between force and structure that subtends this figure remains similar to that of the worker, but the conditions under which it unfolds are markedly different. With the evaporation of the factory worker as the hegemonic political subject of modernity, as Antonio Negri writes in 1975, "the category of the 'working class' goes into crisis but continues to produce all the effects that are proper to it on the entire social terrain as proletariat."[3] The shift of the terrain of the struggle from the factory to society at large, already suggested by the films analyzed in chapter 3, gives rise to a new scene in which the target of antagonism is no longer, or not only, the capitalist exploitation of labor but rather the forms of repression that permeate all aspects of the social sphere: authoritarianism, in the early days of the 1968 movement, and, more in general, the rigidity of a tyrannical society where all roles seem to be perpetually assigned in advance. More than exploitation per se, it is the oppressive and pervasive nature of networks of power that constitutes the new focus of the struggle. With the youth, antagonism undergoes a process of generalization and becomes disseminated into the fabric of the social, with the aim to overthrow the institutions to which the control and reproduction of the status quo is entrusted: the state, the education system, the church, the party, the family, and so forth. The youth is the primary figure of this expansion of the field of the struggle, whose unprecedented novelty is the equivalence he postulates among all struggles for liberation—antipatriarchal, anticolonial, anticapitalist.

This diffused antagonism no longer constitutes itself in the universalist collectivity of the proletariat but finds its root in the irreducible singularity of the individual's desire. The political wager of a movement such as the Autonomia in the 1970s will be precisely that of attempting to establish a dynamic of mutual determination between individual desires and the necessarily collective dimension of political action. As Deleuze and Guattari famously argue in *Anti-Oedipus,* a text that had an enormous influence on the Italian radical movements of the 1970s, any form of "becoming-revolutionary" is fundamentally determined by "desiring-production"—that is, the wholly immanent force of desire as infinite production of connections that must be liberated from the constraints imposed by capitalist society.[4]

The youth as figure certainly incorporates this impetus to free desire from any external limitation or mediation, toward the goal of an unfettered enjoyment. But rather than casting the youth as a vessel for the pure productivity of a desire untethered from the dictates of the system, the figural reading of the films discussed in this chapter will unearth the ways in which this desiring force finds itself in dialectical tension with the reactive feedback of the structure. By presenting the youth as inherently multiple, this chapter will unfold as a sort of taxonomy of the various versions of this figure, with each incarnation articulating a specific variation of the relation between desire and law that marks the terrain of the youth as a possible revolutionary subject.

Horrors of the Sweet Life

More often than not, in contemporary discourses, a vague notion of youthfulness has come to stand in for 1968 as a whole, with an idealizing semantic halo of rebelliousness, impulsivity, and vitality attached to it. However, if Alain Badiou is right in asserting that "every truth is marked by an indestructible *youthfulness,*" then one should resist the temptation to discount the youthfulness of '68 altogether as a cliché and rather ask, what is the truth of which the youth becomes a figure in that specific historical sequence? We will begin to look for an answer in two films released before the events of 1968, yet widely regarded as historically prescient: Bernardo Bertolucci's *Before the Revolution* (*Prima della rivoluzione,* 1963) and Marco Bellocchio's *Fists in the Pocket* (*I pugni in tasca,* 1965). The coupling of these two films is, by now, a critical axiom, and not without reason. At the time of their release, the films were hailed as a historical break in Italian cinema, representing the arrival of a new generation of young auteurs determined to leave the cumbersome legacy of neorealism behind and invent new forms of filmmaking. Their proximity to the events of 1968 certainly contributed to their fortune. How could one fail to see in the two young protagonists, Alessandro and Fabrizio, the embryonic germs of a revolutionary desire that was soon to sweep not just Italy but the entire globe? Bertolucci and Bellocchio were retroactively christened as clairvoyant rhapsodists of the rebellion that was brewing at the heart of the bourgeois world, and the films found themselves crystallized as precursors according to that obstinate critical tautology that subordinates art to history, using the hindsight of the latter to explain the foresight of the former. To be sure, few would deny that a relation between 1968 and the films exists, but any assumption about the obviousness of such relation can be misleading, and at any rate, establishing a biunivocal correspondence in which the films represent 1968 before its time hardly exhausts the complexity of said relation. In a somewhat sacrilegious move, we will put in dialogue this prescient diptych with the later *Come Play with Me* (*Grazie zia*, Salvatore Samperi, 1969), a much less canonical work that nonetheless shows striking similarities to *Before the Revolution* and *Fists in the Pocket* while also offering a singular articulation of the youth as a figure of desire and transgression.

Rebellion as Detour: Before the Revolution and Come Play with Me

Before the Revolution sets its defining impasse right at the heart of the provincial elite in Parma, with its young bourgeois protagonist, Fabrizio (Francesco Barilli), torn between the conformism imposed by his social background and his communist political leanings. This existential rift traverses the entire film. It first leads Fabrizio to call off his engagement to Clelia (Cristina Pariset), a young woman from a well-to-do family, and then pushes him into the arms of Gina (Adriana Asti), his maternal aunt, who is visiting Parma from Milan. The two start a passionate affair, destined, however, to end abruptly when Gina leaves town. His fantasies of another life shattered, Fabrizio returns to Clelia and marries her.

The quote from Charles-Maurice de Talleyrand-Périgord that opens the film and gives it its title ("Only those who lived before the revolution knew how sweet life could be") introduces the motif of the bourgeois sweet life that Fabrizio was born into and longs to reject. The opening scene establishes a tripartite identification among Clelia, Parma, and this sweet life. Aerial shots of the city are interspersed with images of Fabrizio running through the streets, his voice-over declaring, "Clelia is the city. . . . She is that sweet life that I cannot accept." Gina instead constitutes for Fabrizio the horizon of a new, different life grounded in the transgression of bourgeois mores. The split between the two women—one statuesque in her refined fixity, the other whimsical, unpredictable, tantalizing—externalizes the fundamental division at the heart of the figure of the youth in the film: on the one hand, the belonging to a social class where one is, so to speak, condemned to the sweet life; on the other, the desire to relinquish this background and open oneself up to the possibility of change. With his bourgeois past encroaching on his future, Fabrizio looks for a way out. He follows the urge to desire something else—something beyond Clelia, Parma, and the sweet life.

Yet in the film, the object of this desire remains nebulous, irrelevant even, as though the only thing that counted—the real revolutionary horizon Fabrizio is after—were the act of desiring itself. Italian psychoanalyst Elvio Fachinelli detected a similar desire to desire at work on the eve of 1968. He observed that youth rebellion must be understood in conjunction with "an image or fantasy of a society that promises an ever more complete liberation from need, while at the same time threatening the individual with a loss of personal identity. That is, it pairs the offer of immediate security with an unacceptable prospect: the loss of oneself as project and desire. In fact, the liberation from need seems to have as its condition the sacrifice of desire."[5] The figure of the youth in *Before the Revolution* points to this double bind, according to which the generalized satisfaction of needs brought about by the economic boom came with the threat of an annulment of desire. "The loss of oneself as project and desire" means precisely the loss of a future that is not the mere perpetuation of one's past. In his quest for a path away from the sweet life, Fabrizio's desire to desire finds itself split into the intertwined shapes of political militancy and sexual transgression. In the case of the former, Fabrizio models his desire on Cesare's (played by film critic Morando Morandini), an elementary school teacher and communist activist. One scene exemplifies this dynamic. After the mentor chastises him for "talking like a book," Fabrizio retorts, "You're right, I do talk like a book. I have to talk like a book to sound convincing. But don't forget that I speak like the books *you* give me." Fabrizio wants to sound convincing not only to his interlocutor but, first and foremost, to himself. The existence of his newfound political desire depends on it.

The desire to desire embodied by the figure of the youth also follows another trajectory: sexual transgression. Gina, the maternal aunt who, after having sex with Fabrizio, claims that she and his mother "look very much alike," obviously evokes the mother as the lost primordial object of desire. Yet Gina is much more than a simple prop for the dramatization of an incestuous relationship. As opposed to Cesare, who plays the role of the master and offers his own desire to Fabrizio as a legible model to be emulated, she is the sphinx that presents Fabrizio with desire as enigma. Desire, Jacques Lacan famously claims, is always the desire of the Other; we can interrogate ourselves about our own desire only by first asking what the Other wants from us. But it is seldom clear what the Other wants, and the impenetrability of this desire functions as a reminder that one cannot simply appropriate it and be done with it.

Unlike Cesare, Gina offers no indulgence to Fabrizio. Bertolucci closely follows her every expression and sudden mood change with extreme close-ups that make her face a landscape in constant transformation. She discourages Fabrizio from inquiring about what she wants, then admits, "I told you everything without saying a word." Precisely by dissimulating the nature of her desire and presenting it as a riddle, Gina offers Fabrizio the possibility to articulate his own desire in response to what he perceives hers to be. At first Fabrizio doesn't quite know what to do with this enigma. In one scene, clearly marked as Fabrizio's reverie, we see the protagonist looking at Gina while she wears various types of glasses, each time providing a different image of herself—teasing, smiling, shy, frowning. The enigma is therefore transformed into a blank screen onto which the various fantasies associated with Fabrizio's uncertain desire can be projected. Moments of fantasmatic tentativeness like this one seem to suggest that no matter what kind of enjoyment the liberation of desire from taboos promises, a certain form of mediation remains inescapable. With its emphasis on Gina's undecipherable behavior (itself a cliché of feminine enigmatic otherness), *Before the Revolution* reminds us that what the subject wants cannot be simply liberated from its dependence on the Other and the Other's enigmatic desire. The film offers a paradigmatic example of this aspect in the sequence set in the Sanvitale Fortress in the town of Fontanellato, where Gina looks through a camera obscura at Fabrizio as he walks across the square, as though he were the protagonist of a color film (Figure 15).

The contraption of the camera obscura emphasizes Gina's remoteness. Her desire is present (Fabrizio knows she is watching) but illegible (he cannot see her, so he improvises a little performance

Figure 15. Fabrizio's performance for Gina at the Sanvitale Fortress in Fontanellato in *Before the Revolution* (1963).

for her enjoyment). Unheard by her lover, Gina says, "I wish that nothing moved anymore, that everything stopped. Immobile, as in a painting. And we're inside the painting, us too immobile." Is this not a fitting description of how fantasy works, a staged scenario more real than reality itself mediating the subject's relationship to the object of desire? Filtered through a play of light and mirrors, the all-consuming enjoyment and supposed liberating force of incestuous desire becomes domesticated into a stage act. Fabrizio's desire to desire, the film seems to imply, can only find satisfaction within a fantasmatic framework, for what one wants is entirely dependent on fantasy as a mediating factor between the subject and the Other's desire. Years before the 1968 slogans calling for sexual liberation, the youth in *Before the Revolution* posits the relation between desire and fantasy as an open question rather than a mere hindrance on the path to unfettered enjoyment, suggesting that what one loses in freeing desire is in fact desire itself. A liberation *of* desire (from the Other, from fantasy) cannot but be a liberation *from* desire.

In fact, the complex imbrication of fantasies that surrounds Fabrizio in the film points not only to the inevitability of fantasmatic mediation but also, and more importantly, to the possibility that what Fabrizio is looking for is less desire itself than a fantasy capable of framing and sustaining it. In his journey through fantasy, Fabrizio learns how to desire, both politically (with Cesare) and sexually (with Gina). The final lesson will be marked by the emergence of one last fantasy, and one last moment of staged immobility. In the vicinity of the Po River, Gina, Fabrizio, and Cesare visit Puck, an older landowner on the verge of financial collapse and Gina's former lover. The characters converse about the future of the property. Fabrizio, spurred by jealousy as much as political conviction, harshly criticizes Puck and his bourgeois origins. In the meantime, a painter nearby is completing a landscape and, upon seeing his work, Gina observes that all the characters of the scene are in it. At this point, the frame freezes (Figure 16), as though to replicate the painting (which we never see), while Fabrizio's voice-over says, "In that moment I realized that Puck spoke for me as well. I saw myself in him, years later, and I felt there was no way out for us children of the bourgeoisie."

This moment of epiphany marks the affirmation of a fantasy of

Figure 16. The family portrait on the shores of the Po River in *Before the Revolution* (1963).

defeat. The rebellious youth finds himself framed together with the old bourgeois, the communist mentor, and the incestuous aunt, as though in a strange family portrait. The conflicts and divisions that Fabrizio wanted to introduce into his own bourgeois identity by way of his relationship with Cesare and Gina are finally negated, as the possibility of an elsewhere—politics, love, or both—disintegrates. In the end, Fabrizio embraces the desire of the only Other that demanded nothing of him—not the desire of the master (Cesare) nor the desire of the sphinx (Gina), but the desire of his social class: the desire of the father. It is a very specific kind of father that we see in *Before the Revolution*: Fabrizio's is a father that teaches nothing, demands nothing, and, perhaps most importantly, forbids nothing. Consider for instance the scene that takes place immediately after the Easter family lunch at Fabrizio's house, the morning after the couple's first sexual encounter. The sequence is a long take where the camera wanders across the sitting room from one character to the next. After some idle talk, Fabrizio and Gina start dancing to Gino Paoli's love song "Soltanto per un'ora" (Only for an hour). The mother is absent, the grandmother falls asleep on an armchair, and the father turns in for an afternoon nap, unfazed by the promiscuity between his son and his sister-in-law. As the guardians of bourgeois respectability fall off the frame one by one, the camera closes in on Fabrizio and Gina who, after a quick glance around to make sure nobody is watching, kiss passionately.

Interestingly, rather than a daring act of defiance, the scene seems to signal a natural prolongment of the placid festivity that took place just before it. In a family environment utterly unconcerned with enforcing taboos, it takes but a little effort to hide a scandalous relationship in plain sight. But what scandal is there, what glory or tragedy, in spitting in the face of a father that sleepwalks his way through the sweet life? There is no harsh sanctioning by the patriarchal order of a subversive act here, only the father's modicum of lethargic perplexity. "It is forbidden to forbid," the young militants would chant only a handful of years later. Paradoxical as it sounds, if this slogan describes anybody in *Before the Revolution,* it would be Fabrizio's bourgeois family. Fabrizio's yearning for emancipation is but a parenthesis of revolt within a larger social and familial environment that knows nothing of his son's scandals (incest, communism), and that quietly waits for him to do exactly what is expected, namely, marry Clelia and start his own sweet life in earnest. Fabrizio says so himself in one of the concluding scenes, confessing his disillusionment to Cesare: "I don't want to change the present. I accept it, but my bourgeois future is my bourgeois past. For me, ideology was something of a vacation [*villeggiatura*]. I thought I was living the years of the revolution. Instead, I lived the years before the revolution. Because for my sort it's always before the revolution."

Fabrizio's predicament is thrown into relief by another youth in the film: his tormented friend Agostino (Alan Midgette). The only queer character in the film, Agostino shares Fabrizio's bourgeois background but embodies a kind of rebellion that does not conform to his friend's standards. He antagonizes the oppression of his own class status by repeatedly running away from home— something for which he is scolded by Fabrizio, who exhorts him to instead channel his anger politically and become a member of the PCI. Agostino forcefully rejects Fabrizio's sanctimoniousness. Seeing no way out of his situation, he wades into the Po River, only to never return. His apparent suicide provides a stark contrast to Fabrizio's willingness to compromise. For Agostino, rebellion was no vacation. He confronts the same impasse as Fabrizio (how does one rebel against one's own bourgeois destiny?) but repudiates any refuge into the sweet life. Bertolucci has his protagonist ruminate on the meaning of Agostino's demise, which unsurprisingly remains an enigma for him. It seems significant, in this sense, that Agostino's fateful gesture is recounted to a stunned Fabrizio by Enore, a young worker who saw the event unfolding in real time. When revolt is not taken as a vacation, the antibourgeois bourgeois finds by his side in the final moment not the fellow class member but the proletarian.

In a less subtle fashion, Bertolucci also chastises Fabrizio's capitulation by juxtaposing his wedding to Clelia with Cesare reading to his students from *Moby-Dick* about Ahab's tenacious commitment to destroying his nemesis. However, the film suggests that the burden of this defeat does not rest solely on Fabrizio's shoulders. In his final conversation with Cesare, Fabrizio complains about the PCI's lack of a true internationalist vision: "Who is willing to strike for the freedom of Angola today? Tell me the name of someone who went to Algeria to join the fight. Who is going to protest in the streets if they kill a Black man in Alabama?" Fabrizio's surrender is not just an existential issue, the conclusion of a bourgeois quest for his own desire *not* to change the present. It is also, however implicitly, the indictment of a political organization, the Italian Communist Party, that is already showing signs of an inability to read the political present and properly locate the sites of struggle—a master, in other words, whose superior knowledge can no longer be assumed or relied on. It is no mystery that 1968 defined itself as a global movement for emancipation in opposition to the utterly deficient, if not downright reactionary, political framework offered by western communist parties at the time, with the most glaring examples arguably being the PCI in Italy and the French Communist Party, or PCF, in France. In its depiction of political and existential defeat, *Before the Revolution* therefore chronicles the missed encounter between two inadequacies: a bourgeois youth for whom radical change is but a fleeting infatuation, and a political party ossified in its reformist project.

If *Before the Revolution* anticipates anything of 1968, it is not, or not primarily, a generic desire of youth rebellion, with its corollary of intersections between revolutionary politics and demands for sexual liberation. Rather, the film problematizes this idea of revolt by questioning whether a definite desire with an identifiable object exists at all. What is reactivated in *Before the Revolution* is revolt as a nebulous impetus, a desire to desire. The split between the two axes of politics and sexuality allows the film to show the complex structure of fantasmatic imbrication that sustains each, and that the figure of the youth tries to knot together.

It is instructive to compare *Before the Revolution* with another film that deploys the same elements and motifs while displacing and rearranging them. In this sense, *Come Play with Me* can be read as an inversion of Bertolucci's film. Both films are chronicles of a defeat in which the existing structure of the bourgeois sweet life closes in on the youth and its rebellious impulses. In Bertolucci, this defeat is seen from the point of view of the youth; Samperi instead adopts the point of view of the bourgeois sweet life itself. As a result, the ending of the two films is similar (after a disruption, balance is again established and the bourgeoisie can continue to prosper), but the defeat inscribed in the figure of the youth assumes different shapes depending on whence one looks at it.

Come Play with Me revolves around the relationship between a young paralyzed man, Alvise (Lou Castel), and his maternal aunt, Lea (Lisa Gastoni). Alvise's father believes that his son's ailment is psychosomatic in nature, so he sends him to spend a few days at Lea's villa in the countryside to get some rest. As aunt and nephew gradually become infatuated with each other, it is revealed that Alvise is faking his paralysis. The bond between the two strengthens, to the point where Lea breaks off her relationship with her longtime partner, television journalist and intellectual Stefano (Gabriele Ferzetti), and retreats into the house to play erotic games orchestrated by Alvise, who keeps teasing her but refuses to have full sexual intercourse. Eventually, when the two are supposed to play the game of euthanasia, Lea injects an unsuspecting Alvise with poison and kills him.

Whereas in *Before the Revolution* it was Gina who embodied the riddle of the Other's desire with her capriciousness and volatility, leaving Fabrizio to interrogate his own desire through this enigma, in *Come Play with Me,* the roles are reversed. The youth (Alvise) occupies the position of the mysterious Other, seducing Lea with a tightly choreographed oscillation between vulnerability and infantile mischievousness. Alvise's defining dimension—the one he eventually lures Lea into—is that of pretending. He fakes his own paralysis, toys with a gun as he fantasizes about shooting Lea and Stefano, stages his involvement in an accident while Lea is away (so as to have her promptly come back), causes a scene at a dinner party by pretending that someone put one of Lea's earrings in his soup, and so forth. By way of his pretend play, Alvise manipulates Lea, who finds herself in Fabrizio's position in *Before the Revolution*: left to guess what the Other wants, and prompted to interrogate her own desire. The remoteness of Alvise as Lea's Other is exemplified in a scene where he refuses to tell her what he is giggling about with a female friend: "I won't tell you. It's a secret between us young people."

The shift from youth as the desire to desire (Fabrizio) to youth as enigma (Alvise) is revealing in that it displaces the ignorance about the desire of the Other from the protagonist to the spectator. The issue is no longer that the youth doesn't know what he wants. Rather, it is that *we* do not know what he wants. In one scene at a dinner party, Stefano claims that there is something elusive about the contemporary Italian youth, then launches into a garden-variety sociological tirade: "This is the feature of today's youth. . . . Today's generations tend to an emancipation destined to undo the nuclear family, to break it. Right now, for instance, we witness the symptoms: youth becomes autonomous, interconnected by way of ritualistic, fetishistic elements." It is notable that the youth's antagonistic impetus is illustrated in such scholastic terms, as though the youth's otherness were not only to be domesticated by its inscription into the public discourse but also harnessed for the benefit of a nation in which "the senior population . . . is arteriosclerotic" and in desperate need of a transfusion of young blood.

Stefano sees in the Italian youth the same vitality that Alvise's father would like to see in his son. The two characters, it seems, could not be farther apart (Stefano is a public intellectual, the father a wealthy industrialist), yet they constitute two sides of the same coin. While he extols the virtues of the rebellious youth,

Stefano is resolutely committed to celebrating the emergence of the Italian capitalist state on the global scene. Alvise's father, one of the protagonists of such emergence, implicitly encourages this rebellion, as he not only fails to sanction the incestuous relationship between aunt and nephew (similar to *Before the Revolution*) but in fact sets the stage for the incest to occur in the first place. Samperi only shows the father briefly and always from behind. His voice is faceless but overly authoritative when he orders Alvise to spend time with Lea, which only highlights the paradox of a rigid patriarchal despotism that creates the very conditions for this subversive scandal to take place. The supposed undoing of the nuclear family brought about by the youth is revealed by Stefano and the father to be nothing but an injection of obscene vitality needed by a country's capitalist system in rapid development. The secret of the youth is, in this sense, no longer a secret—not thanks to Stefano's platitudes, but because of what the film shows: that the youth's hunger for enjoyment is, in the last analysis, in the service of someone else's desire.

We thus begin to glimpse the silhouette of an emerging kind of superego in which bourgeois respectability only disguises an obscene, vampire-like injunction addressed to the youth to enjoy without restraint. In the scene where Stefano lectures his guests about the state of affairs of the Italian youth, the sound of his voice is silenced as the film's recurrent musical theme fades in. The camera cuts to a series of close-ups of the dinner participants, magnifying their mouths in grotesque detail as Alvise observes them (Figure 17).

The obscene underbelly of the sweet life that is mercifully glossed over in *Before the Revolution* shows itself in *Come Play with Me*. Once the paternalistic, pseudo-intellectual veneer is scraped off, a rough surface of lust, voracity, and narcissism is revealed. Lea, however, is spared this treatment. She is the only one returning the camera's (and Alvise's) gaze, her face congenially framed by a close-up in the midst of a series of shots of lips, teeth, and tongues. With this scene, we get a glimpse of Alvise's fantasy: Lea is presented as different from the others, removed from their rapacious appetites and therefore worthy of his attention as an object of torment and seduction.

Figure 17. Alvise observes the party invitees and Lea in *Come Play with Me* (1969).

As the full reach of the superego's imperative to enjoy becomes apparent, this fantasy proves to be Alvise's downfall. Seemingly in love with Alvise, Lea relinquishes her social role, and with it the assurances of the sweet life. The villa, once the symbol of bourgeois respectability, is now transfigured into the theater of a supposedly liberating game, a playground that becomes increasingly indistinguishable from a prison. But every game must end, and when the enjoyment exhausts itself, the *villeggiatura* is over and it is time to go back to one's routine. So Lea puts an end to the pretense. She murders Alvise and, in the film's last shot, sits at her vanity to apply makeup, ready to return to her pristine bourgeois self as though nothing had happened. The ending reverses the dialectic of desire articulated up to that point. The youth's otherness, the undecipherability around which the film had revolved, is revealed to be the ultimate pretense, a performance put on for Lea's delight, with Alvise's tragic error being not having understood who is caught in whose game. Lea literalizes the vampirization of the youth outlined by Stefano and Alvise's father. By no means a real threat to the status quo, the youth's transgressive impulses are but a fleeting jolt of energy to the stale works of the sweet life.

In *Before the Revolution*, and more explicitly in *Come Play with Me*, the temporary subversion of the existing order is simply a diversion, a vacation. However, the figure of the youth occupies two different positions in the two films, which in turn determine the two different forms assumed by the co-optation of the youth back into the schemata of the sweet life. What in Bertolucci was a surrender to one's own bourgeois past, in Samperi is a sacrifice for the sake of the bourgeoisie's future: in the former, the diary of an existential and political defeat seen from the standpoint of the youth; in the latter, a précis of the instrumental uses of youth by a bourgeoisie in search of renewal. In either case, and against much of 1968 lore, the youth is cast as a fundamentally reactionary figure. In a way, this is the real transgression that the films stage for our times: they think the possibility of wresting the figure of the youth from the hagiography of rebellion to explore the implications of the dialectic of desire that gravitates around it, and the dangerous misreadings that that hagiography might engender.

Acting Out: Fists in the Pocket

The definitive word on many of the grand narratives of 1968 was uttered by a film released well before 1968 actually took place: Marco Bellocchio's *Fists in the Pocket*. The youth at the center of the film is Alessandro (Lou Castel), the epileptic son of a bourgeois family living in the country town of Bobbio (Bellocchio's birthplace), who, wishing to free his older brother, Augusto (Marino Masè), from the burden of their ailing relatives, proceeds to murder their blind mother (Liliana Gerace) and their disabled brother, Leone (Pier Luigi Troglio). Alessandro is also in love with his own sister, Giulia (Paola Pitagora), who in turn is infatuated with Augusto.

Counterintuitive as it may sound, and despite the barrage of critical commentary that the film has spawned since its release, the pseudopsychoanalytical ex post facto clichés about 1968 (parricide, generational conflict mapped onto the Oedipus complex, and the like) have little purchase in *Fists in the Pocket*. The reason for this lies not in the fact that the film predates the event but rather in the argument the film forcefully advances. Bellocchio is not interested in celebrating Alessandro's murderous acts as the allegorical seed of youth rebellion planted at the heart of the bourgeoisie. (The father, for one, is hardly a nemesis to be reckoned with; absent-minded in *Before the Revolution* and invisible in *Come Play with Me,* he reaches here the final stage of his demise: he is dead, unnamed, and referred to only in passing). The truth is much less consolatory. The youth in *Fists in the Pocket* is not the agent of revolutionary change but the last monstrous excrescence of a social class that was dying well before it was murdered.

An epistolary exchange between Pier Paolo Pasolini and Grazia Cherchi (who responded on behalf of Bellocchio) puts into focus the contrast between opposing interpretations of *Fists in the Pocket* as a vitalistic paean to rebellion and a treatise on the terminal condition of a social class.[6] Countering Pasolini's off-target observations about the film as a "celebration of . . . abnormality against the rule of the bourgeois life" reminiscent of "Ginsberg's poetry," Cherchi points out that Alessandro's victims are "already innocuous . . . inert targets, even before he shows up to push them with the strength of a finger into a grave that should have received them way earlier."[7] In *Before the Revolution* and *Come Play with Me,* as we have seen, youth rebellion is nothing more than a digression after which the sweet life can pick up exactly where it left off—with marriage or maquillage, it doesn't matter. Instead, *Fists in the Pocket* tells a story of exhaustion, a condition in which the bourgeoisie has outlived its own life-span. In passing, Cherchi's quote points to a specific aspect that exemplifies this situation of being already dead: the minimal effort required of Alessandro to carry out the matricide and fratricide, the "strength of a finger." In a sense, besides the obvious pervasiveness in the film of a sickness that does not spare bodies, minds, or relationships, what really conveys the idea of the bourgeois family as a walking corpse are Alessandro's gestures. He gently pushes his blind mother off a cliff while she was already walking toward the edge; and, just as gently, he nudges a narcotized Leone underwater when he is taking his bath, drowning him. No weapons, no struggles, no spectacular violence; the camera registers the delicateness of Alessandro's hand gestures with repeated close-ups as death finds its place between the shots, evoked rather than shown.

There is, of course, a stark incongruence here between the minimalism of these gestures—almost a degree zero of aggression—and its effects. The incommensurability between these two aspects is precisely where the enigma of the youth in *Fists in the Pocket* resides. The destruction of the bourgeois family is perceived as scandalous because it is literal, deprived of any allegorical mediation. Indeed, if all one sees in the film is the enormity of Alessandro's actions, then the figure of the youth logically becomes the embodiment of a *passage à l'acte:* a total, abrupt breakdown of every semblance under the pressure of an extreme act of destruction. But the minimalism of Alessandro's gestures seems to point us in a different direction, not that of a *passage à l'acte* that does away with the Other but instead that of an acting out that calls for its restoration.

As an acting out, we can read Alessandro's actions as a call addressed to the Other. It is essential to bear in mind that in the film, the family is oppressive not because of the control it exercises on its subjects as an institution but because it no longer functions as an institution. In other words, the system of bourgeois family values, the only Other Alessandro has ever known, is now dead. Insofar as it has ceased to perform its social function, the family is now nothing but dead weight. Thus, to accelerate this process of decomposition and see whether a new Other will respond to his call and emerge from the ashes of the old one, Alessandro entertains what Italo Calvino called in his review of the film "a very simple idea, an idea that may come to anybody's mind but that nobody expresses, something like, 'why don't we throw the blind mother off the bridge?'"[8] Alessandro is not driven by a political or existential crisis like Fabrizio; nor are his purposes programmatically—if naively—subversive, as with Alvise. He has no clue what this new Other might be; he has no investment in imagining what it might look like. Cherchi and Bellocchio offer a similar interpretation in their exchange with Pasolini (Alessandro "kills if only for the curiosity to know what will happen by introducing into a stale, decrepit order . . . a quantum of irrationality capable of subverting it"), and also indicate money to be one of the protagonist's motivations.[9] Getting rid of the dead weight of the sick relatives would mean fewer expenses, and therefore the possibility for the remaining members of the family to live more comfortably. Spelled out only by Alessandro, this dispassionate, efficiency-driven assessment is implicitly shared by Augusto, who embodies the emergence of a different kind of bourgeoisie, one more modest and utterly indifferent to the cultural and religious framework that shaped the previous incarnation of the sweet life.

Through Augusto, the eminently reactionary nature of Alessandro's fantasy is laid bare; the glimpse of a petty bourgeois life is all that this grand act of rebellion can muster. This is the real scandal of *Fists in the Pocket*—not the violent revolt of the youth, as Pasolini would have it, but the poverty of the fantasies called on to frame it. There are no vacations to be taken from a bourgeois existence here, no aunts to lust after or revolutions to imagine as the sweet life awaits our return. It is as though in *Fists in the Pocket* the bourgeoisie had lost one of its most precious means of subsistence: the ability to produce fantasies of escape from itself. The sense of enclosure that permeates the film, reflected in Bellocchio's use of the house's labyrinthine topography, speaks to this lack of any elsewhere to turn to. However, this entrapment hardly asphyxiates the youth's dynamism. Instead, it imposes a certain curvature to it, bending it enough to turn its trajectory inward. Alessandro wants to restore the family to some sort of vigor by amputating its necrotic appendages, hence his investment in the only semblance of an alternative that he can imagine: Augusto's project of a petty bourgeois life away from the family villa. This is the film's ultimate obscenity. Alessandro's "mask" of "a death project disguised as a 'reasonable' life project" justifies the liquidation of "the weak, the sick, those who impose an unproductive *dépense*" on others.[10] This is what passes for freedom for a bourgeoisie staring at its own rotting corpse.

If we now look back at *Before the Revolution* and *Come Play with Me*, we see that they provide two other distinct versions of this relation between the bourgeoisie and its own demise. In the former, Fabrizio's family do not know that they are dead, which is why they always live before the revolution, in a time outside of time. In the latter, it is the opposite; precisely because it gains perception of its own mortality, the bourgeoisie must devour its children by first construing them as mysterious objects of desire, then consuming them.

Some provisional conclusions may be drawn from our analysis of these three still lifes of bourgeois existence. Desire is not to be understood simply as a positively subversive force that finds itself restrained by external limits imposed on it by the structure of the bourgeois sweet life. On the contrary, it is the structure itself that determines dialectically the form that desire assumes in the various figures of the youth: a poetic longing for escape in Fabrizio, a capricious disruption in Alvise, a desperate acting out in Alessandro. Tourist, saboteur, gravedigger—these three figures of the youth also point to the inconsequentiality of their actions, as the potentially subversive event of the desire of the youth is always reabsorbed into the framework of bourgeois life as, respectively, a vacation, a pretend game, and the natural course of a terminal illness. This is the impasse of the figure of the youth outlined in the three films: a desire to break away from the structure ends up subsumed and put to use by that very same structure.

In an effort to break a new path through this deadlock, Liliana Cavani has tried to reject the notion of the inevitability of the same destiny found in the films of Bertolucci, Samperi, and Bellocchio. With *The Cannibals* (*I cannibali*, 1970), the youth is no longer implicated in the decline of the bourgeoisie as its symptom but rather acts autonomously as an antagonistic agent. No longer limited to the horizon of the family, the youth's desire projects itself into the distance toward revolution, making the youth the subjective figure of a choice: whether or not to be faithful to the event of one's own revolutionary desire.

Bodies in the Streets: *The Cannibals*

A retelling of Sophocles's *Antigone*, *The Cannibals* is set in contemporary Italy, where an authoritarian regime is determined to make an example of young protesters by murdering them and putting their corpses on public display across the city, a thousand Polynices left to rot in the streets. Antigone (Britt Ekland) wants to bury her brother, and is helped by Teiresias (Pierre Clementi), a silent, mysterious man who appeared out of nowhere. Forging a tacit alliance, the two engage in a series of acts of defiance against the government. After burying Polynices, they start removing other corpses from the streets. Their actions set in motion a series of events that will lead to a violent reaction from the state, as Antigone is put in prison and Teiresias is committed to a mental institution. Haemon (Tomas Milian), Antigone's promised husband and the son of a powerful member of the government, tries to intercede with his father to free Antigone, to no avail. He ends up incarcerated himself, and in an act of desperate protest, he starts imitating a dog. After the two protagonists are publicly executed, a group of young men and women recently dismissed from a mental institution begin to pick up bodies from the streets and bury them, continuing Antigone and Teiresias's rebellion.

In *The Cannibals,* the youth's plight assumes an immediately political value, as testified by the unambiguous references to the contemporary student and worker protests as well as the brutality of state repression. At the same time, the recourse to a mythical framework tempers the evident topicality of the film, transfiguring it in part into a more general meditation on the subjective logic of revolt. At once saturated by history and looking to situate itself outside of it in the eternal time of myth, *The Cannibals* shows a certain ambivalence toward the possibility of political subjectivation that the figure of the youth carries. This ambivalence is reflected in the episodic organization of the film. After the initial, heroic decision to bury Polynices, Cavani shows Antigone and Teiresias confronting the state's reaction in various settings, and to various effects. We see a mockery of the impotence of power in the chase scenes, inspired by silent slapstick comedies, with the two protagonists disguised as priests or soldiers trying to elude the police; a matter-of-fact denunciation of the brutality of state violence with scenes of imprisonment and torture; and finally, in the very last scene, the hope for a new collective subject to arise from the event of Antigone and Teiresias's sacrifice, when young men and women pick up their legacy.

As a sort of compendium of possibilities, *The Cannibals* retreads some of the ideas that we have already encountered in other films, even as it envisions new ones. But more than the individual scenarios it presents, the most significant aspect of the film resides in its commitment to not commit, as it were, to any one of these possibilities. Far from a limitation, this is the film's distinctive conceptual strength, namely, the attempt to traverse and encompass all the different and often contradictory facets of the youth as a figure of political subjectivation. In this sense, it would be a mistake to overemphasize the Sophoclean reference in the film. *Antigone* provides the narrative framework, but *The Cannibals* de facto limits itself to listing the tragic heroine's ethicopolitical position as simply one of the possible subjective destinies of the figure of the youth.[11] Cavani is more interested in surveying the larger political field of the figure of the youth after 1968, enumerating the manifold avenues to subjectivation that it presents. Yet more than a celebration of possibility, the film resembles a maze made solely of dead ends. Even the hopeful ending is hardly presented in the film as the necessary outcome of a process of subjectivation. It simply coexists with the other scenarios in the same realm of possibility.

In an interview, Cavani called the film a "happening" in a vein reminiscent of situationist public impromptu performances, especially in the practice, described by the director, of shutting down entire neighborhoods to stage the scenes with the corpses lying on the streets[12]—a veritable traumatic irruption of the political real into everyday life, which would lead one to suggest that if there is a kernel that resists subsumption into the seemingly fluid permutation of registers and scenarios that makes up the film, it is precisely in the images of the dead bodies scattered on the streets.

The imagery of the first part of the film is indeed stunning: a series of shots of Milan's urban landscape littered with bodies even as life in the city bustles on, all but ignoring them (Figure 18).

These images of mass murder coexist, as we have seen, with a number of other possible destinies of the youth, including Antigone's and Teiresias's heroic acts. In fact, one could argue that the film's strange oscillation between history and myth needs to be understood precisely in the terms set by these two images: on the one hand, the corpses scattered in the streets as an explicit reference to contemporary history; on the other, the relentless activity and obstinate silence of the two protagonists as a mythical response not only to state violence, but also to a certain exhaustion of the strategies of revolt of 1968. It is in the ahistorical time of myth, Cavani suggests, that the youth must search for new forms of resistance, away from the dead remnants of defeated

Figure 18. Corpses strewn over the streets of Milan in the opening credits of *The Cannibals* (1970).

struggles—a defeat apparent not only in the images of a corpse-strewn Milan, but perhaps even more in the indifferent countenance of the city dwellers who go about their life as though these bodies never existed. Against the co-optation and neutralization by state and capital of the revolutionary impulses of 1968, Antigone and Teiresias embody the fantasy of a return to some kind of primitive condition of innocence and purity, a sort of mythical prelinguistic existence untainted by the dehumanizing dictates of society.[13] Their silence stands as the sign of an absolute refusal to engage with the system—a refusal that extends beyond the two protagonists to include Haemon, whose transformation into a dog stems from a similar determination to end any dialogue with the powers that be.

The mythical side of the film thus resolves itself into a rejection of a dialectic of political subjectivation in favor of an autonomous self-affirmation grounded in a primitivistic fantasy of innocence. Suspended between the silence of the dead and that of the living, the youth finds himself split between history and myth—a history of compromise and defeat and a myth of revolutionary purity. This division, however, is proven untenable by the film itself. However celebrated by Cavani as a radical path toward liberation, the rebellion of the protagonists remains locked within a dialectical relation with the structure it aims to challenge. After her arrest, a professor lectures Antigone on the interconnection of revolution and reaction: "You need us because it is upon us that you discharge your revolutionary impetus; and we need you, your petty crimes and your exhibitionism. A power without its enfants terribles is an uncivil power, a power destined to perish." Similar to *Come Play with Me,* we see the recognition on the part of the structure of the necessity of harnessing and incorporating the revolutionary impulses of the youth in order to survive, thus shattering any fantasy of primitivistic purity. The impasse that this fantasy points to is, however, absolutely real: how to imagine forms of revolt in a time when revolt itself constitutes the nourishment of authoritarian institutions? The fantasy of pure autonomy of the two silent heroes is precisely a symptom of this impasse, an attempt to solve it by pretending it does not exist.

We return, then, to the images that open the film. Beyond the ultimately reassuring fantasy of Antigone and Teiresias's mythical heroism, these images actually touch on the real of the impasse. They reshuffle the terms of the figural articulation of the youth, who is no longer a potential political subject open to a myriad radical destinies but instead a persistent, lifeless remainder of a once-vital movement. In this sense, the corpses remain on display not only as victims of state violence but also as an ominous literalization of the demise of the youth movement of 1968 as a possible political subject. Cavani seems to suggest that any form of defeat that may befall the mass youth movements of 1968 will have to be thought not only in terms of collective suffering but also, and perhaps more ominously, on a vast generational scale.

Three films from the second half of the 1970s and the early 1980s help clarify the contours and consequences of this defeat: *I Am Self-Sufficient* (*Io sono un autarchico*, 1976) and *Ecce Bombo* (1978) by Nanni Moretti, and *Toxic Love* (*Amore tossico*, 1983) by Claudio Caligari. We can see these films as unfolding from Cavani's images of death. The youthful bodies in Moretti and Caligari may still be breathing, but their agonies of boredom and addiction speak to the historical exhaustion of the conditions under which the project of a liberation of desire and enjoyment could carry a revolutionary potential. Like Cavani's youth-corpses, Moretti's and Caligari's protagonists are tasked with staging, despite themselves, the spectacle of their own defeat.

"The Color of Emptiness": Desire and Drive in Moretti and Caligari

The focus of the three films is symptomatic of the distance that separates Moretti and Caligari, both in terms of their biographical background and their political leanings. In his early diptych, Moretti stages the existential and political disorientation of his generation through loosely connected vignettes of young middle-class types caught in the often comical dead ends and paradoxes of 1970s-era youth culture. Moretti pictures himself as distant from the universe of urban radical leftism—a distance he reclaims in his later films as well, most notably *Dear Diary* (*Caro diario*, 1993). Caligari, on the other hand, was an active participant of the 1977 movement, and his early documentaristic work on the lumpenproletariat as well as the student and worker struggles of those years amply reflects this political engagement. *Toxic Love,* his first feature film, is centered on a group of young heroin addicts in the coastal town of Ostia, on the outskirts of Rome. True to its neorealist inspiration, the film follows the characters (all nonprofessional actors and actresses, many of whom were present or former drug addicts) in a seemingly endless cycle of looking for money, buying heroin, getting high, and starting over again.

The leap from the tedium of urban middle-class life to the epidemic of drug addiction in the suburban underclass is significant, of course, so much so that the juxtaposition of the films may seem dubious, if not outright forced, especially considering the starkly different critical fortunes that the two directors have enjoyed. True, there is the shared sociological relevance (the films as portrayals of a generation), but that angle hardly offers a solid footing for a comparative critical assessment. As with the rest of the present book, such justification can only come from the figure itself, and from the method it imposes on our analysis. So we must ask not only what variation of the figure of the youth is outlined in *I Am Self-Sufficient, Ecce Bombo,* and *Toxic Love* but also, and perhaps more importantly, across what impasses this figure comes into existence.

On the surface, the most conspicuous contrast between Moretti's and Caligari's works resides in the claim that they make on realism and on the question of authenticity. *I Am Self-Sufficient* and *Ecce Bombo* adopt an antirealistic approach in which theatricality and estrangement dominate the scene. Indeed, Michele Apicella (Moretti himself) and his friends are constantly performing, an awkward negotiation between the conformist demands of youth culture and a desire to affirm one's own difference in the form of idiosyncratic narcissism.[14] *Toxic Love* instead opts for a largely naturalistic representation (on-location shooting, natural lighting, the use of dialect and improvisation) whose primary purpose is verisimilitude. These two opposite approaches translate into opposite claims about the figure of the youth. In Moretti, the youth is marked by a kaleidoscopic self-fashioning of identity, where every posture projects a specific image of the self. Michele oscillates between the roles of victim and censor of this collective performance, as he makes fun of its aberrant aspects, but he also fully partakes in this theatrical dynamic. In *Toxic Love,* the constraint of realism generates the opposite figure; the characters are by-products of their material living conditions, their hopes and fears entirely determined by the position they occupy within the social structure. If in Moretti the youth struggles to be (and know) what he wants, in Caligari he can only be what he is.

In Moretti, the pliability of the self as performance is suffused with boredom. In psychoanalytical terms, boredom can be defined as a peculiar indetermination of desire: a "pure desire of enjoyment which does not find any suffering to enjoy"[15] and therefore floats untethered from any concrete object. For Lacan, boredom is the reaction of us moderns to old semblances of love, like Beatrice's divine bliss and Dante's rapt contemplation of it.[16] The root of this bored response is to be found, at least in part, in the youthful liberation of desire that wants to demolish all semblances and sublimations and enjoy without restraint. The figure of the bored youth as a by-product of 1968 is explicitly evoked by Lacan: "If I have talked of boredom, of moroseness, in connection with the 'divine' approach of love, how can one not recognize that these two affects are betrayed—through speech, and even in deed—in those young people dedicated to relations without repression."[17] These "relations without repression"—the fantasy of a pure, unrestrained enjoyment beyond the Oedipal prohibition—aim at annulling the fundamental kernel of impossibility that is sex itself: the traumatic real of the sexual nonrelation. As a society, we confront this real through processes of mediation and sublimation that allow us to rationalize its impossibility: "the sexual impasse exudes the fictions that rationalize the impossible within which it originates."[18] What Lacan calls "discourses" are one such fiction: forms of organization of social relations designed to offset the sexual nonrelation. One particular discourse, however, abdicates this task: the "capitalist discourse." As Colette Soler writes,

> Unlike the preceding discourses, [the capitalist discourse]
> thus does not make up for the real nonrelationship and leaves
> it exposed for all the world to see. This does not mean that it

sheds light on the fact that there is no such thing as a sexual relationship; it simply deprives subjects of the symbolic resources that tempered it in other eras, leaving them more exposed than ever to the consequences of solitude and of the precariousness of the sexual nonrelationship.[19]

This is where youthful boredom finds its origin; the collapse of all forms of mediation between the subject and the object results in the impossibility of forging viable libidinal ties that, while not solving once and for all the problem of the sexual nonrelationship, would at least manage to make it tolerable for the subject. Soler again: "Boredom, in essence, is one of the affects of the desire for something else . . . a desire for another jouissance."[20] In the case of Moretti, the mirage of a direct access to enjoyment has as its obverse the impossibility of locating an anchoring for desire. The result is boredom, that peculiar situation in which desire drifts untethered from one object to the next, in search of another type of enjoyment. The bored youth in Moretti, then, is a mask that simultaneously disguises and reveals its own determining impasse, one of the "fictions that rationalize the impossible" of the sexual nonrelation.

If Moretti is primarily concerned with boredom as the "desire for another jouissance," Caligari situates the youth in a territory beyond desire altogether. The cycles of high and low that Caligari's youths go through point to the insistence of an irreducible surplus to the logic of desire, a compulsion to repeat that evokes the dimension of the drive. As responses to a structural impasse, boredom and addiction are two sides of the same coin. Both driven by fantasies of immediacy, they establish subject–object relations that are equal and opposite. To the impossibility of stable libidinal attachments in boredom, addiction opposes the promise of a unique, steadfast tie to an object capable of maintaining the subject in a continuous state of enjoyment. But while the logic of desire in Moretti still presupposes the fantasy of attaining the object, the drive that dominates *Toxic Love* projects no sense of futurity, only repetition.

Éric Laurent defines toxicomania as "the quest . . . for the verification of the color of emptiness."[21] The expression "the color of emptiness" is taken from Lacan, who identifies it as the fundamental "coloring" of the drive, which is "suspended in the light of a gap."[22] This gap is the limit imposed on desire by the symbolic—that is, the unattainability of the object of desire, or, in other words, the fundamental impossibility that is enjoyment itself. The young addicts in *Toxic Love* verify the color of emptiness by covering up this gap (through access to heroin, enjoyment becomes possible) while at the same time testifying to its irreducibility. The very act of covering up the gap installs a time of unceasing repetition, for the drive endlessly circles around its object without ever attaining it. In fact, the enjoyment associated with the drive only derives from missing the object, so that the cycle of the subject's self-sabotage can be repeated once more.

Beyond the stereotypical portrayals of a defeated generation, the figure of the youth that emerges in Moretti and Caligari reveals a structural situation in which the fantasy of a direct access to enjoyment runs aground in the interconnected forms of boredom and addiction. Yet not only the proximity of but also the distance between the former and the latter, along with their attendant logics of desire and drive, register politically. In Moretti, the youth's inability to forge viable libidinal ties translates into a deeply atomized world in which characters seem to float untethered from each other, refractory to any idea of collectivity, be it based on love, friendship, or solidarity. In Caligari, the dominance of the drive, often described as antisocial, generates the opposite effect. When understood as a universal condition of the human subject, the insistence of the drive—the gap—becomes the background against which social bonds can be created. One example of this is the subterranean motif of solidarity that traverses the film. Caligari makes a point to emphasize minor moments in which the characters, faced with the opportunity for selfish or even predatory behavior, opt for the opposite. For instance, after a botched robbery, one of the main characters, Cesare (Cesare Ferretti), insists that his partner in crime take all of the meager score; later in the film, Cesare steals a pack of cigarettes from a sleeping homeless man, only to then take one cigarette and put the pack back. Not only does solidarity become a form of resistance against a shared condition of marginalization, it also signals the episodic reintroduction of the Other (the heist partner, the homeless man) as the agent capable of regulating the access to enjoyment (renouncing one's cut, taking one cigarette instead of the whole pack).

In *Toxic Love,* the structure constantly interpellates the characters as lumpenproletarian addicts. They are assigned the role of idlers and deadbeats, their behavior as predictable as the recurrence of the impulse to shoot up. However, these instances of unprompted solidarity speak to a refusal of this interpellation, little moments of heroism in which the drive is temporarily kept at bay. One scene vividly presents this refusal of interpellation. Sitting at a table in a friend's apartment, Cesare reminisces to his girlfriend, Michela (Michela Mioni), about an episode from two years earlier. We hear the story of a heroin injection in the backseat of a cab that knocks Cesare out. When he comes to, he finds that the taxi driver has taken him to a hospital. When he notices two orderlies running toward him with a stretcher, Cesare flees: "I left them without their junkie corpse *[il loro cadavere di drogato]*." This leads him to briefly ponder suicide, a motif that returns in the following scene, where Cesare, after having had sex with Michela, puts a gun in his mouth and then to her head while she is sleeping. When she wakes up, she looks at him and calmly asks, "Why, Cesare?"

Why indeed? Beyond any psychologizing explanation that would cite hopelessness and existential despair as the reason, the answer to Michela's question resides in Cesare's previous gesture of refusal: "I left them without their junkie corpse." Similar to his suicidal fantasies, Cesare's escape from the hospital speaks to a desire for withdrawal. But withdrawal from what—or rather from whom? Someone, it seems, is watching. Cesare's words suggest the scene of a spectacle in which the addicted youth fulfills the role of the sacrificial outcast. "They," therefore, doesn't simply refer to the orderlies but also to the entirety of so-called civil society that takes pleasure from the spectacle of self-destruction staged by the addicted lumpens. The "junkie corpse" would then be precisely the ultimate object of desire that this spectacle would have to offer, and that would unfailingly be met by "them" with a mixture of distant compassion and reproving paternalism.[23] This, however, would be nothing more than a veneer of respectability papering over a collective enjoyment derived from this spectacle of death. Lacan clearly identified this aspect when he admonished the students protesting at Vincennes in 1970 that the powers that be were in fact taking pleasure in the spectacle of their rebellious appropriation of enjoyment: "You fulfill the role of the helots of this regime.... The regime puts you on display; it says: 'Watch them fuck.'" Does not the invisible "regime" of civil society in *Toxic Love* put the youth on display and say "Watch them die" or, more precisely, "Watch their own enjoyment kill them"?

In fact, more than addiction itself, Cesare's tragedy is that of awareness—the awareness of performing for an audience whose enjoyment comes in equal measure from the sanctioning of addiction on a social and moral level and from the spectacle of devastation unleashed by drug abuse among the rebellious youth of the long '68. Cesare's dogged refusal to give "them" anything to enjoy is the last, desperate political gesture of the figure of the youth. In this sense, we could read the tragedy of Cesare in Caligari as the obverse side of the comedy of Michele Apicella in Moretti. Michele shares with Cesare the awareness of being on a stage, but in contrast to the protagonist of *Toxic Love*, he fully embraces the performance. Boredom then becomes a way to turn the tables on the regime by exposing the absurdity of the spectacle of enjoyment that it forces the youth to interpret. It is not surprising, then, that the end point of the youth's arc would coincide with a meticulous portrayal of "them," those who are loudly applauding at the spectacle of the youth's demise: Mario Monicelli's *An Average Little Man* (*Un borghese piccolo piccolo*, 1977).

The Cloven Youth: Fantasies of Reaction in *An Average Little Man*

The life of Giovanni Vivaldi (Alberto Sordi), a cynical, opportunistic white-collar employee nearing retirement, revolves almost exclusively around his son, Mario (Vincenzo Crocitti), a dim-witted accounting graduate looking to follow in his father's footsteps and secure a job in the public sector. Giovanni goes to great lengths to make sure his son is hired (including joining a Masonic lodge), yet his dreams of a solid middle-class future for him are shattered when Mario is accidentally killed during a bank robbery. Stunned, Giovanni nurses ideas of revenge while his wife, Amalia (Shelley Winters), is left paralyzed and mute by a stroke. Convinced he has identified the murderer (Renzo Carboni), Giovanni springs into action: he severely injures the young man and abducts him to a shack in a swampy area at the outskirts of Rome with the idea of torturing him. The prisoner, however, dies from his wounds. Disappointed, Giovanni prepares to enjoy his retirement, but Amalia too passes away, overcome by her illness. The film ends with Giovanni caught in an altercation with a young man. The two exchange insults, and as the young man walks away, Giovanni starts following him in his car, presumably ready to kill again.

At first sight, *An Average Little Man* seems bent on rejecting the type of dialectical positioning of the youth that we found in the films discussed so far in this chapter. Monicelli depicts neither the creature of desire, caught in a wrestling match with the Other, that one finds in Bertolucci, Samperi, and Bellocchio, nor the outcasts lured by the mirage of free enjoyment we encountered in the films by Moretti and Caligari. What we see in *An Average Little Man* is a sort of Januslike figure made up by two diametrically opposed faces: that of the purely familiar object of love (Mario) and that of the purely foreign object of envy and hate (the bank robber). Monicelli emphasizes this duality by arranging the film around the split between these two faces of the youth, with the death of Mario occurring exactly at the halfway point. In formal terms, while the first part is reminiscent of the Italian-style comedy, the second takes on a considerably more somber tone, as the one-liners and surreal imagery give way to protracted silences and a more austere mise-en-scène.

Like any clear-cut division in which the two parts are found in a position of inoperative externality, this seemingly self-evident presentation of the two-faced youth should give us pause and prompt us to look at these two faces in detail. Mario is unassertive and obedient, his aspirations perfectly aligned with those of his father, who sees his son as a mere extension of himself. There is no conflict to speak of between the two, no contrasting worldviews or any trace of generational hatred. Mario, in this sense, embodies the revisionist fantasy of a world in which 1968 never happened. This timid, infantile son poses no enigma; his desire is, quite simply, his father's. The other face of the figure of the youth in the film, the bank robber with no name or backstory, is Mario's obverse. In Giovanni's eyes, he embodies an unchecked, socially unacceptable drive that stands in open defiance of the law. While Mario is a conformist entirely absorbed into his middle-class existence, the bank robber is pure antisocial otherness, the photographic negative of Mario as a family man–to-be.[24]

The crux of Giovanni's reactionary fantasy resides in the relation between these two faces of the youth. On the surface, it might seem as though Mario's murder is the cause of Giovanni's desire for revenge. But perhaps the terms should be reversed. What if Giovanni's desire for revenge came first, and the scenario that the film depicts is nothing but the fantasmatic enacting of that desire? In other words, it is not the case that the murder triggers the fantasy of revenge but rather, inversely, that the fantasy of revenge—in order to be acted on—requires Mario's sacrificial murder. In this sense, the split in the figure of the youth is a by-product of the father's fantasy. Mario's death is as much an integral part of the unfolding drama of Giovanni's desire as the kidnapping and torture of the bank robber.

Reactionary fantasies are, at their core, always fantasies of ressentiment. Giovanni is hardly seeking justice. Instead, he is envious of what he thinks is the youth's enjoyment and wants to pry it from him. Uninterested in simply handing down a death sentence (Giovanni is visibly disappointed when he discovers that his prisoner has died), the *borghese piccolo piccolo* (petty petty bourgeois) wants to put the unruly youth under his control and deprive him of his source of enjoyment: that freedom that, according to Giovanni, is a "good thing" but, he also says, has become too widespread, too readily available by the time of the late 1970s. Selfishness and envy of the Other's enjoyment go hand in hand. Giovanni's petty acts of abuse (such as taking advantage of a situation and then lamenting a disregard for the common good when others do the same) speak precisely to the cynical intersection of freedom (for oneself) and normativity (for everybody else), which makes the petty bourgeois a figure simultaneously of victimhood and hostility.

However, there might be an even more sinister aspect to Giovanni's project of revenge. In the attempt to keep his captive alive, we can see a co-optation of the bad son, who has now been tamed, into a newly minted familial nucleus in which the father can once again exercise total control. Giovanni's is not only a fantasy of revenge; it is also, more subtly, a fantasy of fatherly omnipotence affirming the idea that as history unfolds and different figures of the youth emerge, paternal authority remains unchanged and unchallenged. Giovanni is, after all, a former member of the Resistance who admiringly quotes Mussolini and, it is safe to assume, traversed the past two decades of Italian history unfazed by the momentous events that transformed the country—unfazed thanks to his chameleonic ability to blend in, to become whatever fits any given historical moment (the obverse of this compulsive adaptability being, of course, a reactionary faith in the immutability of the existent).

Giovanni's fantasy persists even after the death of the bad youth, as the film's ending demonstrates. There is something ridiculous and at the same time horrifying about the image of an old man in a small, ramshackle car stalking a young bully, ready to pounce at any moment. Every private fantasy, seen from the point of view of an external observer, appears laughable and infantile, and Giovanni's reverie is no exception. However, this individual fantasy evokes a larger, collective desire for revenge as reappropriation of enjoyment from the youth that takes on a distinct shape in the late 1970s. Giovanni enacts the fantasy of the so-called silent majority, the moderate middle-class electorate seething in anger at the radicalism of youth militancy and secretly longing for a return to order and discipline.[25] With *An Average Little Man,* the youth is observed from the standpoint of this silent majority and co-opted into the fantasy that sustains its reactionary desire. This reification of the youth into the false contradiction of good versus bad renders the figure politically inert, de facto putting an end to the exploration of the vicissitudes of desire and their attendant subjective potentialities that we traced in the films examined in this chapter. The youth in *An Average Little Man* has no desire to call his own. Instead, he seems to throw into relief the desire of the structure, an ominous foreshadowing of the mounting tide of reaction and alienation that will sweep Italy in the years of the *riflusso*.

5 The Saint

An Ethics of Autonomy

I side completely with the saint.
—Pier Paolo Pasolini, *Letter to Don Emilio Cordero*, June 9, 1968

The more saints, the more laughter.
—Jacques Lacan, *Television*

A Figural Surplus

If there is a kinship between the figures of the saint and the youth analyzed in chapter 4, it finds its most imaginative articulation in the work of Pier Paolo Pasolini. Repeatedly throughout his oeuvre, Pasolini associates the young body to sainthood and the dimension of the sacred. In his cinema alone, the Christlike apotheosis of the protagonists of *Accattone* (1961) and *Mamma Roma* (1962), the depiction of Jesus in *The Gospel According to Saint Matthew* (*Il Vangelo secondo Matteo*, 1964), and the divine nature of the Visitor in *Teorema* (1968) all testify to the recursivity of this figural coupling between the youth and the saint. Perhaps because of its seeming ubiquity, this coupling is often taken as a given, one of many Pasolinian idiosyncrasies whose obvious artistic—and autobiographic—significance overshadows the elusiveness of its exact articulation. To be sure, the youth stands as the primary, openly avowed object of Pasolini's desire, not only from the standpoint of sexuality but also from artistic and political ones.[1] In relation to this centrality of the youth, the saint seems to function as a sort of figural surplus, either in the form of a becoming-saint of the youth or as a separate figure that nonetheless relays back to the youth, putting it into relief. But how are we to understand this surplus? What originates it?

It is well known that Pasolini saw in the youth (in particular the lumpenproletarian youth) a promise of authenticity in a world of vile conformism, an innocence untainted by the malaises of contemporary neocapitalism and simultaneously a reservoir of intractable antagonistic energies that resist co-optation into dominant social structures. However, this redemptive vision is not without its ambivalences, emerging at first in Pasolini's own thorny relationship to '68, then detonating dramatically in his famous repudiation of the Trilogy of Life. In this brief introduction to the 1975 Italian edition of the screenplays for *The Decameron* (*Il Decamerone*, 1971), *The Canterbury Tales* (*I racconti di Canterbury*, 1972), and *The Arabian Nights* (*Il fiore delle mille e una notte*, 1974), the filmmaker famously reconsiders his artistic and political investment in the youth, whose sexualized yet "innocent" body he previously saw as "the last bulwark of reality."[2] In a handful of terse lines, Pasolini comes to terms with his own misconception: "Sexual liberalization, rather than bringing lightness and happiness to youths and boys, has made them unhappy, closed, and consequently stupidly presumptuous and aggressive."[3] The ambiguity of the figure of the youth in the long '68 discussed in chapter 4 is cast into stark relief. Manipulated by the "false tolerance" of the establishment, the pursuit of a free enjoyment reveals the rebellious youth of the long '68 as a symptomatic by-product of the system, rather than its antagonist.[4]

The omnipresence of the youth in Pasolini's work is therefore haunted by a fantasy of radical emancipation of which the young body would be both a site and an agent—a fantasy whose misguided, even reactionary, nature became apparent to Pasolini only after having traversed it in the form of the unapologetic vitalism of the Trilogy of Life. Indeed, one could argue that what drives the proliferation of young bodies in Pasolini's works is, in fact, the very limitation of the youth's political horizon; the quest for an accurate representation of the elusive radical subjectivity of the youth reinscribes this limitation at every turn. This is what propels Pasolini's pursuit forward, shifting focus to other young bodies precisely to disavow the fact that the pitfalls of the youth as a subject of emancipation were there from the start, ingrained into the very fabric of this figure: "The youths and the boys of the Roman proletariat—the ones I have projected in the old and resistant Naples, and later in the poor countries of the Third World—*if now* they are human garbage, it means that potentially they were such also *then*."[5]

It is within the context of Pasolini's conflicted relationship to the youth that the appearance of the figure of the saint must be understood. Precisely because of its absolute centrality in Pasolini's life and works, the youth as object of desire can only be represented directly at the price of a certain loss, in the form of a defusing of this figure's political potential. To seize this potential, the mediation of a third term is needed. While the youth maintains its centrality, he becomes supplemented by a figural surplus. In a way, it is precisely when Pasolini is not depicting the youth as a revolutionary subject per se but rather is displacing its political dynamism across other figures that he can truly capture the scope (and limitations) of this figure's political dimension. This happens most prominently with the figure of the saint, whose presence in *Teorema* and *Pigsty* we will discuss in this chapter. But, as we will see in chapter 7, this figural surplus also marks Pasolini's last completed film, *Salò*, where the withering political horizon of the youth emerges precisely in contrast with the rise of another figure: the tyrant.

It is therefore crucial to formulate the separateness of the figure of the saint in Pasolini as something that must be maintained not in opposition to the youth but rather precisely due to the youth's centrality in Pasolini's work. No doubt this seems like a deliberately perverse reading of an author widely associated with the political significance of the youth. But if so, this perverse reading is warranted by a perversion inherent in the work of Pasolini himself, in the psychoanalytical sense of a detour away from the object of desire in order to seize it where it is not, displaced and disguised as something else. This reading also offers one way to understand Pasolini's own uneasiness with respect to the event of 1968, since it allows us to grasp this uneasiness as an attempt to find some distance from an object of desire that is otherwise too close for comfort. In Pasolini, as we will see, the saint is presented as the bearer of a singularly radical ethics of subjective autonomy. As such, the saint stands in close alliance to the figure of the youth while signaling a qualitative leap. The saint magnifies the impasse we detected in chapter 4 (the youth's impossible quest for a liberation of enjoyment within a parasitical system that feeds off rebellion) and simultaneously takes its subjective consequences to the absolute extreme, thus transforming the entire situation in which this impasse appears.

A final note about the objects of study for this chapter. A discussion of the role of sainthood in Pasolini's vast body of work, and a comprehensive critique of his conception of the sacred, lie outside the scope of this book.[6] Our focus here will be at once more modest and more partisan: Pasolini alone seems to have been able to elevate the saint to the level of a figure, capable of revealing fundamental impasses of a historical sequence and point to the possible emergence of a political subjectivity.[7] Therefore, we are interested in a sort of circumscribed inquiry into Pasolini's cinema aimed at unearthing the fundamental logic of the saint as a tension-figure. Consequently, the scope of this chapter is intentionally limited. I only discuss two of Pasolini's films released in the immediate proximity of 1968, the aforementioned *Teorema* and *Pigsty* (*Porcile*, 1969). The hope is that our findings will open up the possibility for a figural reassessment of other appearances of the saint in Pasolini's cinema, in films like *La Ricotta* (1963), *The Gospel According to Saint Matthew*, *The Hawks and the Sparrows* (*Uccellacci e uccellini*, 1966), and beyond.

A "Little Secular Manual" of the Event: *Teorema*

A theorem is a statement that can be logically demonstrated on the basis of another, already accepted truth (an axiom, or another theorem). It is a truth that proceeds from truth. The axiom from which Pasolini begins in his 1968 film is one that the films discussed in chapter 4 have made explicit, and that we could formulate as follows: any equilibrium reached by the bourgeois family in the historical sequence of the long '68 is rooted in crisis. In *Before the Revolution* and *Come Play with Me,* the equilibrium is fostered by a crisis (the incestual relation) that allows the status quo of the sweet life to perpetuate itself, while in *Fists in the Pocket,* the death of the bourgeois family simply coincides with its fantasized resurrection in another, yet unknown form. In either case, crisis paradoxically becomes a condition of equilibrium. Pasolini takes this situation of equilibrium in crisis as verified and sets out to prove that, given the current situation of the bourgeoisie, the introduction of an external force into the family would neither leave the status quo untouched nor induce a transformation that would let the status quo attest itself at another level of equilibrium. Instead, the only observed outcome is chaos—chaos in the sense of a heightened level of entropy that ultimately leads to the collapse of the family altogether. Pasolini formulates the starting point of the theorem thus: "The question is this: if a bourgeois family were visited by a young god, whether Dionysus or Jehovah, what would happen?"[8]

The proof the theorem hinges on has to do precisely with a repositioning of the figure of the youth as "a young god." No longer a member of the family, the youth here assumes the shape of the Visitor (Terence Stamp), a divine presence without a name or a backstory that visits a Milanese bourgeois family, which includes the unnamed Father (Massimo Girotti), an industrialist; Lucia (Silvana Mangano), his wife and mother of his children; Pietro (Andrés José Cruz Soublette) and Odetta (Anne Wiazemsky); and Emilia (Laura Betti), the maidservant. The visit, announced by an arm-flapping mailman unequivocally named Angiolino ("little angel," played by Ninetto Davoli), provides the film with its formal structure, systematically organized in different sections.

The initial introduction of the characters is shot in a lifeless sepia tone, suggesting that their world is one of pure repetition. The shots of Pietro leaving school and joking with his schoolmates, or of the Father being driven in his Mercedes around his factory, evoke a quotidian routine deprived of any specific marker of uniqueness. It is the emblem of a bourgeois sweet life seemingly impermeable to change. The film explicitly invites the spectator to look at the characters as generic types whose existence is illustrative of the prescriptions and privileges of their social class.

In the novel of the same name written while he was shooting the film, Pasolini calls the description of the characters "data," noting, "Every preliminary detail about the identity of the characters has a purely indicative value: it serves the purpose of concreteness, not the substance of things."[9] As Maurizio Viano has pointed out, the characters are "signs."[10] For a film that, in the words of Pasolini himself, wants to be "emblematic," it is imperative that this data have the highest degree of generality.[11]

The arrival of the Visitor marks a shift to a vivid color palette and inaugurates the section on seductions. One by one, the members of the family succumb to an irresistible attraction toward the mysterious man. From one character to the next, the scene repeats itself with minor differences: after a moment of hesitation or futile resistance, they all give in and offer themselves to the Visitor.[12] When Angiolino delivers a second telegram, prompting the Visitor to announce his imminent departure, the section on confessions begins. The characters speak to the Visitor about the collapse of their previous worldview and the need to find a new one. The Father questions a life accustomed to possession; Lucia acknowledges the emptiness of her existence; Pietro comes to terms with his homosexuality; and Odetta relinquishes her obsessive love for her father. Emilia remains conspicuously absent from this section, as Pasolini does not grant her a last word with the Visitor. Instead, in a silent parting gesture, she is shown carrying his suitcase to the cab waiting at the villa's gates.

After the Visitor departs, the family implodes. The Father divests himself of all his possessions (including his factory, which he donates to his workers) and is last seen wandering naked and screaming in the desertlike, otherworldly landscape of Mount Etna; Lucia seeks reprieve from her existential pain in casual sex with young strangers who vaguely resemble the Visitor, but finds no satisfaction in it; Pietro takes up painting as a way to recapture the Visitor's image but is deeply frustrated with the results; Odetta frantically tries to reconstruct the scene that led to her intercourse with the Visitor, but when she understands the futility of her endeavor, she falls into a persistent catatonic state. As for Emilia, Pasolini sets her apart again. She returns to her rural home, where she becomes a silent, saintlike mystical figure, subsisting exclusively on nettle soup and performing miracles, to the townspeople's awe. Finally, accompanied by Pasolini's mother, Susanna, she buries herself alive at a construction site and weeps out of joy, promising her companion that her tears will generate a new spring of life.

Given its pervasive biblical connotations, it would be tempting to look at the film as a statement about the role of the sacred in contemporary society.[13] By the same token, and at the other end of the spectrum, it would be just as easy to read the irrational irruption of sexuality in the film along the lines of a celebration of sexual liberation and its revolutionary consequences. But a theorem is not a parable or a manifesto. There is no moral lesson to be evinced at the end; nor does it lay out strategies and objectives for a political program. The film's avowed generality and abstraction position it at a distance from both empirical referents and explicit political or religious messages. So although it would be an oversight to simply dismiss the role played by religion in *Teorema,* any uncritical assumption of the film's being about religion would be just as misleading. In the introduction to the novel, Pasolini defines his work in a way that could easily be applied to the film as well: it is "a little secular manual *[manualetto laico]* . . . about a religious irruption into the order of a Milanese family."[14] As a "secular manual," we would argue, *Teorema* mobilizes religion not as content but as form. The religiosity that qualifies the event at the heart of the film—the "irruption" of the Visitor—should therefore be understood not as the essence of the event but as the formal principle that determines its appearance.

Of all the Christian elements in the film, the reference to Saint Paul offers the most useful paradigm for grasping this event and its logic. It is known that for Pasolini, Saint Paul was a figure of the utmost philosophical and political relevance, as testified by the film project on the life of the saint he pursued right after wrapping up production for *Teorema.*[15] Paul provides Pasolini with the formal paradigm for thinking the complex relationship between the occurrence of an unforeseen irruption tearing asunder the fabric of the status quo and the fidelity of a subject to the consequences of that occurrence, which, in turn, retroactively confirms its eventual, revolutionary character. In philosophy, Alain Badiou was the first to attempt to release Paul from his assigned place within the history of Christianity and elevate him to the level of a "poet-thinker of the event": "If Paul helps us to seize the link between evental grace and the universality of the True," Badiou writes, "it is so that we can tear the lexicon of grace and encounter away from its religious confinement."[16] It is thus no surprise that Badiou's admiration for Pasolini would be grounded in a shared fascination for a figure whose relationship with truth stands as a conceptual model for any kind of militancy worthy of its name.

The crux of Emilia's character resides precisely in her (and only her) fidelity to the encounter with the "young god" and her commitment to the truth that his advent introduces into the mundane repetitiveness of bourgeois life. Like Paul, she becomes the subject of a revelation, which prompts her to renounce her assigned place within the status quo, and with it any attachment to her identity. For Badiou, this is precisely Paul's lesson. Because it is addressed to all, the universality of the truth associated with the evental grace supersedes any "communitarian" separation and can only result in the radical indifference of its subjects to the existing law.[17] This is in stark contrast to the other members of the family, for whom the encounter with the Visitor only reveals an inability to become subjects and let go of the law. In their own individual ways, the family members find themselves stuck in a melancholic impulse to replicate the image of the event, a form of repetition that resembles the quotidian routine the film depicted before the arrival of the Visitor.

What is at stake in all these forms of bourgeois destitution is nothing less than the repetitive character of desire. Jacques Lacan and Badiou credit Paul for having articulated before Freud the logic of this specific formation of the unconscious. The family members in *Teorema* are prey to an automatism of desire that is entirely dependent on the law, for there is no desire without prohibition. As such, the only opposition to the law that they can conceive is that of transgression, which in turn generates the automatism and sustains the regime of law itself.[18] This is the tragedy of the bourgeois family in the film; the initial equilibrium in crisis grounded in repetition is shattered by the event and results in the implosion of the family nucleus. Yet this implosion hardly signals a radical overturning of the law or the trace of a new beginning. The family members are still prisoners of their identities, only now in solitary confinement. Quod erat demonstrandum: as we have seen in chapter 4, the family had survived the assaults brought from within by a tourist of the revolution (*Before the Revolution*), a devious provocateur (*Come Play with Me*), and a scheming murderer (*Fists in the Pocket*). Nothing less than a divine entity is needed to break it apart.

The difference between the maidservant and the other members of the family is made even more explicit in the novel. In a poem titled "Complicity between the Lumpenproletariat and God," the Visitor addresses Emilia in the first person: "You will be the only one to know, when I am gone, / that I will never come back, and you will look for me / where you will have to look for me."[19] Indeed, the problem of the family members is not only that they don't understand that the Visitor "will never come back," but also that they do not look for him where they should. Their attention turns inward in hope of finding a new identity to replace the one that the event stripped away. In the film, an extended circular pan shot of Odetta staring at the camera in a close-up drives the point home. Odetta's dance with the camera evokes a bourgeois narcissism that leads the characters to turn their attention inward and makes their response to the Visitor a question of individual identity and imaginary self-recognition, an emblem of a bourgeoisie that "no longer has a soul, but only a conscience."[20] In Emilia, in contrast, we can discern the outline of a Pauline figure. She professes her fidelity to the event by relinquishing her identity (maidservant for Emilia, like Jew for Paul), thus pointing to the kernel of a possible political subjectivization.

In one of his passing remarks on the topic, Lacan defines the saint as a remainder—a reject, an outcast who is at the same time produced by and excluded from the (supposedly) functioning mechanisms of society.[21] The abjection of the saint is specifically configured as useless. The saint is the fragment that doesn't produce anything but that is itself the waste of the process of production.[22] Again, the implicit reference here is Saint Paul in the First Epistle to the Corinthians: "We have become, and are now, as the refuse of the world, the offscouring of all things." Emilia embodies precisely this idea of saintliness as abjection. First she abandons her assigned place in the hierarchy of bourgeois society and generates a little cult following in her hometown; then, in a second departure, she gives herself over to abjection completely by leaving the farm and burying herself at a construction site at the city's outskirts.

Commenting on Pasolini's choice to set Emilia's final act in this liminal space, Cesare Casarino brings the political significance of the character's stance into focus:

> [Emilia] refuses to choose between the city and the country, between the dominant history of progress and the residual myths of a lost golden age, between the economic miracle of modernization and the mystical miracles of pre-modern religion, between blind acceptance of modernity and faithful return to tradition, as well as—one might say—between so-called secularisms and so-called fundamentalisms of all sorts. In the end, neither of these options is viable, neither of these worlds has much to offer—and hence she tries to imagine and produce another space, another time, another history altogether different from both.[23]

It is precisely by becoming useless that the saint proves useful. By occupying the position of the castoff of society, the saint rejects the false dichotomy between a "blind acceptance of modernity" and a "faithful return to tradition," opting instead to generate a new space—a new event site—that is autonomous from either option. As Stefania Benini puts it, "the Pauline word ... transfixes—lacerates and crucifies, we can say—the fabric of the present with the announcement of a liberated future that appears obsolete (*inattuale*) but is invoked in our present time."[24] It is in this sense that we should read Lacan's remark about the saint's laughter ("the more saints, the more laughter") being nothing less than a "way out of the capitalist discourse."[25] In the capitalist discourse, the subject is prey to the peculiar illusion that the solution to the problem of her own division resides in the surplus of gratification or enjoyment she attains by obtaining the objects she seeks. The Father, the prime representative of the capitalist discourse in the film, follows precisely this logic in his act of donating his factory to the workers. He thinks that simply attaining a certain desired condition (dispossession) will provide a solution to the rift caused by the encounter with the Visitor. As a consequence, he understands the possibility of the new only in the terms of an individual, isolated adjustment of the structure's functioning. The justice he is looking for amounts to little more than mere fairness, a discolored simulacrum of Emilia's commitment to radical autonomy.[26]

This is the family's fateful error: believing that there would be an identitarian—and therefore imaginary—solution to a condition of division that is inherent to the human as such, and that the Visitor confronts them with. To the Father's Franciscan gesture of surrender, Pasolini juxtaposes Emilia's Pauline fidelity to the event, which follows a properly saintly path that consists in "not giving a damn for distributive justice."[27] Instead of looking for a solution to the division of the subject introduced by the encounter with the Visitor, Emilia's character posits the absolute inescapability of that division and of its correlate surplus of enjoyment. As a saint, she becomes "the refuse of *jouissance*," the embodiment of its excess.[28]

This is only one side of the matter, however. In becoming the refuse of jouissance, Emilia fashions for herself a way not to succumb to the family's destiny of subjective collapse. She becomes what Lacan calls the sinthome. A symptom (of which *sinthome* is an archaic spelling) situated beyond the workings of the symbolic and beyond meaning altogether, the sinthome is not a message to be deciphered but rather the marker of an individual subjective enjoyment that resists interpretation absolutely: "I define the symptom by the fashion in which each enjoys [*jouit*] the unconscious insofar as the unconscious determines him."[29] But the sinthome is also a survival strategy concocted by the individual in a situation where symbolic structures and imaginary identifications falter, and one's own subjectivity runs the risk of collapsing into psychotic dissolution. This is precisely what happens to Odetta and the Father in *Teorema*. They are unable to forge their own singular, viable way of maintaining a modicum of subjective consistency after the event, and as a result, they succumb to psychosis.

The sinthome can then be understood as a self-fashioned artifice that allows one to live in the face of the threat of constant subjective destitution. Emilia's arc makes clear that the only way to deal with surplus enjoyment without being swallowed by psychosis is to develop some sort of individual know-how, a singular savoir faire that rejects any positivistic attempt at finding a permanent solution to the problem of surplus enjoyment (and its attendant subjective split) embodied by the Visitor.[30] In Lacan's puns, the sinthome is not only a saint (*saint homme*—or *femme*, in this case) but also a "synthetic man" (*synth-homme*)—that is, the artificial by-product of one's own act of self-creation.

The deliberate gesture of the saint as sinthome carries fundamental ethical implications. "The saint doesn't see himself as righteous," Lacan says, "which doesn't mean that he has no ethics. The only problem for others is that you can't see where it leads him."[31] There is no sense of generic righteousness that motivates Emilia's actions, no desire to impart a lesson or repent for her sins. Emilia simply behaves in the only way she considers possible after encountering the Visitor. Her sinthomatic behavior follows an inscrutable but steadfast trajectory that leads to the extreme gesture of self-sacrifice. In *Teorema*, enjoyment and ethics find an enigmatic alliance in the saint. The logic underpinning this alliance, and the pitfalls of reactionary subsumption to which it is vulnerable, are explored in even greater detail in *Pigsty*.

Annihilation/Assimilation: *Pigsty*

The film is split into two story lines. One takes place in a nondescript antiquity, possibly in the fifteenth century, where a young man (Pierre Clementi) roams a barren landscape (Mount Etna, again) in search of victims to murder and devour. A small following gathers around the young man as the violence continues, until the government of the nearby city manages to capture the group of cannibals. Betrayed by his followers, the young man is sentenced to death and eaten alive by a pack of dogs. The second story line revolves around Julian (Jean-Pierre Léaud), the young heir of the Klotz industrial empire on the eve of the *Wirtschaftswunder* in postwar Germany. To his father's bafflement, Julian is apathetic and indifferent to everything that surrounds him, including his politicized fiancée (Anne Wiazemsky). His only source of solace (and sexual gratification) are the pigs that live on a nearby farm. The father (Alberto Lionello) is gathering intelligence about an emerging competitor, the mysterious Herdhitze (Ugo Tognazzi). When the latter unexpectedly pays a visit to Klotz, it is revealed that Herdhitze was in fact a Nazi officer directly responsible for the death of hundreds of thousands of Jews. In response to this revelation, Herdhitze hints that he is aware of Julian's zoophiliac inclinations. On the basis of this reciprocal blackmail ("a tale of pigs for a tale of Jews"), the two industry titans agree to a merger of their corporations. But on the day of the gala celebrating the merger, Julian throws himself to the pigs, who devour him instantly. As the news of the tragedy reaches Herdhitze, he orders the witnesses to not say a word to Klotz, thus preserving the value of his bargaining chip.

The idea of saintliness outlined in *Teorema* with the character of Emilia returns here in the redoubled form of the cannibal and the zoophile, both abject refuses of jouissance condemned to a life at the margins of the community. Julian and the cannibal can only satisfy their desire in a marginal space removed from the city and the villa as seats of power—the desert and the pigsty, respectively. As with Emilia, the saintliness of the cannibal and the zoophile hinges on an identification with the useless waste that translates into a certain suspension of, and autonomy from, the Other as symbolic law. Emilia's fidelity to the event in *Teorema* persists in *Pigsty*, but refracted through the prism of a new historical situation determined by the advent of 1968 itself, understood not as a mere set of factual occurrences but rather as a moment of radical reorganization of discourses around desire and enjoyment. The shift from *Teorema* to *Pigsty* is clear. In *Teorema,* Emilia's saintliness is a "way out," the autonomous affirmation of a third space that rejects the dichotomy between melancholic attachment (Lucia, Pietro) and psychotic break (the Father, Odetta). Emilia's extreme gesture of fidelity to the event is ultimately an affirmation of life, as her becoming waste opens up the possibility of a new, unforeseen future. In *Pigsty,* however, the apostasy of the saint only leads to obliteration and defeat. In the opposite and specular forms of unchecked aggression and unconditional love, the cannibal's and the zoophile's commitment to their desires pushes them toward a similar fate of isolation and death. Yet, we should not assume that the film's two story arcs are simply reflections of each other. In fact, if the figure of the saint is fundamentally similar in the cannibal and the zoophile, the way in which they are defeated is markedly different, as the law asserts its dominance over these two refuses of jouissance in two distinct ways. The discontinuity between the two parts of *Pigsty,* then, should be read as signaling a fundamental shift from one regime of enjoyment to another.

Let us consider the cannibal first. His enjoyment is emphatically cast as foreign, inaccessible. It is not only antisocial, but also—like Teiresias in *The Cannibals,* also played by Clementi—unspeakable; the cannibal only speaks at the moment of sentencing, repeating three times: "I killed my father, I've eaten human flesh, I tremble with joy." The anti-Oedipal cliché omnipresent in the discourse around '68 receives here a stark literalization: with his taboo-breaking embrace of cannibalism, the young man has removed paternal prohibition as the obstacle toward full enjoyment and can now "tremble with joy." This enjoyment is framed as a surplus, an unruly excess that threatens the nearby city. Pasolini frames the city's reaction to this unsettling surplus in a very precise manner. The sentence is passed through the voice of an invisible judge as the townspeople gather at the public spectacle of the trial and the young cannibal occupies center stage. The disembodied, acousmatic voice (the judge) is none other than the old Master's voice, the archaic mode of sovereign power that holds what Foucault calls "the right of life and death" over its subjects.[32] However, this sovereign power doesn't quite know what to do with this refuse of jouissance that is the cannibal-saint, so it simply frames it as a form of criminal deviance and deals with it accordingly—that is, outside the city walls—in hope of making it disappear without a trace. In Pasolini's mythical precapitalist time, the form of defeat of the youth-saint is annihilation. Surplus enjoyment is a threat that needs to be eradicated for the good of the community.

Not so in postwar Germany, where Julian, whom Klotz Senior describes as "an embalmed saint," is literally digested by a new discursive organization—one in which surplus enjoyment is counted and appropriated by the capitalist. No longer a threat to the community but rather a source of wealth, the zoophile-saint as refuse of jouissance is fully recaptured and put to use by the productive machine. Again, saintly uselessness becomes of the utmost utility, but in an inverted form. Rather than indicating "a way out of the capitalist discourse," like Emilia, Julian and his secret enjoyment become their precondition, the bargaining chip that allows for a new monopolistic conglomerate to come into existence. The defeat of the saint here is marked not by annihilation but, more pessimistically, by subsumption. The refuse of jouissance embodied by the saint is assigned a specific exchange value ("a story of pigs for a story of Jews") and thus becomes counted, and accounted for, in the capitalist discourse. In this new regime, everything can be digested, even saintliness.[33]

It is precisely through this process of digestion of the saint that Klotz and Herdhitze can attain what they call their "new youthfulness" (*nuova giovinezza*). Lacan foresaw precisely this situation when he declared, "It's not as if the smart alecks aren't lying in wait hoping to profit from [the saint's enjoyment] so as to pump themselves up again."[34] The separation of the figure of the saint into the cannibal and the zoophile thus illustrates a shift in the way power deals with the intractable refuse of jouissance: annihilation at the hands of a sovereign power in precapitalist times for the former, and assimilation facilitated by capital's strategic flexibility for the latter. While the destinies of the two saints are ultimately similar, the structural conditions in which they live and die are remarkably different.

This logic of enjoyment as a persistent refuse or waste prompts a more general consideration about the figure of the saint and the distance that separates it from its figural next of kin, the youth. In a truly Pauline gesture, Pasolini breaks with the dialectic of law and transgression that informed the films analyzed in chapter 4. We can see how the position assumed by Pasolini's saints has little to do with the dialectic at work in *Before the Revolution* and *Come Play with Me*. There is no tactically subversive intent in the figures of the cannibal and the zoophile, no calculated decision to infringe on the rules, be it taking a vacation from the sweet life, as in *Before the Revolution,* or playing a game of pretend, as in *Come Play with Me*. In this sense, Fabrizio and Alvise, the protagonists of these two films, are no saints. They do not share the commitment to one's own desire and the radical suspension of the symbolic Other that we see emblematized by Emilia in *Teorema* and the two protagonists of *Pigsty*. In fact, all the instances of the youth discussed in chapter 4 cannot separate themselves from the unavoidable presence of the Other, for it is precisely this presence that gives meaning to their rebellion in the first place. This is certainly the case for Bertolucci, Samperi, and Bellocchio, but even in Cavani and Caligari the symbolic remains as the inescapable pole of a dialectic of transgression. In *The Cannibals,* the collection and burial of the protesters' corpses appears as a rebellion against the Other of the state; in *Toxic Love,* drug addiction fulfills the role of a spectacle of defeat staged for the enjoyment of the Other of civil society.

This is the fundamental difference between the saint and the youth. Pasolini believes in the possibility of an ethical subjectivity that comes into existence on the basis of a radical postevental commitment, and he puts the saint at the center of this process of subjectivation. In doing so, *Teorema* and *Pigsty* leave behind the dialectic of law and transgression proper to desire, instead situating the figure of the saint at the level of enjoyment and drive. By positing a suspension of the symbolic order, Julian and the cannibal affirm their existence beyond the pleasure principle, beyond any measure of the good and the appropriate, beyond law itself. This uncompromising assertion of autonomy sets the saint apart from the youth. While the saint opens up—like Emilia—a third space for herself, the youth's rebellion always takes place within the horizon of the Other.

This is also why the saint may be a figure of defeat but never of surrender. There is no returning to the sweet life for Emilia, Julian, or the cannibal. Yet the pessimism that permeates *Pigsty* can hardly be overlooked; in fact, even the apparent hope associated with the character of Emilia in *Teorema* takes on a slightly different nuance in the darker light cast by the later film. The protracted silences, the enigmatic miracles, the final gesture of self-effacement—could we not read Emilia's arc as a retreat into a certain mysticism of the ineffable? As a mystic, she only offers a nebulous promise of redemption, gesturing toward the possibility of a new beginning rather than assuming onto herself the pragmatic burden of militancy. After all, Saint Paul himself—Emilia's alter ego—was seen by Pasolini also as a figure evoking a crisis of militancy. The screenplay for the film on Saint Paul that was never made, published after the author's death, depicts the transformation of the saint from militant to priest—that is, from a subject of the event to a high-ranking, power-hungry functionary of church bureaucracy.[35]

The priest, the mystic, the cannibal, the zoophile: in Pasolini, the saint as a figure can only emerge in the form of a failure to live up to the ideal of pure saintliness. The circumstances of these failures are different in each case; for Saint Paul it is a deviation, for Emilia a retreat, for the protagonists of *Pigsty* a defeat against an all-powerful structure. Yet there seems to be one limitation that all these Pasolinian figures share: the lack, or loss, of a universalistic address in their ethical commitment. The form of commitment that defines all these saintlike figures fails to produce a true political subject because it renounces the possibility to turn a singular experience of the event into a universal claim about humanity as such—in other words, it renounces the possibility to be militant. Emilia shuns the collectivity of the townspeople to withdraw into a solitary sacrifice; Saint Paul abandons his mission and enters the church hierarchies; Julian and the cannibal reduce their quest for autonomy to an individualizing, existential gesture. Yet this might be precisely what the films think about the historical sequence of 1968: the ambiguous politics that stem from the quest of a pure liberation of enjoyment, a quest that the youth pursues within the coordinates of desire, and that the saint expands into the territories of the drive. Julian's case is in this sense emblematic. His failure to attain some level of a political subjectivization is inextricable from his individualizing ethical stance, which Herdhitze exploits to his own advantage. This is why, in the last analysis, even saintliness can be digested by the structure. The lack of a universalistic horizon that is rooted in, yet reaches beyond, fidelity to one's own desire allows the capitalist to make a quick meal of this refuse of jouissance.

Lorenzo Chiesa has credited Pasolini with the intuition that the injunction to emancipate oneself sexually goes hand in hand with the imperative to appropriate and consume economic surplus—a confirmation, if needed, of Lacan's intuition that surplus value and surplus enjoyment are in fact homogeneous.[36] In the long run, the existential revolution of the youth in 1968 ended up serving the reproductive apparatus of "tolerant" late capitalism—a tolerance whose obverse is the obscene superegoical imperative to enjoy. In the words of Pasolini, "A kind of society that is tolerant and permissive is the one in which neuroses are most frequent, insofar as such a society requires that all possibilities it allows be exploited, that is, it requires a desperate effort so as not to be less than everybody else in a competitiveness without limits."[37]

It is important to clarify that what *Pigsty* thinks is not some cynical dismissal of 1968 as a nonevent, or an inability of 1968 to generate its saintly subjects, which would amount to the same. Saints exist, as do witnesses to their acts, like the peasant Maracchione in *Pigsty* (Ninetto Davoli), the transhistorical presence that mourns the deaths of the premodern cannibal and the modern zoophile, in a role similar to the one fulfilled by Pasolini's mother, Susanna, who bears witness to Emilia's self-sacrifice in *Teorema*. It is not surprising that Pasolini would resort to these subproletarian characters to suggest the possibility of reactivating the latent universality of the saint's acts. But do these witnesses indicate the rise of a new subject, interpellated by the encounter with the saint? Pasolini does not give us any clear indication one way or the other. Yet it is precisely in this undecidability that the evental nature of 1968 resides: "a series of obscure events," as Badiou called it—that is, a historical sequence to which we cannot ascribe a proper unity.[38] With his obstinate and lost saints, Pasolini undertakes the arduous work of thinking the possibilities of subjectivation amidst this obscurity, between the horizon of subjective autonomy and the pitfalls of reactionary assimilation.

6 The Specter

Totality as Conjuration

> The specter is always a sworn conspirator [*conjuré*].
> —Jacques Derrida, *Specters of Marx*

> The demonstrations and festivals in the square were a thing of the past the movement was like a great ghost absent withdrawn sheltering in its ghettoes.
> —Nanni Balestrini, *The Unseen*

"The Hidden Figure of All Figures"

The visibility of the figure of the specter constitutes a paradox. Specters appear as suddenly as they vanish, yet these manifestations indicate a constant, invisible presence in the form of haunting. For this reason, the specter is an erratic figure in a twofold sense. On the one hand, spectral apparitions are erratic in that they are unpredictable and intermittent; on the other hand, the specter occupies spaces by endlessly roaming, in a movement that is aimless yet confined. At its most basic phenomenological level, then, spectrality names at one and the same time a fleeting encounter and an obstinate haunting, neither of which can be classified as pure presence or pure absence.

The fact that the specter can hold together these two seemingly contradictory features gives it an ambiguous ontological status, which has been famously investigated by Jacques Derrida across several of his works, but most comprehensively in *Specters of Marx:*

The State of the Debt, the Work of Mourning, and the New International. Derrida says of the specter that it is "neither substance, nor essence, nor existence, [it] *is never present as such.*"[1] The specter's phenomenology is inseparable from its ontology (or, to use Derrida's pun, hauntology), for the specter's appearance and being are defined by the same undecidability which perturbs any antinomy: neither present nor absent, neither dead nor alive, neither being nor nonbeing.

The specter's phenomenological and ontological undecidability also marks its relationship to time. Unlike figures like the worker (whose history is inextricable from that of capital) or the youth (who is a datable sociological invention), the specter is a figure without history, in the sense that it does not belong to historical time per se. The specter's distinctively uncanny traits instead derive from the fact that it dwells in a peculiar temporal dimension; the specter has always already been there, so its first appearance is, in fact, always a return. This ghostly appearance thus opens up a rift within the living present, revealing a fundamental noncontemporaneity of time with itself, a point of undoing of established temporal coordinates. However, if spectrality is "what makes the present waver," can we then not see in the specter a sort of degree zero of the Blochian tension-figure described in chapter 1?[2] "The figure of the ghost," Derrida writes, "is not just one figure among others. It is perhaps the hidden figure of all figures."[3] One way to understand this enigmatic statement is precisely in the terms outlined by Bloch, who takes figures to be symptoms of the present in crisis. If figures for Bloch are always tension-figures that make visible the noncontemporaneity of the present with itself, then the specter—following Derrida's pervasive references to *Hamlet* in *Specters of Marx*—can be regarded as the ur-figure of this "time out of joint."

Perhaps by virtue of it being a sort of degree zero of figurality, the specter's politics remain considerably more amorphous than those of the figures analyzed up to this point. This opaqueness, however, should not lead us to the conclusion that the only possible politics attached to this figure is that of a "messianism without religion, even a messianic without messianism," as Derrida would have it.[4] Within this framework, communism takes the form of a promise—something that is always to come, but without any ultimate guarantees as to which concrete shape it might assume, or whether it might come at all. The political subject of this spectral communist promise is one of open-ended waiting, "hospitality without reserve."[5]

Is this all there is to it? One has to wonder whether the undoing of any stable ontology and the fetishization of undecidability attached to the specter in the wake of *Specters of Marx* actually exhaust its figural possibilities. The definition of figure presented in this book proposes that we look at figures as sites of a dialectical tension and coimplication between two terms: a structural situation, and a force born within it and bent on transforming it. But to what extent is it possible to redialecticize the figure of the specter after *Specters of Marx*? Not, to be sure, in the sense of a rigid dialectics resolved in a positive synthesis, but rather as the ability to discern in the specter a series of variations of the dialectical tensions between force and structure, and to see how this redialecticized figure might relay to a different form of political subjectivity than the one Derrida saw as possible—and desirable—after the fall of the Soviet Union in 1989.

In this chapter, I will trace these tensions across five films, organized in three sections. The first section explores the relationship between the specter and state power in the historical context of the Italian 1970s, characterized by the proliferation of interlocking national and international conspiracies orchestrated by state apparatuses, foreign powers, and agents of global capital. By revisiting Fredric Jameson's understanding of conspiracy as a form of cognitive mapping, we will trace the shifting position that the specter occupies vis-à-vis the state in Francesco Rosi's *The Mattei Affair* (*Il caso Mattei*, 1972) and *Illustrious Corpses* (*Cadaveri eccellenti*, 1976), and Elio Petri's *Investigation of a Citizen Above Suspicion* (*Indagine su un cittadino al di sopra di ogni sospetto*, 1970).

The second section, devoted to Petri's *Property Is No Longer a Theft* (*La proprietà non è più un furto*, 1973), centers on the question of real abstractions (private property in particular) by examining the interconnections between on the one hand capitalism as a system predicated on abstraction, and on the other state power as the enforcer of the reality of those abstractions. The section links the spectrality of the film's protagonist to a certain surplus of enjoyment that permeates real abstractions. The dominant social structures, unable to fully absorb this excess, find themselves haunted by it. The film's spectral protagonist, however, also foreshadows a certain unraveling of revolutionary subjectivity in the late 1970s, when the dangers of disillusionment, withdrawal into the private sphere, and loss of a sense of collectivity become painfully evident.

Verifying Petri's diagnosis of political disengagement, the coda on *To Love the Damned* (*Maledetti vi amerò*, Marco Tullio Giordana, 1980) puts into focus the consequences of the collapse of radical movements at the turn of the decade. Still haunting empty factories and universities long after that demise, the specter of the militant in the film lives his anachronism with shame. This is not a shame for what he did (or did not do) in the years of the revolutionary struggle. Rather, it is the more fundamental shame of being alive—of being *de trop*—in a historical moment that has no place or use for him. The coda concludes the chapter with a discussion of this fading of subjectivity in the end of the 1970s in the context of the argument put forth in *Specters of Marx*.

Haunted States

Technocratic Utopia: The Mattei Affair

In the immediate postwar period, Enrico Mattei helmed an unprecedented attempt by a state-owned company (ENI [Ente Nazionale Idrocarburi], of which Mattei was founder and plenipotentiary) to unsettle the oligopoly of the global oil cartel, the so-called Seven Sisters: the Anglo-Iranian Oil Company, Texaco, Esso, Socony, SoCal, Gulf Oil, and Royal Dutch Shell. Under Mattei, ENI strongly advocated for abandoning the predatory practices of old and establishing a more equitable business relationship between oil-producing and oil-consuming countries. The film documents the origin and subsequent unfolding of this strategy in a meticulous account of events: Mattei's appointment in 1945 as chief liquidator of the fascist oil agency AGIP, which he refused to liquidate and instead transformed into ENI; his early exploits in Northern Italy, where he located vast deposits of methane gas; the rapid expansion of ENI's economic and political interests on a global scale, toward North Africa (Egypt, Morocco, Libya, Tunisia, Algeria), Sudan, Somalia, and Iran; the tensions with the Seven Sisters oil cartel, who saw in the Italian newcomer a suddenly dangerous competitor capable of upsetting the geopolitical balance; and finally Mattei's death in a mysterious plane crash in Bascapé, near Milan, on October 24, 1962.

The economic and political implications of the relation between Mattei's individual arc and the larger system of the global oil market constitute the fundamental object of inquiry of Rosi's film. The concrete terms of this relation, however, remain nebulous. As formal inquiries and newspaper investigations multiply, so do rumors and ambiguities. As one of the journalists investigating the network of interests and influences around Mattei puts it in the film, "We have the impression of putting our hands on something concrete, that then suddenly vanishes." The hard facts of Mattei's biography are known, and the film duly chronicles them: his participation in the partisan struggle, his political sympathies for the Christian Democrats' left current, his strong-minded temperament, his unorthodox methods. What remains somewhat abstract—what vanishes—is the totality of the economic and political system in which Mattei operated.

The ambition to bestow concreteness on such elusive yet overpowering abstractions is the driving desire of the genre of the Italian *film-inchiesta* (film inquiry). The genre, for which *The Mattei Affair* can serve as a paradigmatic example, is defined by a fundamental tension. On the one hand, there is the historic, factual dimension the film aims to illuminate through its investigative approach, proposing plausible hypotheses about its most obscure developments. On the other hand, as a corollary derived from the factual aspect, there is the attempted outlining of a larger picture, a totality of interconnected occurrences, actors, and interests that emerges in the background, and that in turn reframes the individual affair as the fragment of a much vaster network of institutional and corporate strategies and competing powers.[6] In this sense, one could argue that Rosi's primary concern is with representation. How does one seize and put into form the immense and elusive networks that envelop reality as we know it? To borrow Fredric Jameson's widely influential concept, it is certainly possible to argue that *The Mattei Affair* attempts a cognitive mapping of the postwar global oil market. The film tries to capture aesthetically the interpenetration of neocolonial practices and financial machinations that make up a transitional phase in the history of capital.[7]

Focusing on the Hollywood paranoia thriller of the 1970s in his landmark essay "Totality as Conspiracy," Jameson argues that conspiracy is to be understood as one such form of cognitive mapping—or, at the very least, as the signal of a desire to map totality, for this attempt proves inadequate, as the totality that the films wish to capture remains ultimately out of grasp.[8] This is to be regarded, however, not as the individual shortcoming of the film but rather as the structural limit imposed on representation by the vastness and complexity of the object to be represented. In this sense, the paranoia thriller offers the example of a failure to map that is nonetheless revelatory. The motif of conspiracy predominant in those films works precisely as a lesser form of cognitive mapping, its inadequacy a means of representation of the global system of financial capitalism pointing simultaneously to a desire to map that the films register and to the unmappability inherent in the object itself that the films can put into relief only negatively.

The conspiratorial theme is also central in Rosi's film inquiries, particularly in *The Mattei Affair*. In the film, it is intimated that Mattei died at the hand of a conspiracy orchestrated by the Seven Sisters, who were concerned by their competitor's plan to establish ENI's presence in the newly independent Algeria and build a direct oil pipeline to Sicily. Yet the way in which conspiracy is presented in the film prompts us to ask whether the interpretive paradigm of cognitive mapping deployed to analyze the Hollywood paranoia thriller also offers an adequate framework in this case. While the thematic and stylistic affinities between *The Mattei Affair* and its American counterparts are evident, there seems to be something that Jameson's conceptualization of conspiracy, centered as it is on the problematic of representation, does not seem to be able to account for, and that is the ghostly presence of the film's protagonist himself, Enrico Mattei. Jameson accounts for characters in paranoia thrillers primarily as Greimasian actants; their agency (or lack thereof) vis-à-vis the conspiratorial network is determined by the structural position they occupy in the narrative. Unbeknownst to the characters themselves, this actantial position often shifts in the course of the film, thus transforming a protagonist's role from heroic seeker of truth to unwitting tool in the hands of the conspiracy. *The Mattei Affair* adopts a different approach. Rather than reorganizing actantial positions, the film subverts narrative linearity by supplementing it with the spectral surplus embodied by its protagonist.

The film opens with a fatal plane crash, then unfolds as a series of flashbacks and flash-forwards that cut back and forth from three distinct time lines: 1962 (Mattei's death and his aftermath), 1948–62 (the rise of ENI), and 1972 (Rosi's investigation into Mattei for his film, set in the present day). As the present disintegrates across three different time lines, Mattei's presence also becomes tenuous, spectral. The film opens with his demise, so he is cast from the beginning as a revenant ("a specter is always a *revenant*... it *begins by coming back*"[9]) who installs a dimension of time out of joint, a certain blurring of the distinction between what is present and what is not. This spectrality effect, to borrow Derrida's formulation, pervades the film. More than simply represented, Mattei is evoked after death by journalistic investigations, memories of other characters, old TV interviews, newspaper articles, pictures, and, of course, Volonté's characteristically mimetic performance. But how does the film's conjuration of Mattei's ghost relate to the other conjuration—namely, the conspiracy in which, to paraphrase the *Manifesto,* "all the powers" of the global oil market "have joined into a holy hunt against the specter"?

The connection, Derrida observes, is in the word itself—the French *conjuration*—which "has the good fortune to put to work and to produce, without any possible reappropriation, a forever errant surplus value."[10] This surplus value, ghostly in its own right, is produced by the word's two distinct and opposite meanings. On the one hand, it means "conjuration," a conspiracy sealed by an oath, and also the magical evocation of a spirit; on the other hand, it means "conjurement," which in white magic is an exorcism aimed at conjuring the malevolent spirit away. A spectral effect is thus already inscribed in *conjuration,* as it is also in the etymology of "conspiracy," where the Latin word *conspirare* (literally, "to breathe together") has the same root as *spiritus* (spirit, ghost).

This ambivalent spectral effect of conspiracy captured in the French *conjuration*—to conjure a ghost and to conjure it away—seems to offer the possibility for a conceptualization of conspiracy that is alternative to Jameson's. What if conspiracies could not be separated from the specters they evoke because, on a structural level, the very existence of a conspiracy depended on a ghostly surplus? What is at stake in the shift from Jameson's "totality as conspiracy" to totality as spectral conjuration is a different conception of totality itself, as well as the way cinema seizes on this totality. If we look at conspiracy as conjuration, then the question of totality shifts away from the Jamesonian problematic of representation and instead reorients itself toward the question of ontological consistency. In order to attain such consistency, any hegemonic totality—imagined in the form of conspiracy—must rely on some form of exclusion or repression of one of its elements, which then returns in the form of the specter. The impossibility of totalization, then, is not simply ascribable to the vastness and complexity of the object the film tries to represent, as is the case in Jameson. Rather, the form of the conspiracy as spectral conjuration itself points to the totality's immanent incompleteness. In *The Mattei Affair,* totality as conjuration is not a zero-sum game; in order for the totality to present itself in the form of conspiracy, a spectral remainder must be produced. This specter is what we might call the symptom of a totality that is constitutively not-all. "Haunting," writes Derrida, "belongs to the structure of every hegemony."[11] The figure of Mattei as a specter arises precisely as a reaction to the hegemonic practices of the cartel, as what is structurally excluded from the global harvesting and capitalization of natural resources returns as a force bent on transforming the status quo. Mattei himself publicly pointed out that it was the monopolistic agreement between the Seven Sisters grounded in their vertical organization (total control over the oil trade from extraction to refinement to distribution) that "has provoked and is provoking a reaction of new forces interested in breaking the system."[12]

This articulation of a structural situation (the global oil market, dominated by the Seven Sisters) with a force born within it and bent on transforming it (Mattei's ENI) delimits the field of subjectivation of the figure of the specter in the film. As the antagonistic surplus of the strategies of the cartel, the specter of Mattei marks a point of internal contradiction within the structure of the global oil market, one that—through the subjective torsion represented by ENI's political project—simultaneously opens up the possibility of a transformation of the status quo. In this sense, Mattei's deliberate attempt at a reconfiguration of the geopolitical situation indicates a subjective effort and creativity that, however embryonic or opportunistic, we may indeed qualify as utopian. Cast as the patriotic defender of the country's independence (Rosi repeatedly reminds the spectator of Mattei's involvement in the Resistance), Mattei is a synecdoche for the state itself as on the one hand the last line of defense against the mounting tide of globalizing economic interests, and on the other the agent of a possible reorganization of the geopolitical relations between oil-producing and oil-consuming countries.

Of course, Mattei was no anticolonial guerrillero. As the CEO of a state-owned energy company, he was bent on pursuing Italy's economic interests. Under his leadership, however, those interests repeatedly aligned with those of anticolonial forces (the FLN in Algeria in particular). On the planetary stage of the Cold War, characterized by the appearance of unprecedented forms of extrastate influence and neocolonial practices, Mattei's spectral figure is subjectivized by the film into the leader of a state-driven national resistance to forms of imperialism old and new, and as a force able to single-handedly reshape the precarious Cold War equilibrium.[13]

To be sure, the political limitations of the vision Rosi attributes to Mattei remain evident; they have been aptly summarized by Goffredo Fofi, who calls the film a "technocratic dream."[14] We could further qualify this "dream" as a return to a simpler situation where economic interests could be mapped onto the spatially delimited and politically defined entity of the nation-state (and a certain idea of the common good for its citizens) against the unmappable and rapacious voracity of the global oil cartel. The subjectivation of Mattei as Italy's savior thus points back to the question of mapping, but seen obliquely from the perspective of the specter. In a situation in which the increasing complexity of the global oil market makes any attempt at a mapping unrealistic, the state is summoned to provide a more reassuring fantasy of mappability in which agents, beneficiaries, and the framework of their interactions are more readily identifiable.

The Mattei Affair, then, looks at totality from this inherently partial figural perspective. The specter functions as a reminder that there is no supposedly objective depiction of totality, for the coherence of any such depiction is guaranteed by the foreclosure of some kernel of subjective antagonism—in this case, Mattei's fight against the oligopoly of the Seven Sisters. First conjured and then conjured away by the oil cartel and its network of allies, the specter of ENI's antagonism is the surplus that threatens the existence of the structure; yet, at the same time, the specter allows the structure to find a new internal consistency precisely in the act of violently repressing this antagonism (Mattei's assassination). In turn, it is the persistence of this ghostly surplus after Mattei's demise that makes the outline of the larger conspiratorial networks of the cartel visible. The question raised by a reading of totality as conjuration is thus not one of incommensurability between individual perception and the complexity of a totality, as is the case in Jameson. Rather, it prompts a revisited conceptualization of totality itself. As the gap inscribed at the heart of totality, the specter constitutes at the same time the limit and the condition of possibility of cognitive mapping. The specter is not a distortion that needs to be corrected in order for an objective totality to emerge. Instead, it is in this ghostly distortion itself, and in the subjectivation of antagonism to which it points, that we can glimpse the logic governing the totality as not-all.

Rules of the Game: Illustrious Corpses

If *The Mattei Affair* shows an attempt to subjectivize the specter in order to elevate the Italian nation-state and its publicly owned energy company to the level of anti-imperialist bulwarks, then *Illustrious Corpses* adopts a considerably more ambivalent stance, with the state taking on the ominous shape of an authoritarian and conspiracy-driven machine. Adapted from a 1971 novel by Leonardo Sciascia, *Equal Danger (Il contesto)*, the film is set in an unnamed, "wholly fictional country; a country where ideas were obsolete, where principles—still proclaimed and acclaimed—were ridiculed, where political ideologies were reduced to pure denominations in the roleplay of power, where only power for power's sake mattered."[15] The protagonist, Amerigo Rogas (Lino Ventura), is a police detective tasked with investigating a string of assassinations of high-profile judges as the country is roiled by a wave of far-left street protests and strikes. The investigation focuses on Cres, a pharmacist unjustly convicted for the attempted murder of his wife. His motive seems obvious: the murdered judges were all part of the panel that passed his sentence. However, as the investigation progresses and the bodies pile up, Rogas begins to suspect that Cres's vendetta is a cover-up to justify an authoritarian coup by the upper echelon of the government, the judiciary, and the armed forces. Rogas, determined to expose these machinations, meets with the left-wing opposition leader, but they are both murdered by an unknown killer. As the media pin the responsibility of the deaths on Rogas and tanks are revving their engines in the streets, the leadership of the left-wing party (informed by Rogas about the imminent coup) opts to remain silent in fear of precipitating events.

The influence of the Hollywood paranoia thriller in *Illustrious Corpses* is even more evident than in *The Mattei Affair*, as Rosi adopts many of the conventions of the genre outlined by Jameson: a deliberately convoluted narrative; a protagonist whose righteous desire to expose the scheme leads him to become an unwitting tool in the hands of the conspiracy itself; and, finally, a certain fetishistic fascination with surveillance and communication technology as the allegorical stand-in for an invisible and all-pervasive network of power. The historical reference for this depiction of sprawling conspiracies and authoritarian undercurrents is obviously the Italian political conjuncture of the 1970s, which saw the institution of a permanent state of exception that lasted for over a decade and came to be known as *strategia della tensione*. This "strategy of tension" combined state-sponsored terroristic attacks and brutal police repression of radical movements in order to stoke fears about an imminent communist takeover and push public opinion toward support of increasingly authoritarian measures.[16]

This occurred in the international context of a vast, multiyear economic crisis, what Robert Brenner has famously named the long downturn. An increase in competition and decline in profitability in the global manufacturing sector dating back to the mid-1960s forced national governments in industrialized countries to adopt extreme measures, including unilateral monetary policies, such as Nixon's cancellation of direct convertibility of the U.S. dollar to gold in 1971.[17] The global economy's downward spiral, compounded by the oil crisis of 1973, resulted in the stock market crash of 1973–74. In this situation of economic recession and heightened political uncertainty, the U.S. empire undertook decisive measures to curb the threat of a communist rise to power in allied countries. In Italy, this took the form of military and intelligence support for the creation of fail-safe authoritarian plans that would install a junta in the presence of the threat of a communist overthrow.[18]

No longer the embodiment of an external enemy encroaching on the country's autonomy as it was in *The Mattei Affair,* the conspiracy in *Illustrious Corpses* is now nested within the state, an overt reference to the current events of the time. However, it is important to note that *Illustrious Corpses* is not, nor wishes to be, a factual account of the historical occurrences that punctuated the years of the strategy of tension. It should rather be read as a tract on the conspiratorial logic that defines the rule of law in the so-called democratic state when the state finds itself under attack from within.[19] At the center of these labyrinthine machinations we again find a specter—that of Cres, the elusive pharmacist turned killer. If Mattei's spectrality was suggested by the disjointed temporality of the film, then Cres's is openly avowed. Of the three suspects that Rogas investigates, Cres is the only one who remains faceless. During a visit to his residence, Rogas notices a number of photographs with Cres's silhouette cut out (Figure 19).

While Sciascia describes the atmosphere of the house as haunting ("there lingered something sinister, as though in a convent, or a prison"[20]), the image of the cut-out pictures is entirely Rosi's,

Figure 19. A picture of Cres with his face cut out in *Illustrious Corpses* (1976).

testifying to the specific significance that the figure of the specter bears in the film.

As was the case with Mattei, Cres's spectrality marks the uncanny return of an originally foreclosed element. The victim of a plot organized by his wife to take his money (a conspiracy within a conspiracy), Cres is sentenced to jail in the absence of definitive evidence, only to then return as vengeful ghost. He stands as the embodiment of a miscarriage of justice, whose foreclosure reveals the fundamentally divided nature of the rule of law. On the one hand is the avowed pursuit of justice by way of impartial procedures; on the other is the unspoken principle of the absolute unimpeachability of the judiciary, embodied by the supreme court president, Riches (Max von Sydow). In one scene, Riches explains to Rogas that there is no such thing as a miscarriage of justice, for "a judge may have doubts, he may question himself . . . but at the very moment he delivers his sentence, no more. At that moment, justice is done." Regardless of any shortcomings of the individual officiant or the investigative process, the institutionalized performance of a ritual establishes a reality that possesses its own autonomy from factual considerations or objections.

The postulate of the infallibility of the court conjures a figure like Cres who is (factually) innocent and (legally) guilty at once. His predicament is exemplified by the ancient Roman army practice of decimation evoked by Riches. In this disciplinary measure, designed to punish and discourage mutiny, one randomly selected soldier out of every ten is executed. Riches reasons that times of social and political turmoil warrant such extreme recourses, whereby a punishment meted out unjustly yet legally serves the purposes of the raison d'état. Cres's predicament is thus presented not as an accidental occurrence but as the necessary by-product of the inner logic of the state. The foundation of state power thus reveals its obscene underside. The arbitrary interpellation of innocents as criminals as a form of self-perpetuation of the state points to the authoritarian excess that is intrinsic to democratic power. As Žižek writes, "The law can only sustain its authority if subjects hear in it the echo of the obscene unconditional self-assertion.... Laws do not really bind me, I can do *whatever I want,* I can treat you as guilty if I decide so."[21]

As the film progresses, however, another dimension of state power becomes apparent—what we might call its proper political dimension, coinciding with the shift in the film setting from the periphery to the capital. This dimension emerges by way of a further displacement of the specter. After the murder of a judge unrelated to Cres's case, the president of the republic addresses the nation, framing the murders as a "revolt against order, authority, and the law" whose responsibility lies with the far-left groups, guilty of instigating impressionable individuals to challenge state authority. Previously cast as the return of the repressed in the authoritarian logic of judicial power, the specter is now weaponized politically. The president's speech announces the state's project to make itself into a political subject—that is, an antagonistic (and in this case reactionary) force against the perceived threat of an imminent revolution.

Similar to *The Mattei Affair,* in *Illustrious Corpses,* the conspiracy functions as a conjuration. In the film, state agents participate in both evocation and exorcism of the ghost. Yet one cannot fail to notice that the development of the conspiracy in the film proceeds in a remarkably fortuitous manner, as many turning points in the advancement of the conspiratorial plans are either determined by chance or are left utterly unexplained. One such example is Rogas's unplanned visit to a party hosted by foreign billionaire Pattos (Alexandre Mnouchkine). Chasing someone he suspects could be Cres, Rogas ends up at the party but loses track of him. Rogas is then greeted by Pattos and the Minister of Safety (Fernando Rey) and invited to stay and enjoy himself. The gathering is the capital's who's who of the political, economic, and intellectual elite; in attendance are high-ranking functionaries of the state, industrialists, renowned leftist writers, and even one of the leaders of the so-called radical groups.

In a conversation that mirrors Riches's lecture on the infallibility of the law, the Minister of Safety educates Rogas on what he calls "the game": everybody participates in it, playing a role, whether they are aware of it or not. Rogas does too. His impromptu appearance at the party, the Minister explains, will be taken by some of the players as a calculated move to instill the doubt that the police are surveilling them. This game, in which the players are asked to constantly guess the opponent's (or ally's) moves, reminds us of the other game evoked in the film's title: *cadavre exquis,* the surrealist pastime in which participants are asked to collectively assemble a text or a picture by each adding one element, but without knowing what the previous contributions are. The picture of the conspiracy painted in *Illustrious Corpses* greatly resembles such assemblages. In the film, the schemers are presented as loosely linked to one another and often lacking a proper cognitive mapping of the general situation—*cadavre exquis* as statecraft. The party scene suggests a fluid and contradictory situation in which the interests represented by the guests are shown as sometimes colluding and sometimes conflicting, but always in the context of a struggle in which the ultimate motives and aims of the counterparts remain obscure. The game's participants are forced to operate in a regime of heightened contingency and reciprocal blindness, taking advantage of unanticipated eventualities such as Cres's murderous spree and Rogas's unplanned visit to the party.

This reactive opportunism of the conspirators, while certainly presupposing a general authoritarian design, nonetheless suggests the lack of an all-encompassing master plan. Conspiracies are often invoked to provide an identifiable intentionality to otherwise obscure and anonymous processes (what Jacques Lacan would call the Other of the Other). The dimension of the game in *Illustrious Corpses,* however, complicates such a proposition, for the players

198   The Specter

operate in the absence of an ultimate transcendental guarantee of their actions. In light of this aspect, we can now better grasp the import of Riches's position discussed earlier. Riches and the Minister—the judiciary and the executive—are two sides of the same coin. The judge's belief in the existence of the supreme infallibility of the law (when passing a sentence, the judge embodies justice itself) is the obverse of the Minister's awareness of its absence (everybody is playing a game). The spatial organization of the film speaks precisely to this duality between the somberness

Figure 20. The police headquarters, Riches' house, the president's palace, and the museum where Rogas is assassinated in *Illustrious Corpses* (1976).

of quasi-religious state rituals and the playful theatricality of the game. The places where the liturgy of state power takes place (the supreme court, the ministry, the police archives, the prison) are captured by Rosi with wide-angle lenses, lending a staged quality to the action (Figure 20). The characters never seem to dominate the scene. Often dwarfed by the grandiosity of baroque architecture and brutalist buildings, they simply perform in these environments like puppets against a backdrop that had been set for them by someone else.[22]

The point here is not (solely) that democracy structurally bears within itself the seed of authoritarianism. Rather, it is that the field of authoritarianism in democracy is precisely defined by these two

seemingly contradictory coordinates: the law as absolute necessity and the game of statecraft in its radical opportunism. Most importantly, the two are intertwined in a dialectical relationship. In the vertiginous feedback loop that echoes throughout the film, it is the fiction of a transcendental guarantee of state rule created by the judiciary that allows for the relative free play of conspiratorial plotting. When the rule of law comes under attack by the spectral by-product (Cres) of its own inflexible logic of infallibility, the state intervenes by weaponizing the specter for its own authoritarian objectives while simultaneously revealing the incompleteness of the totality it purports to represent.

What is deliberately left obscure in *Illustrious Corpses* is the link between this Januslike manifestation of the strategy of tension and the global economic and geopolitical framework in which it occurs. In his famous "Article on the Fireflies" (originally titled "The Void of Power in Italy"), Pier Paolo Pasolini seized on the elusiveness of this invisible global hand and the general unawareness on the part of the Italian establishment of the epochal shift that occurred concomitantly to the economic miracle. The Christian Democrats, writes Pasolini, have been deluding themselves about their leadership role and are now mere "death masks" covering up a real power void.[23] "Of this 'real power,'" writes Pasolini, "we have images that are abstract and ultimately apocalyptic: we cannot picture what 'forms' it would assume by substituting itself to the slaves [*servi*, the DC] who took it for a mere 'technical' modernization."[24] In *Illustrious Corpses*, while the "slaves" play their game, a new master announces its presence not only in the relatively marginal figure of the billionaire Pattos but also, and more ominously, in the ubiquitous white Mercedes-Benz—and its unknown occupant—that materializes at all key narrative junctures in the film. (The car is a ghostly presence in its own right, with its Swiss plates unsubtly adumbrating the stateless nature of the interests it represents.)

We thus arrive at the last twist in the intricate labyrinth that is *Illustrious Corpses:* from the unequivocal belief in the Other of the Other (Riches's religious mindset), to the acknowledgment of its inexistence (the Minister's emphasis on the gamelike nature of statecraft), to the vague insinuation that there in fact might be a grander plan in place, one orchestrated by the mysterious forces of global capital. As we have seen, the split between the former two conspiratorial paradigms (Riches's and the Minister's) maps out the division at the heart of the law itself: the fact that law is not-all, and that a surplus of arbitrary violence is needed to disavow—and simultaneously reaffirm—this lack. The latter paradigm (global capital's invisible hand) functions as a solution to the problem posed by the other two. Not only does it fill the historical void behind the death masks of the judge and the Minister, but it also bridges the structural gap nested at the heart of the state itself. The hint to a global conspiracy enveloping the other two local plots offers a way—however unresolved or merely suggested—to overcome the division that haunts the state, thus providing it with a modicum of internal consistency.

The specter cuts through the three paradigms obliquely, as both a condition of possibility of the interlocking conspiracies and the index of a totality that is not-all. Created by the judiciary as collateral damage, fortuitously weaponized by the executive, and finally reabsorbed into a vast global conspiracy, the specter is the pivot around which the subjectivation of the state revolves. This subjectivation occurs dialectically; the state evokes the specter as the externalization of its own internal split, only to then attempt to exorcise it, attaining subjective consistency in the process. The specter then becomes the vanishing mediator that allows the disparate, if not outright contradictory, spirits of the state to come together in one large authoritarian design.

It is significant that in the context of the globalizing world of the 1970s, it is only in the presence of some form of extrastate influence that the state can attain its own subjectivation, as though it could only find its own coherent self-image outside of itself—a perspective shared by both Pasolini and Rosi that has to do with Italy's peculiar geopolitical position in the postwar period. In both *The Mattei Affair* and *Illustrious Corpses,* the key factor seems to be the distance that separates the center of power from the peripheries, and the attendant freedom to maneuver that political and economic actors may have within such liminal spaces. In *The Mattei Affair,* the limited control that U.S. companies had over Italian geological resources after World War II permitted Mattei's efforts toward the country's energy independence, and with them the rise of a credible threat to the oligopoly of the Seven Sisters. Inversely, *Illustrious Corpses* depicts a situation in which Italy's geopolitical positioning as a frontier—part of the U.S. empire, yet home to the largest Communist Party in Europe and close enough to the Soviet bloc to be susceptible to their influence—warranted the planning and deployment of military countermeasures aimed at containing and neutralizing the communist threat. The important shift between the two films is in the diverging conceptions of the state in a similar context of U.S. imperialist interference. Subjected to immense pressures by the global geopolitical situation, the state, once imagined as protector of national interests, reveals itself in the economic recession and political instability of the 1970s as a repressive apparatus completely enmeshed in the networks of influence that are coming into being in a globalizing world.

Dividing the Law: Investigation of a Citizen Above Suspicion

With *Investigation of a Citizen Above Suspicion,* Elio Petri opens up the logic of state authority to a more abstract examination. While obviously redolent of the historical context of the strategy of tension, *Investigation* aims for a proper formalization of the logic of state authority in the form of a general symptomatology that takes as its starting point the figure of the specter. The film revolves around the murder of libertine bourgeois Augusta Terzi (Florinda Bolkan) by her lover, an unnamed police chief in the homicide division (Gian Maria Volonté, referred to by the honorific title *Dottore* in the original version). Eager to test the limits of his own impunity, the Chief covers his tracks only haphazardly, while the investigation zeroes in on a young anarchist, Antonio Pace (Sergio Tramonti), with whom Augusta was also having an affair. As the Chief is promoted to helm the political division and sets out to prosecute radical leftist groups, a series of flashbacks paints the picture of a perverse relationship between the victim and the murderer in which the Chief's authority—and, by proxy, his virility—was now revered, now ridiculed by Augusta, who shows a bemused fascination with the Chief's line of work, prompting her to reenact crime scenes with him for sexual arousal. In the surreal ending, the Chief decides to turn himself in, but he falls asleep and dreams of his colleagues coercing him into the most paradoxical of admissions: a confession of innocence. The film ends with the Chief, now awake, welcoming the same group of colleagues into his apartment in a near-exact replica of his dream.

Plenty of analyses of *Investigation* to date have focused on the character of the Chief, and for good reason.[25] However, the spectral presence of Augusta—murdered in the first scene and turned revenant through the series of flashbacks—has scarcely received the same critical attention. After the murder, Augusta first re-appears as a disembodied voice, visiting the Chief in his sleep as the dreamlike reminiscence of their first contact: a phone call in which Augusta introduces herself as an admirer of the Chief's public persona. From then on, the flashbacks chronicle the progressive trajectory from, at first, a shared fetishistic attachment to violence (the crime scene reenactments) and the superegoical authority of the law ("I love when you question me," confesses Augusta. "You're so suspicious, you remind me of my father"), to a contentious affair in which the Chief's jealousy, mocked by Augusta, reveals his fundamental insecurity.

The stereotypical traits of hypersexualization, sophistication, and elusiveness seem to point to a reading of Augusta as a male fantasy. In the film, these traits are suffused with the stereotypical sociocultural nuances of '68 counterculture: with her ethnicizing clothing, emancipated sexuality, carnivalesque penchant for masquerade, and ambiguous distaste for authority, Augusta is framed by Petri as an assemblage of the kind of liberties (sexual, political) that the state apparatus helmed by the Chief is designed to repress, thus making her at the same time the good object and the bad object of the Chief's desire. First, she bolsters his delirium of omnipotence by giving herself over to him; she gleefully plays the victim in the crime scene reenactments, offering herself as the object of the Chief's voyeurism, amplified by the omnipresent prosthesis of the photo camera. But she also pokes holes in the Chief's facade of authority and respectability, constantly reminding him—and the spectator—that his power is ultimately nothing but a fiction. In this sense, Augusta performs for the Chief the spectacle of state law itself, whose paradox is that of being inherently split, simultaneously omnipotent and impotent.

The recurrent theme of immaturity in the film shows precisely how these two aspects are linked. "The people are underage," explains the Chief during his inauguration speech at his new post, and the police, as representatives of the fatherly power of the state, have "the duty to repress" any and all forms of subversion. But the Chief also reveals his own childish inanity when his presumed omnipotence is exposed as a fiction by Augusta and the anarchist Pace. The mask of authoritarianism quickly falls off when Augusta mocks the Chief's virility and Pace refuses to be intimidated by his interrogation tactics. From fascist, hypermasculine enforcer of the status quo, Volonté masterfully switches registers to portray a sniveling man-child prone to tantrums. Like Lulù in *The Working Class Goes to Heaven* discussed in chapter 2, the Chief oscillates between the position of the pervert (the tool in the hands of the law as Other) and that of the hysteric, who is tortured by a fundamental uncertainty as to why the law assigned him to his position of power ("Why am I what the Other says that I am?").

The doubt instilled by Augusta's mockery is precisely what triggers the Chief's probing of the foundations of his authority. Being "above suspicion," then, means being beyond the doubt of the hysteric. To dispel this doubt, the Chief must test the boundaries of his own power, and in doing so, he reveals the split nature of law itself: "eternal, sculpted in time" for the pervert, as the Chief says in his inauguration speech; elusive and enigmatic for the hysteric, who must launch an "investigation" on suspicion itself. The repeated return of Augusta, however, prevents the film from solving the problem of this internal fissure in terms of a simple separation between autonomous dimensions. As is often the case in Petri, there is a surplus that haunts the split, an enjoyment that does not let itself be fully captured by the side of the pervert or the hysteric but rather creeps into the gap between the two. Augusta frames this surplus for the Chief by acting as a *fantasma*—in Italian, a word meaning both "fantasy" and "ghost." The fantasy of Augusta as the rebellious sexual object infatuated with authority frames the desire of a law that can enjoy its omnipotence only by finding itself powerless—or, put differently, a law that can only enjoy in the gap between its omnipotence and its impotence.[26]

It is the specter of Augusta, with her insistent questioning of the Chief's lawman persona, who hystericizes the perverse Chief, thus opening up for him the possibility to find enjoyment in the compulsive probing of his own unaccountability. This possibility to find enjoyment, it should be noted, seems precluded to all the other characters in the film; the other police officers are perverts without hystericization, having power but experiencing hardly a doubt about their symbolic mandate, whereas the citizens (Augusta's gay ex-husband, Pace's anarchist comrade, the plumber played by Salvo Randone) are hysterics without perversion, interpellated by the state (they are all subjected to interrogations) and forced into the agonizing exercise of guessing what the Other wants from them.

This surplus enjoyment, figured by the specter, is what makes state authority not-all. The totality of the state is structurally incomplete because it is tied to enjoyment. In *Illustrious Corpses,* the state attained its subjectification into an authoritarian agent thanks to the specter acting as a vanishing mediator in a concrete, historically situated geopolitical context. In *Investigation,* Petri provides a more general formalization of the logic of state power by starting from the police and charting the dynamics of the excessive pleasure that haunts the state's repressive apparatuses. Not-all and split from within as in Rosi, state authority in *Investigation* is held together—and simultaneously kept in its divided form—by this surplus enjoyment. This is the paradox of state authority as Petri sees it: there can be no enjoyment without the division at the heart of state law, just as there can be no unitary notion of state law without the enjoyment that splits it apart. The hysteric and the pervert are two sides of the same cop.

In Petri, as opposed to Rosi, the conspiracy functions as a deus ex machina, manifesting itself at the end to operate a compulsory dehystericization of the Chief, a cure for what he calls the "occupational hazard" of being a cop—namely, the questioning of one's own mandated power. The final apparition of Augusta reveals her as *conjurée* in that she participates in the conspiracy to cover up her own murder by providing the most liberating of absolutions, the one bestowed by the victim: "You killed a worthless person," she tells the Chief in his dream; "somebody else would have killed me. Sooner or later, I was destined to die that way. Do what they tell you. Think of your colleagues. Think of your career." Augusta's last words seal her fantasmatic destiny. Just like the postulate of the infallibility of the law explained by Riches in *Illustrious Corpses* was made possible by the specter of Cres as the founding exception, the ultimate unaccountability of law enforcement is sanctioned by Augusta, the specter of the victim conjured by the police officer who absolves her murderer and exhorts him to return to his assigned place in the symbolic order.

This question of enjoyment haunting state law is hinted at in another film by Petri, *Property Is No Longer a Theft* where a police detective (Orazio Orlandi) confesses that what he likes most about his job is the liberty to arrest whomever he wants, because "to arrest someone is the most beautiful thing" (*arrestare è bellissimo*). In *Property*, however, the scope of Petri's symptomatology enlarges considerably to encompass not only the question of state authority but also that of capital's rule over the individual and, most significantly, of the mutually reinforcing relationship between the two.

Real Abstraction and Enjoyment: *Property Is No Longer a Theft*

Property Is No Longer a Theft follows Total (Flavio Bucci), a young bank clerk with a peculiar allergy to money, as he persecutes a wealthy and boorish butcher (Ugo Tognazzi). A self-professed follower of the "Marxist-Mandrakist" current (from the name of comic book character Mandrake the Magician), Total steals the butcher's knife, his hat, his jewels, and, eventually, his mistress Anita (Daria Nicolodi) in a crescendo that leaves his victim baffled and furious. The film ends with the butcher murdering Total, after the latter's staunch refusal to be bribed into subservience.

Total, the aspiring thief, haunts spaces like a ghost and is referred to by other characters as *malocchio* (evil eye, curse), hinting at his preternatural status. His most prominent spectral traits—omnipresence and elusiveness—are framed by Petri as the implicit conjuration of the butcher's fantasy. As the detective explains to Tognazzi's character, "Without the fear of theft one doesn't enjoy one's own wealth." Later, he adds that the butcher "wants to be persecuted." The capitalist needs to conjure the ghost of the thief in order to frame his own drive toward the accumulation of wealth and derive enjoyment from it. Just as Augusta in *Investigation* is the police officer's fantasy, here the thief is the capitalist's fantasy. Total and the butcher, then, are two sides of the same coin. The thief is the criminal exception to the rule of private property that constitutes the foundation of capitalist accumulation, while the capitalist can only ever enjoy his wealth under the threat that someone might take it away.

In the film, the ghostly thief is presented as the personified correlate of the structural spectral surplus that haunts capitalism. Derrida draws attention to the role played by specters in the capitalist relation of production and to the obsession with ghosts evident in Marx's writing. From the critique of Max Stirner's reduction of social institutions to mere figments of the imagination in *The German Ideology* to the dancing table in the section on commodity fetishism in the first volume of *Capital,* Marx attempts a spectrography of the abstract yet concrete "non-sensuous sensuous" presences that hover around social and economic relations under capitalism.[27] These spectralities have a name: real abstractions, of which private property is one instance. As we have seen in chapter 3 in our discussion of *Red Desert* and *Dillinger Is Dead,* real abstractions do not idealistically precede the concrete manifestation of things; nor can they be simply inferred, ex post facto, from that manifestation. Rather, they haunt human relations in a properly spectral mode of manifestation—abstract yet concrete, absent yet present. It is in this sense that spectrality is inherent in the operations of capital: "capitalist production is the production of ghosts," in Antonio Negri's succinct formulation.[28]

In the specific case of private property, properties in their physical existence—the things one owns—are inseparable from the abstract logic that asserts the inviolability of ownership rights. Similar to the logic that subtends commodity fetishism, private property is a quality of things that is not intrinsic to them and yet defines all social relations that revolve around them, in a superimposition between the dimension of being and that of possession—a predicament literalized in a scene where Total's destitute father (Salvo Randone) tries to conjugate "to be" and gets confused, mixing it with "to have." As Total corrects him, he clarifies that the dilemma of the age of capitalism is no longer between "to be or not to be," as it was for Hamlet, but between to be and to have—a dilemma that causes Total to battle with his incurable illness. The cause of this peculiar illness must be traced back to the process of alienation that man is subjected to in a regime of real abstraction. While social relationships like private property gain an autonomous existence from the individual, the individual also undergoes a process of equal and opposite abstraction. Marx describes the nature of private property in these terms in the *Manuscripts:* "This *material, immediately sensuous* private property is the material, sensuous expression of *estranged human* life."[29] Private property for Marx is the expression of the fact that man is alienated from himself ("man becomes objective for himself and, at the same time, becomes an alien and an inhuman object for himself").[30] This alienation, in the form of the impasse between to be and to have, is what ails Total—and society as a whole, for private property stands as one of the preconditions of all the other real abstractions that determine human existence under capitalism: "The positive supersession of *private property*, as the appropriation of *human* life, is therefore the positive supersession of all estrangement, and the return of man from religion, the family, the state, etc. to his *human*, i.e. *social* existence."[31] The "supersession of *private property*" is of course the horizon of the communist project, whereby "man appropriates his integral essence in an integral way, as a *total man*."[32] One can only wonder whether Petri, an avid reader of Marx, was familiar with this passage from the *Manuscripts*. The name he gave to his protagonist surely suggests the mockery of someone who will never be a "total man," irredeemably torn as he is between being and having.

But why this fate? What is it that keeps the horizon of communism—of the total man and the supersession of private property—forever out of reach for the protagonist of Petri's film? The answer lies in the praxis of thievery itself, adopted by Total as a political response to the real abstraction of private property. To understand the intrinsic inadequacy of theft as a political response under capitalism, we must first consider the way in which capital and its logic of accumulation are represented in the film. This task is bestowed on the butcher, in an example of what Alberto Toscano and Jeff Kinkle call "capitalist shamanism."[33] As though possessed by the spirit of capital itself, the butcher addresses the spectator directly, against a dark background, in one of the monologues that punctuate the film. With a shrug, the butcher admits to being consumed by a yearning for wealth that far exceeds what is required for the satisfaction of his needs: "My fundamental need [*bisogno*] is to make money.... If capital is not growing [*non lievita*] in my hands thanks to my uncontrollable desire to amass wealth, I feel like I'm rotting, like a carcass. Capital keeps me alive." He concludes by lamenting his unhappiness, because he longs to be eternal, "like money." One can discern in the butcher's unquenchable thirst for wealth the contours of the drive. As the constant tension of an urge that cannot be satisfied, the drive possesses the vitality of the undead. The capitalist's demand for surplus value has a life of its own, which takes hold of and vivifies his "carcass," because a capital that does not valorize itself is no capital at all. This "uncanny excess of life"[34] informs the fundamental fantasy of capital itself—namely, that of an endless, death-defying cycle of wealth accumulation whereby money organically engenders money.[35]

The drive toward the expansion of value personified by the butcher attaches itself to a certain surplus, which Marx identified as surplus value. Lacan, noting the proximity on this point between the Marxist critique of political economy and psychoanalysis, likens this surplus value to surplus enjoyment.[36] This surplus has no use value whatsoever (the butcher's desire for accumulation has nothing to do with his material needs), but the drive endlessly seeks after it for the sake of enjoyment itself. This is why Petri can surmise that private property is no longer a theft; what is being stolen—from the worker by capitalism, from the capitalist by the worker turned thief—are not just things but something more elusive: enjoyment itself. Long before Petri's humorous negation,

Marx himself had noted the fallacy of Pierre-Joseph Proudhon's famous motto, "La proprieté, c'est le vol!":

> The upshot [of Proudhon's motto] is at best that the bourgeois legal conceptions of *"theft"* apply equally well to the *"honest"* gains of the bourgeois himself. On the other hand, since *"theft"* as a forcible violation of property *presupposes the existence of property,* Proudhon entangled himself in all sorts of fantasies, obscure even to himself, about *true bourgeois property.*[37]

Chief among these fantasies is the fact that bourgeois property is a legal matter and not, as Marx argues, part of a relation of production deserving "a critical analysis of *'political economy.'*"[38] The bourgeois also figures as a thief in this relation, thus implying that the circulation of surplus in conditions of capitalism can only ever take place within the framework of forcible appropriation.

What complicates this circulation—and the capitalist relation of production as a whole—is the fact that the surplus is not merely a substance or a commodity that can be passed from one subject to the other. Rather, it is itself the crystallization of a split, appearing in a different guise depending on who is looking at it. This split is captured in the original French used by Lacan, *plus-de-jouir,* which translates as both "surplus enjoyment" and "no more enjoyment." These two sides of *plus-de-jouir* account for the butcher and Total's relation to enjoyment in the film. Seen from the standpoint of the butcher, this *plus-de-jouir* looks like surplus value that must be appropriated, in observance of capital's imperative of growth. From Total's standpoint, it is perceived as a lack of enjoyment triggering an attempt to recuperate it by the compulsory taking of private property from the capitalist. The two positions, however, are not in a symmetrical relation. While the butcher, true to the drive that he represents, makes a profit out of the thefts by insurance fraud, Total collects the butcher's properties only to discover their worthlessness. His thefts function according to a logic of reappropriation that is oblivious to the intricate abstractions that innervate the capitalist mode of production.

The pitfalls of Total's political struggle can be described by using

Marx's cutting critique of a "wholly crude and unthinking communism"[39] that, instead of abolishing the condition of the salaried worker, universalizes it: "Physical, immediate *possession* is the only purpose of life and existence as far as this communism is concerned; the category of *worker* is not abolished, but extended to all men; the relation of private property remains the relation of the community to the world of things."[40] With his attempt to take the butcher's properties for himself, the spectral thief fails to recognize the real abstraction of private property as the dominant form of social relations under capitalism. Indeed, what remains unthought in Total's "unthinking communism" is the fact that private property is a real abstraction—or, in other words, the irreducibility of private property to private properties.

Indeed, the idea of private property, along with its material consequences, remains as operative as ever, even when—especially when—one steals. Total's thievery is animated by an idea of distributive justice, in the sense of a reallocation of properties and resources that would leave the system fundamentally unaltered. Ironically, it is the butcher who illustrates to Total the dead end of his "crude and unthinking communism:" "For someone like me, an owner, to be forced to give up everything, one would need a revolution, which is nowhere in sight. . . . For you to take everything away from me, you would have to destroy the land register, kill all the notaries, burn down all police precincts, occupy the parliament, take control of television broadcasting!" This is also the point where the mutual relation between state and capital comes to the fore. It is the state, in the form of the institutions designed to defend property rights, that guarantees the continued functioning of the capitalist relation of production and the ever-expanding accumulation of wealth by the capitalist class.

It is no surprise that Petri would baptize *Property* "a film on the birth of despair [*disperazione*] within the left."[41] The roots of this despair are indicated in Total's opening monologue, where he claims that "class hatred [has] decomposed into selfishness, and has therefore been rendered innocuous." In the film, this "selfishness" takes two specular forms: the butcher's greed and its inverse, the thief's envy. In the words of Marx, "Universal *envy* constituting itself as a power is the hidden form in which *greed* reasserts itself and satisfies itself, but in *another* way."[42] In *Property*, the *plus-de-jouir* as surplus enjoyment (greed) and no more enjoyment (envy) are woven in and out of the narrative, reflected in the various monologues as little Brechtian tales of enjoyment that can only be told somewhere else, in a metafictional nonworld away from the diegetic universe of the film. The film's formal structure, in this sense, becomes itself a symptom of the way in which real abstractions tend to elude direct representation as a result of the exorbitant component of enjoyment that permeates their logic of functioning. In Petri, the figure of the specter indexes this elusiveness. It makes the circulation of this *plus-de-jouir* visible while at the same time demarcating the narrowing field of possibility for the rise of a radical political subjectivity under these conditions.

Coda: The Ashamed Specter

Under the "despair within the left" diagnosed by Petri in *Property*, we can recover the vaster, historically determined configuration of affects that start taking hold of the left by the late 1970s. This historical phase, characterized by a retreat into the private sphere and a relinquishing of mass politics often referred to as *riflusso* (ebb), possesses its own "emotional situation": Paolo Virno has defined it not merely as a "a bundle of psychological propensities" but rather as "those modes of being and feeling so pervasive as to be common to the most diverse contexts of experience, to the time given over to work as much as that dedicated to what is called life."[43] Heightened contingency, diffused precarity, rampant individualism, and marketization of public and private life are only some of the traits that define the years of *riflusso*, and that Virno sees reflected in the viral spreading of cynicism, opportunism, and fear throughout the social fabric.

This peculiar form of leftist despair in the years of the *riflusso* has its own history—one intimately connected with a history of specters. In the very partial genealogy of ghosts presented in this chapter, we have followed a trajectory of what we might call a decreasing spectral agency, understood as the specter's ability to determine or influence the situation in which it manifests itself—what Mark Fisher called the "agency of the virtual," the ghostly property of "that which acts without (physically) existing."[44] From the prefiguration of a challenge to the status quo (*The Mattei Affair*), to a pivot around which to consolidate the authoritarian subjectivity of the state in the years of the strategy of tension (*Illustrious Corpses* and *Investigation*), to a symptom of leftist despair under the regime imposed by the alliance between state and capital (*Property*), one notices the decreasing level of agency associated with the specter from one film to the next. Nostalgically imagined in pre-1968 times as the savior of the nation (Mattei), the specter becomes an unruly and elusive entity co-opted by competing authoritarian designs (Cres, Augusta), ultimately surrendering to the futility of its own antagonism (Total). As agency vanishes, despair sets in.

Arguably, no film has been able to capture this lived experience of disorientation, withdrawal, and disenchantment of the years of the *riflusso* in a more convincing way than Marco Tullio Giordana's *To Love the Damned* (*Maledetti vi amerò*), his debut feature from 1979. The film follows Riccardo, aka Svitol (Flavio Bucci), a communist militant in the long '68 who returns to his hometown of Milan after spending five years in Venezuela, where he fled to presumably avoid arrest for seditious activities. Svitol struggles to come to terms with the momentous changes that occurred in his absence. Some of his friends from the years of militancy have embraced bourgeois life, becoming entrepreneurs and stockbrokers. Others, like *Lotta Continua* editor Beniamino (David Riondino), have held on to their political beliefs but are left to register the despair and anxiety of a defeated movement. Still others, like Gigi (Pasquale Zito), have fallen victim to heroin addiction. Lonely and disoriented, Svitol ends up striking an unlikely friendship with a police detective who looks just as lost as he is.

Svitol's awkward encounters with old acquaintances are interspersed with oneiric sequences of him wandering around the deserted sites of the radical struggle of 1968, including the cloisters of the Università Statale and the shop floor of an abandoned factory (Figure 21). In a seeming echo of the ending of *Germany Year Zero* (where the young protagonist plays alone in a bombed-out building before committing suicide), these scenes are at once playful

Figure 21. Svitol wanders through an abandoned factory in *To Love the Damned* (1980).

and mournful. Clapping his hands to the rhythm of strike chants and loudly invoking a working class that is nowhere to be found (*"Classe! Classe!"* he repeats), Svitol haunts these places as a specter, the untimely remainder of a militant struggle that has now faded.

Through the spectrality of his protagonist, *To Love the Damned* draws our attention to one of the "modes of being and feeling" in times of disenchantment with radical politics that eludes Virno's taxonomy: shame. In part, the film frames this shame as regret for the protagonist's involvement in the violent political struggle of the long '68. The ideological position of the film in this respect remains somewhat ambiguous. This position is crystallized in another instance of spectrality in the film: Svitol's personal "wall of ghosts" (*parete dei fantasmi*), a collection of nameless silhouettes of victims of political violence stenciled from magazine photographs. "Without the captions," says Svitol, "they all look the same." One of the most obvious risks of this revisionism in which all victims are lumped together is the wholesale erasure of the specificity of the historico-political context of the time. Giordana's temptation here seems apparent; it is that of a dehistoricized account of that moment hinging on an abstract—and ultimately moralistic—condemnation of political violence within the context of a spurious ideology of national reconciliation. This results in an ultimately reassuring snapshot of

Italy's recent history where the fundamental political fault lines of the time, along with the meaning political violence assumed along those lines, are all but expunged.

While the film feigns a certain ambivalence ("I asked myself if I should feel pity for everyone," says Svitol, "but I haven't decided yet"), a more fundamental kind of shame insinuates itself in the interstices of this vague revisionism: the shame of being a relic of radical militancy in a time and a place—Italy at the turn of the decade—that no longer has any place for it. This shame points directly to Svitol's spectral ontological status. In psychoanalysis, shame has been defined by David Bernard as an "ontological affect," for it has to do with the foundations of subjectivity itself, and in a double sense.[45] Shame arises in the confrontation with the subject's own lack in being as a result of castration, but also, as is the case with Svitol, from the simple fact of being there as a body that does not fit in and sticks out, thus garnering unwanted attention. These two aspects are not independent from each other but rather intertwined around a point of vanishing. Bernard has argued that the Lacanian matheme of shame would be the same as the matheme of fantasy: $\$ \lozenge a$, where the shameful subject ($\$$) vanishes in front of the signifier of her lack (*a*), while the *a* constitutes the point of objectification where the subject fades. We thus have, respectively, a subjective side and an objective side of shame: a lack of being ($\$$) and a too much of being there (*a*), which coincide at the point of vanishing.[46]

One could argue that Total in *Property Is No Longer a Theft* and Svitol in *To Love the Damned* (incidentally, both played by Bucci) embody these two interrelated aspects of shame. For the former, it is the shame of his own lack in being, as an individual who is alienated from himself because he cannot reconcile the split between "to be" and "to have" imposed by the real abstraction of private property. For the latter, it is the shame of being *de trop*, an objectified surplus that has no proper place and is simply there, as a foreign body. Ironically, total will always be haunted by lack (and will therefore never be total, or whole), while Svitol—who bears the name of a brand of industrial lubricants—is incapable of participating in the smooth functioning of the capitalist machine.

In *To Love the Damned,* the ontology of the specter is not only a hauntology. It is also, to borrow a term from Lacan, a *hontologie*—a study in shame.[47] The time out of joint that Derrida identified as one of the foremost symptoms of hauntology returns here suffused with a peculiar affective tinge. At the cusp of the decade, after the murders of Pasolini in 1975 and the Christian Democrats' president, Aldo Moro, in 1978, Svitol lives his condition of exclusion as a reason for shame—shame of his own anachronism, of no longer serving any purpose, of being left out of the capitalist logic of profit that has seized society as a whole (as it becomes apparent to Svitol when he tries unsuccessfully to reinvent himself as an alpaca fleece salesman).

Following Lacan, Colette Soler has observed that it is rather uncommon for someone to die of shame nowadays, referring to more heroic times when the inability to fulfill the duties prescribed by social norms made death preferable to dishonor.[48] We now live in a time in which the imperative to die of shame has been inverted into a generalized low-intensity "shame at being alive," of living a life in which nothing is really worth dying for—not even one's own shame. "You will see," Lacan quips, "that this shame [at being alive] is justified by the fact that you didn't die of shame."[49] Lacan maps the transition between the two regimes of shame onto a shift between dominant discourses—that is, from the master's discourse to the university discourse, a formal configuration of social relationships that began in earnest during the revolts of 1968 and presided over the *riflusso*. Lacan frames the university discourse as a perversion of the master's discourse:[50]

$$\frac{S_1}{\$} \to \frac{S_2}{a} \qquad \frac{S_2}{S_1} \to \frac{a}{\$}$$

Master's Discourse University Discourse

The latter, predicated on Hegel's master–slave dialectic, has the master (S_1) in the dominant position, exploiting the slave and his know-how (S_2)—of which the master knows nothing—to produce the object of the master's enjoyment (a). The university discourse introduces a fundamental shift: knowledge (S_2) is extracted and appropriated from the slave. Now formalized as a set of scientific procedures and abstracted from any individual know-how, knowledge becomes episteme and comes to occupy the dominant position that once was the master's. The tyranny of episteme as the modern master has its proper subjects, which Lacan alternatively calls proletarians or students (*a*), in the position of the addressee previously occupied by the slave. Proletarians and students are to be considered coextensive, for they both find themselves reduced to units of value (salary for the proletarian, college credits for the student). The shame of being alive, then, is the fundamental affect that defines the proletarian/student in this position of objectification, a *honte de vivre* dictated by the quantification of one's worth. This shame, however, is twofold. It is not just the shame of being objectified (*a*) but, perhaps even more agonizingly, of not being objectified enough (of being worthless, of not having any quantifiable value) and therefore always on the verge of vanishing ($).

Svitol's former comrades' shameless transition into this brave new world as entrepreneurs and stockbrokers allegorizes the former part of objectification: the reification of the creative antagonistic energy of the long '68 and its subsumption by capital in the context of its endless quest for extraction of surplus value, which, in the conjuncture of the *riflusso*, happens to double as the strategic neutralization of endogenous threats. The remainder produced by this dialectic of capitalist development (Svitol, Beniamino, Gigi), however, points to the other side of objectification: the systematic marginalization of that which cannot be subsumed. While Svitol's spectral wandering is certainly the most striking emblem of this insistence of the remainder, Beniamino's inertial commitment to *Lotta Continua* and Gigi's heroin addiction fulfill a similar function, offering an ever more literal representation of the despair that seized the left in the years of the *riflusso*.

In a conversation with Svitol in the decrepit offices of the magazine, Beniamino bemoans the sense of loss and disorientation—registered in hundreds of letters to the editor—among the members of one of the biggest radical leftist group in the Italian long '68. The shock of Moro's death and a pervasive sense of impotence contribute to a generalized affective situation that resembles what Wendy Brown has famously called "Left melancholia": "It is a Left that has become more attached to its impossibility than to its potential fruitfulness, a Left that is most at home dwelling not in hopefulness but in its own marginality and failure, a Left that is thus caught in a structure of melancholic attachment to a certain strain of its own dead past, whose spirit is ghostly, whose structure of desire is backward looking and punishing."[51] One can locate the beginnings of Brown's situation, ghostly in their own right, precisely in the tail end of the long '68, when the last of radical collective movements met their demise. The Italian left, in particular, begins to develop in the years of the *riflusso* not only a habit of regret and recrimination, but also, and relatedly, a libidinal attachment to its own lack of agency. As Beniamino puts it, "The Christian Democrats run the country, and we write and we cry." No longer a real threat to the status quo after the institutional and political realignment after Moro, the left sinks into self-doubt as the very idea of collective action disintegrates into a myriad of individual agonies. "Depression" Beniamino deadpans, "is deadlier than repression."

Yet it is not only radical antagonism that is relegated to impotence under these psychohistorical conditions. The foil of revolutionary movements for the better part of the long '68—the apparatus of surveillance and repression of the state we saw portrayed in *Illustrious Corpses* and *Investigation*—meets a similar fate here, finding in the worn-out detective, as baffled and helpless as anybody else, its most conspicuous representative. While the uneasy friendship between Svitol and the detective unfolds under the aegis of the discourse of national reconciliation we outlined earlier, it also signals, more subtly, the vanishing of a certain organization of the field of struggle, with once-competing actors now left to interrogate themselves about their own historical role. "It was much better when you could recognize the enemy": Svitol's nostalgia for neater lines of demarcations between friends and enemies signals the advent of a new social, economic, and political order in which the antagonism that defined the long '68—with state and capital on one side and the diverse front of revolutionary forces on the other—becomes blurred. As pockets of resistance to the status quo shrink into irrelevance, the years of the *riflusso* see a generalized marketization of everyday life, driving a diffused situation of isolation, competition, and precarity. Often summarized under the umbrella term neoliberalism, this process is also an exorcism of sorts. It aims to shame out of existence all those lingering specters of revolution that haunt society after the defeat of radical movements.

This situation in which no revolutionary politics seems possible inaugurates a historical sequence defined by the withering away of "communism" as the name of a universal emancipatory project, a sequence that found a late culmination with the fall of the Soviet Union and, one might suggest, stretches to the present day. Derrida exhorts us not only to interrogate this sequence as a "latency period" that links the post-1968 situation to the end of state socialism, but to do so in terms of its "event-ness."[52] Written in the immediate aftermath of 1989, *Specters of Marx* casts the collapse of the Soviet Union as the condition of possibility for distilling a "spirit" of Marxism purified from the tactical choices made by communist movements in the concrete historical circumstances of the twentieth century, including those that go under the name of long '68. Derrida conjures this specter to provide the ultimate hauntological refutation of any stable ontologization of Marxism—that is, its crystallization into concrete and nameable entities, be they theoretical or historical, as "philosophical or metaphysical system, as 'dialectical materialism,' [. . .] as historical materialism or method, and [. . .] [as] Marxism incorporated in the apparatus of party, State, or workers' International."[53]

Can we not read in this liberation from ontology celebrated by Derrida also the torture of the militant subject after the defeat of the radical movements of the long '68—a militant doomed to aimlessly wander through factories and universities in the absence of any quilting point that would secure, however precariously, its being to the signifier "communism"? Caught between melancholia and *cupio dissolvi*, the communist militant in the *riflusso* is an awkward and worthless remainder. We can understand shame, then, as one possible subjective consequence of the hollowing out of the name "communism" invoked in *Specters of Marx*. The question Derrida poses of spectrality, then, may need to be reversed. Instead of starting from the event of an institutional collapse to derive from it an abstract form of spectral subjectivity (of waiting, of openness), we should start from concrete historical subjectivities and interrogate their spectralization as it relates to—but is not entirely determined by—state politics.

This is, in part, the position articulated by Alain Badiou. Rejecting the connotation of the fall of the Soviet Union as an event, Badiou has argued that existing socialism actually died well before its official death certificate was signed in 1989 because it was predated by a far more consequential crisis of communist militancy. Hardly an event that calls for a reinvention of the spirit of Marxism, as it was for Derrida, 1989 for Badiou is simply a secondary reverberation of a larger crisis of political subjectivity that began after the historical sequence of 1968: "The dislocation of the Soviet party-State is merely the objective crystallization [. . .] of the fact that a certain thought of 'we' is inoperative and has been for more than twenty years."[54] The communist "we" that originated in the aftermath of October 1917 has been obsolete, according to Badiou, "at least since May '68 as far as France is concerned."[55] *To Love the Damned*—and to a similar extent *Property Is No Longer a Theft*—allow us to discern the signs of the fading of this "we" of militant subjectivity in the Italian context: the loss of a sense of collectivity, the lack of agency, the increasingly elusive terrain of antistate and anticapitalist struggle, the melancholic attachment to the past.

It is in this larger context that the question of the specter emerges in all its historical and political complexity. In Italian political cinema, the specter is the figure that more than any other signals the weakening of radical political subjectivities at the end of the long '68. This weakening has to do with the progressive drawing of the antagonism into the machinery of state politics we have traced throughout this chapter. The figure of the specter makes visible this weakening and the ultimate demise of political subjectivity. It does so by outlining a shrinking field of possibility for the affirmation of radical emancipatory projects, a field progressively colonized by the reactionary forces of state and capital. As the relative autonomy of revolutionary political subjectivities fades, the remaining forms of struggle become increasingly characterized by an intensification of demonstrative violence and the proliferation of terroristic organizations—itself a spectral lingering of revolutionary desire, yet a desire that has become impotent, bereft as it is of any subjective horizon of mass mobilization. The new world order announced in the 1980s—and ratified after 1989—managed to do away with all these specters. Yet times that are not visibly haunted by specters are not times without specters. They are simply times that have managed to keep them at bay, exorcising them in more effective ways. One can chase specters, even chase them away, but one is never done with them.

7 Apocalypse with Figures
The Tyrant, the Intriguer, the Martyr

> This age drunk with acts of cruelty both lived and imagined.
> —Walter Benjamin, *The Origin of German Tragic Drama*

> I readjust my commitment to a greater legibility (*Salò?*).
> —Pier Paolo Pasolini, "Repudiation of the Trilogy of Life"

An Informal Triptych

To sketch out a possible conclusion of the figural arc of Italian political cinema, this chapter will center on three films that, despite their chronological and thematic proximity, are seldom mentioned in the same breath: *Salò, or The 120 Days of Sodom* (*Salò, o le 120 giornate di Sodoma,* Pier Paolo Pasolini, 1975), *Todo Modo* (Elio Petri, 1976), and *La Grande Bouffe* (Marco Ferreri, 1973). The lack of a sustained comparative analysis between these films is perhaps due to the directors' differing critical fortunes and the disparity of their respective positions in the Italian cinematic canon. Yet it is also, and just as importantly, a matter of sheer visibility, if one considers the Italian censors' ferocious attacks on the films and, in the case of *Salò* and *Todo Modo,* the outright attempt to consign them to perpetual oblivion.[1]

Salò remains substantially faithful to its literary inspiration, the Marquise de Sade's *120 Days of Sodom,* while changing its setting to 1944. During the fascist last stand of the Republic of

Salò (1943–45), four lords—the Duke (Paolo Bonacelli), the Bishop (Giorgio Cataldi), the Magistrate (Umberto P. Quintavalle), and the President (Aldo Valletti)—have a group of local teenagers kidnapped and taken to a villa near Marzabotto.[2] For four months, the teens are subjected to acts of extreme physical and psychological violence, all for the pleasure of their kidnappers. The highly ritualized cadence of orgies, tortures, and rapes to which libertines and victims must adhere unconditionally is regulated by a group of four prostitutes, who organize a series of storytelling interludes between acts of violent debauchery.

Also based on a novel (*Todo Modo* by Leonardo Sciascia), Petri's film applies spatial seclusion and the ritualization of time to a secretive retreat. While a mysterious epidemic is ravaging the country, the establishment of the political party governing Italy—which remains unnamed but is immediately identifiable as the Christian Democrats (DC)—gathers at an underground hotel to perform a series of spiritual exercises inspired by the teachings of St. Ignatius of Loyola, in which they are led by a mysterious priest, don Gaetano (Marcello Mastroianni). The exercises are repeatedly interrupted by mysterious acts of violence targeting the notables, while plots and intrigues are orchestrated by the President (Gian Maria Volonté, impersonating Aldo Moro, then the president of the DC) in order to save the party from an irreversible crisis. The film ends with the massacre of all the hotel guests at the hands of an unspecified governmental agency.

Finally, in *La Grande Bouffe,* four friends—a chef (Ugo Tognazzi), a television producer (Michel Piccoli), a judge (Philippe Noiret), and an airline pilot (Marcello Mastroianni)—organize a retreat to a villa with the purpose of eating themselves to death. Halfway through the weekend, they are joined by four women, three prostitutes and a schoolteacher (Andrea Ferréol), with whom they have sex. As the feast continues without interruption, the prostitutes leave in disgust and the friends die one by one, with the only survivor, the schoolteacher, assisting them in their final endeavor and watching over their demise.

The initial wager of this chapter is that *Salò, Todo Modo,* and *La Grande Bouffe* may be usefully read as an informal triptych. The approach I follow will be to consider this triptych as a single entity made up of three components, the figural significance of which is best elucidated by looking at them at a glance. The effort, different from a more standard comparative analysis, will be to understand the differences between the three films as central to the figural economy of the triptych as a whole. A triptych, after all, is not only predicated on harmony among its parts; it is also, and perhaps more importantly, an object made up of discontinuities and heterogeneity, as the unity of a triptych can only originate from the disunity among its components. This disunity is most readily perceivable in the fact that each film sketches its own figure. Borrowing from Walter Benjamin's figural analysis in *The Origin of German Tragic Drama*, this chapter revolves around the tyrant (*Salò*), the intriguer (*Todo Modo*), and the martyr (*La Grande Bouffe*). This proliferation should itself be regarded as a symptom: what is it that these films wish to think collectively that cannot find articulation in any one individual figure?

Echoes of the Baroque

A glance at the films' shared features points us toward the beginning of an answer. The three films are defined by two fundamental conditions: seclusion and ritualization. The two are functions of each other. Seclusion institutes what we might call a state of exception in which the rule of the law is suspended and substituted by a new, ritualistic set of rules—a routine of torture and violence for the sadistic pleasure of the lords in *Salò*, spiritual exercises of penance for the ruling class in *Todo Modo*, and the repetition of cooking, eating, and fucking in *La Grande Bouffe*. These rituals are enforced with a great deal of "scrupulosity," which Roland Barthes, in *Sade, Fourier, Loyola*, associates to a certain theatricality ("a powerful impression . . . of performance").[3] This highly regulated performance of repetition is underpinned by a desire to control time itself—harnessing the passing of time to ultimately bring it to a standstill in the form of eternal torture, eternal penance, and eternal consumption. The state of exception portrayed in the triptych would thus not only be a legal one but also a temporal one, a regimented attempt at being excepted from history itself.

What is the ultimate rationale of this Sisyphean task? What is all this staged repetition designed to ward off? In all three films, we sense the pervasive omen of a world coming to an end. In *Salò*, the spectacular ferocity of the libertines in their secluded quarters not only reeks of the stench of decomposing fascism but also prefigures the future of a world without redemption, a hell on earth where suffering—and the pleasure that the lords derive from it—extends itself into eternity. (It is thus not surprising that Pasolini would structure the film on the topography of Dante's *Inferno*.) In *Todo Modo*, Petri depicts the collapse of the contemporary political establishment, as the President's attempts to stave off the decline of his party in the midst of a pandemic are cut short by the extermination of all its members. In *La Grande Bouffe*, the physical and psychological toll of the four friends' endless gourmandizing makes itself felt in increasingly alarming fashion, tracing the progressive annihilation of the social order imposed by the bourgeoisie in the wake of World War II. The form of appearance of history in the triptych, then, is that of decay.[4] The films record the dying whispers of an era, but they do so in intaglio—not directly, but through the protagonists' inhuman efforts to stave off the seemingly inevitable deterioration of their world.

The origins of this idea of a naturalization of history as organic decay and the capacity of the work of art to give it form was located by Walter Benjamin in the genre of German baroque drama, or *Trauerspiel*:

> Nature remained the great teacher for the writers of this period. However, nature was not seen by them in bud and bloom, but in the over-ripeness and decay of her creations. In nature they saw eternal transience, and here alone did the saturnine vision of this generation recognize history. [. . .] In the process of decay, and in it alone, the events of history shrivel up and become absorbed in the setting.[5]

The baroque is marked by what Samuel Weber calls a "confusion" between history and nature.[6] In the *Trauerspiel*, historical change—represented by the transience of sovereigns—follows a methodical pattern of growth and decay reminiscent of the natural cycles of organic life. This destiny of the baroque sovereign, however, should not simply be read as the demise of an individual but rather as the "dislocation of sovereignty as such."[7] As a result of the process of secularization that began with the Renaissance and concludes in the baroque, the seat previously occupied by a divine principle of law, embodied by the sovereign and around which society coalesces, now finds itself empty. In Benjamin's account, this "dislocation of sovereignty" is the epochal crisis that German baroque drama stages through the figures of the tyrant, the intriguer, and the martyr.

At the center of the question of sovereignty stands the conceptual linkage that unites the sovereign to the state of exception. In the work of Carl Schmitt, sovereignty is understood first and foremost as the power to decide on the state of exception—that is, the suspension of state law in the presence of an existential threat to the state itself. As such, the state of exception transcends the state and at the same time constitutes its ultimate guarantee: "the state of exception appears as the legal form of what cannot have legal form."[8] Interestingly, Benjamin adopts the opposite position on the matter. In the *Trauerspiel*, the Schmittian sovereign decision no longer obtains:

> The antithesis between the power of the ruler and his capacity to rule led to a feature peculiar to the *Trauerspiel* which is, however, only apparently a generic feature and which can be illuminated only on the basis of the theory of sovereignty. . . . The sovereign, who is responsible for making the decision on the state of exception, reveals, at the first opportunity, that it is almost impossible for him to make a decision.[9]

The baroque dislocation of sovereignty, then, consists in this split between power and its exercise that defines the position of the sovereign. This position, according to Giorgio Agamben, marks the opening of an unbridgeable fissure in the law itself: "between *Macht* and *Vermögen* . . . a gap opens which no decision is capable of filling."[10] In this decaying world in which no transcendental guarantee is bestowed on the sovereign's decision, the state of exception becomes the rule. This is the ultimate task of the baroque sovereign for Benjamin: not to safeguard state law by ensuring the existence of what transcends it (the state of exception), as it was for Schmitt, but to make that transcendence immanent to the state—to make the state of exception become part of the law. Under these conditions, the sovereign decision finds itself emptied of its function. No actual decision on an interruption of the law can be made when interruption has become immanent to the law itself.

The dislocation of sovereignty, however, is not a historico-political feature uniquely inherent to the baroque. The *Trauerspiel* gives it a particular historical form, but it is important to remind ourselves that Benjamin's argument is less a historicist than a formalist one. His perspective is not that of an antiquarian, bent on identifying in baroque drama a lifeless relic of the past. Rather, as György Lukács observes, Benjamin strives to read this art form "from the perspective of the ideological and artistic needs of the present."[11] Benjamin himself surmises that eras of decadence tend to resemble each other, and furthermore that all art in eras of decadence look alike, to the point that modernism "reflects certain aspects of the spiritual constitution of the baroque, even down to the details of its artistic practice."[12] Benjamin's analysis of the *Trauerspiel*, then, outlines the possibility of a formidable paradigm to interpret art in times of decay in general.

The hypothesis that we will attempt to verify here is not just that the triptych of *Salò*, *Todo Modo*, and *La Grande Bouffe* "reflects certain aspects of the spiritual constitution of the baroque." The argument is, in a stronger sense, that the complexity of their figural dimension cannot be fully accounted for if not examined in the light cast by Benjamin's analysis of the *Trauerspiel*. Indeed, do we not recognize the situation of Italy in the years of terrorism in Benjamin's description of the becoming-rule of the exception? Agamben makes an unequivocal case for this interpretation. He traces the history of the prominence gained by the executive over the legislative in Italy after the unification of the country through fascism, a process that culminates in the law decrees (*decreti-legge*) designed to repress terrorism in the long '68. These were issued by the government autonomously from the parliament and thus de facto plunged the country into a permanent state of exception.[13]

However, a crisis of sovereignty is never simply a legalistic matter. It certainly wasn't in the baroque described by Benjamin, where the becoming-rule of the state of exception is but the symptom of a larger crisis of the symbolic order caused by the collapse of the master signifiers that hitherto organized the collective life of monarchic states, the most significant of which is the divine nature of the sovereign, now fully secularized. We can detect a similar decline in symbolic efficiency during the long '68, which also stems from a historical crisis at the heart of the law. The libertarian and antiauthoritarian impulses of the long '68, as we have seen in chapter 4, strove to do away with prohibition to enjoy without constraints, with the figure of the youth providing a mapping of the revolutionary overtures and dead ends that defined this quest. Likewise, the figure of the specter in chapter 6 introduced the idea of a division immanent to the law, split between the belief in a transcendental guarantee of state sovereignty and the games of political conspiracy.

As early as 1968, Jacques Lacan observes a symbolic collapse occurring in contemporary society, whose origin he identifies in the "evaporation of the father" (*évaporation du père*).[14] This evaporation—suggesting a process of progressive dematerialization—causes a weakening in the Oedipal prohibition inherent in the Name of the Father (in French, *le Nom-du-Père* is also a pun for "No of the Father"), which, Lacan claims, leaves a "scar" in our society that "we could classify ... under the heading and general notion of segregation."[15] The term Lacan uses is highly specific. Etymologically, "to segregate" means "to separate from the flock," and it defines an act whose immediate effect is the isolation of a group of individuals from the rest. "What characterizes our century," Lacan continues, "is a complex, reinforced, and constantly overlapping form of segregation that only manages to generate more and more barriers."[16] *Salò, Todo Modo,* and *La Grande Bouffe* offer one way to understand Lacan's sibylline remark, in that the triptych literalizes precisely such a situation of proliferating segregation, in which the lords' estate, the Jesuit hotel, and the friends' villa represent the "barriers" that separate the characters from the rest of the world. The evaporation of the father as a crisis of sovereignty, then, has two intertwined effects: it generalizes and makes permanent the state of exception, and it establishes a regime of widespread segregation in which a multitude of local states of exception can be born.

Already in the *Trauerspiel,* this evaporation presents itself as the correlate of a void. The immanentized sovereign, banished from his transcendental seat of power, returns as an absence; the exclusion of transcendence in the baroque only makes the sovereign appear on the side of immanence as a "cataract."[17] Paradoxically, the sovereign acquires an even mightier aura in this emptied-out form, as Weber notes: "Far from doing away with transcendence ... such emptying [of transcendence] only endows [the sovereign] with a force that is all the more powerful: that of the vacuum, of the absolute and unbounded other, which, since it is no longer representable, is also no longer localizable 'out there' or as a 'beyond.'"[18] What Weber describes here is, in Lacanian terms, a confrontation with the insubstantiality of the big Other. In chapter 6, we saw how the figure of the specter in Italian conspiracy thrillers lays bare the lack of a transcendental legitimation to the series of semblants of sovereignty that are involved in endless interlocking conspiracies: the executive, the judiciary, law enforcement, capital, and so on. If the specter revealed the brittleness of the Other floating untethered from any transcendental guarantee, the tyrant, the intriguer, and the martyr enumerate the consequences of this revelation.

Père-version: The Sadistic Tyrant in *Salò, or The 120 Days of Sodom*

A tyrant is, in essence, a despotic ruler whose range of action and decision is unrestrained by any law or constitution. In fact, he comes into existence by establishing a new law in the form of the state of exception. This moment is captured in the opening of *Salò*, in which the lords sign an agreement with each other: for 120 days, they will engage in all sorts of debauchery and violent excesses. As the covenant is sealed by a shared vow to marry each other's daughters, the four notables find themselves united in a single monstrous figure, a four-headed tyrant.

Commenting on the nature of regulation in the autarchic worlds of Sade, Barthes pithily quips: "Law, no. Protocol, yes."[19] The distinction is subtle but significant. As a mere code of conduct, however inflexible, the protocol agreed on by the four libertines is but a pale copy of the sovereignty they embodied with their titles under the fascist regime: the Duke (aristocratic power), the President (sometimes identified as the President of the Central Bank, thus indicating economic power), the Bishop (religious power), and the Magistrate (judicial power). Reduced by Pasolini to mere types, these characters renounce their symbolic position in the outside world in favor of a new form of whimsical yet highly regulated sovereignty—a Sadean contradiction Barthes did not overlook: "The most libertarian of writers wants Ceremony, Party, Rite, Discourse."[20] As an emptied-out version of sovereignty, this protocol has the traits of a compensatory fantasy. While the lords' world— the world in which they could be lords—crumbles outside the villa's walls, they engage in a theatrical exercise of what we might call a surplus sovereignty whose figure is that of the tyrant. In Benjamin, the rise of the tyrant presents itself as the obverse of the crisis of the sovereign; the surplus of authoritarianism embodied by the tyrant is a symptom of the void left by the loss of the sovereign's transcendental dimension. In *Salò*, this surplus serves a specific function. Faced with the irreversible crisis of sovereignty, the four-headed tyrant relies on an exaggerated despotism to cover up and disavow the crisis itself. The four lords' peculiar way of staving off decay is thus pretending that the crisis never existed in the first place.

It may come as little surprise for a film inspired by Sade's work that the tyrant in *Salò*, in his obstinate attempt to ignore the crisis of the symbolic order, displays a distinctly perverse inclination. As we know from Lacan, perversions are defined at their core by a disavowal of the lack in the Other. This is the remedy that perversions offer in the moment of crisis of sovereignty: behave as if the lack in the Other did not exist. This is why perversion for Lacan is also a "*père*-version"—that is, a version of the father; to counter the "evaporation" of the paternal metaphor, the pervert conjures up the all-powerful authority of an Other without lack.[21] The sadist, specifically, annuls this lack by asserting his knowledge of what the Other wants: it wants to be tortured, and the sadist is only too happy to oblige. But—and here is the remarkable twist of sadism—the sadist's victims are not the Other. A split, in fact, occurs. The victims are reduced to others—that is, dispensable objects in the hands of the sadistic torturers—while the Other as law is elevated to a transcendental guarantee of the torturer's acts. For the four libertines in *Salò*, the Other has never been more whole or coherent. The bureaucratic protocol of rape, torture, and murder admits no deviations, and the tyrant, for all his autocratic posture, is but the Other's instrument—and a rejoicing one at that. This is the perverted structure behind the lords' absolute control over their victims in the film: under the aegis of a law degraded to a protocol that demands total submission from the torturers as much as the tortured, the otherness of the latter—the obscurity of their desire—is obliterated, their lack manipulated against them.

However, in the film, this schema of perversion has another side, one that has often gone unnoticed. One must agree with French film critic Serge Daney, who writes that *Salò* has less to do with a "triumphant fascism" than with the fundamental disconnect between two heterogeneous dimensions.[22] One, which we have outlined above, speaks to the sadist's enjoyment in his knowledge and control of the victim's desire. The other has to do with another form of enjoyment: that of the teenagers themselves, who, as opposed to the lords, know nothing of their own desire and simply enact it in the interstices of the film. Consider the lesbian lovers (Antiniska Nemour and Olga Andrei), or the collaborationist Ezio (Ezio Manni), who has sex with the Black servant (Ines Pellegrini). In both cases, while the sadistic rule over life in the estate is supposed to be absolute, we witness the formation of pockets of antagonism within and against the protocol. The desire embodied by Ezio and the lesbian lovers marks a dimension of enjoyment that the lords do not have access to, something they can neither know nor control. Indeed, one of the most revealing moments of the film occurs when the lords, guns in hand and ready to kill Ezio for his transgression, experience palpable hesitation when confronted with his fist raised in the communist salute (Figure 22).

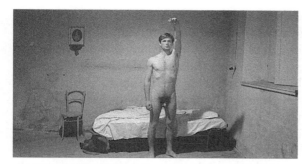

Figure 22. The lords punish Ezio for his transgression in *Salò, or The 120 Days of Sodom* (1975).

The surplus sovereignty of the tyrant suddenly reveals its ineffectuality in the form of an inability to decide. To be sure, it is only a fleeting moment of paralysis, but it stands out as a unique occurrence in the film. However transitory, this indecisiveness of the tyrant (which, as we have seen, Benjamin identifies as one of the features of the *Trauerspiel*) opens up a fissure in the facade of the pervert's Other. The separation, foundational for the sadist, between the victims as others and the law as big Other is no longer tenable. The inscrutable Other is now embodied by one of the teenagers, who confronts the lords with an enjoyment they will never know or manipulate. In psychoanalytical terms, this breakdown of tyrannical sovereignty reminds the tyrant of his own lack as a lack in the Other—a lack their perversion was designed to disavow at all costs, and that now resurfaces carrying a surplus of anxiety. The lords' ultimate reaction is telling. In contrast to the controlled demeanor they otherwise display throughout the film, the rather un-sadist-like fury with which they unload their guns on Ezio is symptomatic of a certain anxious disorientation.

This asymmetry splits the film in two along the axis of enjoyment. On one side is a totalitarian fantasy of sovereign power that encounters its own failure; on the other is the episodic emergence of fragments of antagonistic enjoyment that threaten to undo the protocol presiding over the estate. The repetitive enjoyment of knowledge associated with the lords (who believe they know what the Other wants) is juxtaposed to the transgressive enjoyment of ignorance embodied by the teenagers. It is certainly tempting to read the teenagers' blithe pursuit of pleasure as a properly political stance against the law, and Ezio's raised fist appears to attest to that. But what are we to make, for example, of the final vignette, in which two collaborationists converse amiably about a girl and dance to the tune of a waltz while victims are being tortured and mutilated in the nearby garden? Isn't their obliviousness to the horror that surrounds them yet another form of the enjoyment of ignorance that we have just described? And yet we would hardly count it as an active resistance against the powers that be—quite the contrary.

One possible key to understanding the status and function of this mysterious enjoyment is provided by the Lacanian concept of the *sinthome*, discussed in chapter 5 in relation to *Teorema*. However sparse and episodic, the youths' private affirmations of their individual enjoyment in *Salò* would seem to make them precisely into *synth-hommes*. Ezio and the Black servant, the lesbian lovers, and the collaborationists chatting and dancing in the last scene all enjoy in such a way as to create for themselves a minimum of subjective consistency, which in turn allows them to survive in the aftermath of the evaporation of the father—a chance not afforded to the pianist, for instance, who takes her own life in a *passage à l'acte* after witnessing the horrors taking place in the garden at the end of the film. From the standpoint of the lords, this sinthomatic enjoyment remains forever obscure, either figuratively (because they cannot interpret it, like Ezio) or literally (because they do not see it, like the dancing collaborationists).

But the youths know nothing of their own enjoyment either. Lacan explains that there is a certain aspect of ignorance tied to the sinthome; even James Joyce himself (whom Lacan cites as an example of a sinthome created through literary writing) "didn't know that he was fashioning the sinthome. . . . He was oblivious to it and it is by dint of this fact that he is a pure artificer, a man of *savoir-faire*."[23] This "*savoir-faire*" "is art, artifice, that which endues a remarkable quality to the art of which one is capable, because there is no Other of the Other to perform the Last Judgement."[24] Beyond Joyce, these lines seem to offer a fitting description of *Salò* as much as Benjamin's analysis of the *Trauerspiel*. If, as Benjamin suggests, all times of crisis and their art resemble each other, they do so, Lacan adds, as historical moments of revelation that there is no Other of the Other. *Salò* offers two intertwined yet irreconcilable answers to this situation of crisis: the *père* version of the sadistic tyrant, who disavows the crisis altogether, and the self-fashioned artifice of the sinthome as a singular, unanalyzable path to the survival of the subject in a time of the crisis of the symbolic.

Seeking the Divine Will: The Intriguer in *Todo Modo*

In *Todo Modo*, the crisis of sovereignty generates a different figure, which we can identify with Benjamin's intriguer or plotter (*das Intrigant*). What sets the intriguer apart from the tyrant and the martyr in the *Trauerspiel* is his readiness to come to terms with a new situation marked by the collapse of the universal principles that had hitherto governed society, with the consequent elevation of the state of exception to a rule. While the tyrant dissimulates the crisis of sovereignty by way of a surplus of authoritarianism, the intriguer recognizes it and acts accordingly by embracing the performance of power as nothing more than a game (similar in this to the Minister's plotting in *Illustrious Corpses,* discussed in chapter 6). The intriguer understands better than anyone that the workings of power possess a fundamentally theatrical quality, in that roles are always assigned in advance, and any action or decision takes place within the boundaries of a set of predesigned rules: "Unlike the sovereign . . . the plotter 'knows' that the court is a theater of actions that can never be totalized but only *staged* with more or less virtuosity."[25]

This theatrical dimension is evident in *Todo Modo,* where the irreversible crisis of the hegemony of the DC in postwar Italy is ruthlessly exposed. The film weaves an extraordinarily intricate web of internal conspiracies and plots, all unfolding within a unity of space (the Jesuit convent-hotel) and time (the three-day retreat). This complex choreography of power, in which alliances are unceasingly forged and broken and party notables meet their untimely demise, indicates what we may call a surplus of theatricality. The frenzied performance of political intrigue reveals what it is supposed to disavow: the fact that the DC establishment no longer knows its historical role. This doubt at the heart of the figure of the intriguer signals the rise of a different subjective position vis-à-vis the crisis of sovereignty, namely obsessional neurosis. As opposed to the pervert, the obsessional neurotic recognizes that there is no Other of the Other. Because of this awareness, the obsessional neurotic takes it upon herself to prop up the Other in order to stave off a complete collapse of the symbolic order. The elaborate and repetitive rituals associated with obsessional neurosis are precisely aimed at mastering this lack in the Other and preventing such a catastrophe.

According to Barthes, Ignatius's spiritual exercises exhibit the exact structure of obsessional neurosis, in that they involve a repetitive accounting and enumeration of one's sins that, crucially, engenders its own errors. Because the exercitant will always account for his sins in a faulty, incomplete way, he is guilty of a new sin that must itself be added on to the original list. The list thus becomes infinite, as the very fact of accounting for one's sins is itself a source of sinful behavior: "It is the neurotic nature of obsession to set up a self-maintaining machine, a kind of homeostat of error."[26] In *Todo Modo*, the DC count its mistakes and crimes, but precisely to commit an error and thus create the need to continue with the count and avoid having to personally do anything about the mistakes. The spectacle of penance in the film is thus a defense mechanism that aims at leaving the status quo untouched. Guilt, one of the central affects of the obsessional neurotic, becomes irredeemable: one must live with it, and keep adding sins to an endless list. Petri, who was familiar with Barthes's text, paints Moro in an explicit comparison with Ignatius, ascribing to both a certain pursuit of a "movement that could develop into immobility":

> For many years Moro carried his power like a cross on his shoulders, and the torment of this sort of exhausting spiritual exercise was clear in his emaciated face, in his somewhat lost behavior, in the bitter grimace of his mouth, in his sickly gaze. He took onto himself the impossible endeavor of mediating between the utopian and opportunistic souls of his party, between his party and the Left, between the poor and the rich, between the exploited and the exploiters.... Moro too, like Loyola and Sade, conceived of the unconceivable: a change that did not change anything, a movement that could develop into immobility, a whole that seemed empty, a Left that would go Right, and a Right that would go Left.... In the meantime, the cultural and social fabric of the country... was falling apart, rotting, and dying, and it is still dying.[27]

In the film, Volonté's caricature of Moro carries the power of mediation and reconciliation not only as a cross, but also as an endless source of sin for which atonement is required, as don Gaetano repeatedly preaches. To fully grasp the nature of Moro's balancing act in *Todo Modo*, one must consider the formal logic of the Jesuit spiritual exercises. We can describe Ignatius's central preoccupation as follows: to conform one's own behavior to God's will. But how does one identify divine will? The title of the film evokes the famous Ignatian motto, "Todo modo para buscar la voluntad divina" (One must use every means to seek the divine will); the spiritual exercises are to be understood precisely as one such means. This is why the exercises possess an "interrogative structure":[28] they ritualize the act of asking a question addressed to God. The question, however, is not open-ended ("What should I do?"); rather, it assumes the form of a binary choice: "To do this or to do that?"[29]

This is what Ignatius calls the moment of election—which counterintuitively requires an effort on the part of the exercitant *not* to choose. Barthes explains this conceptual layer of the Jesuit discourse most lucidly:

> The exercitant must strive not to choose; the aim of his discourse is to bring the two terms of the alternative to a homogeneous state so pure that he cannot humanly extricate himself from it; the more equal the dilemma the more rigorous its closure, and the clearer the divine numen, or: the more certain it will be that the mark is of divine origin; the more completely will the paradigm be balanced, and the more tangible will be the imbalance God will impart to it.[30]

The highest achievement of the exercitant, then, is creating a balance between the two terms of the binary choice that is so perfect as to preclude the very possibility of any decision, thus throwing divine intervention into relief as the overriding principle capable of breaking the stalemate. This rigorous pursuit of the inability to decide—the Ignatian principle of indifference—has obvious echoes in the crisis of sovereignty we identified in the *Trauerspiel* as the monarch's defining indecisiveness regarding the state of exception. In the case of the figure of the intriguer in *Todo Modo*, however, this inability to decide is not considered a hindrance to the exercise of state power; rather, it is elevated to its ultimate goal. The President engages in a rigorous accounting of his sins so that he would not have to stop atoning for them. He does the same in relation to his political positions, seeking an impossible reconciliation of opposites in order not to have to take a side. Consider for instance the programmatic monologue he delivers at dinner:

> I feel the time has come to think back on the thirty years during which we've led the country. Thirty years during which we've carried out a difficult, painful, maybe agonizing conciliation.... I mean reconciliation between past, future, and present. Between religious faith and political practice. Reconciliation between public and private enterprises, stasis and development, North and South, Left and Right, the rich and the poor, wages and prices... between us and them. Now nobody wants to recognize the need for any reconciliation with our own role. They ask for clarity. What should we do, then? We can no longer dilly-dally. New orientations are necessary.[31]

The President casts the historical role played by the DC in the postwar period as one of mediation and compromise at the political, social, and economic level. "Between us and them," in particular, seems to refer to the Historic Compromise (Compromesso Storico), a decade-long alliance established in 1973 by the Moro-led current in the DC and the PCI that aimed to fend off the risk of an authoritarian turn in the country. But the President's sibylline expression could also be read in the context of foreign policy: not the DC and the PCI, but Italy and the United States, with the former's unwavering Atlanticism as the guarantee of American influence on one of the strategic outposts in the Cold War. This project of national and international reconciliation, however, reaches a point of exhaustion in the second half of the 1970s, primarily as a result of shifts in global geopolitics and the historical trajectory of capital from postwar expansion to a phase of stagnation and recession. "Clarity" is needed in this situation of crisis, and "new orientations are necessary"—hence, in *Todo Modo,* a renewed interrogation of divine will.

As the President also suggests, what the DC establishment is looking for in the Jesuit retreat is a confirmation of their party's historical role in the developmental trajectory of capitalism ("Now nobody wants to recognize the need for any reconciliation with our own role"). History is the God that must be interrogated as to what it wants. However, if in the past the obsessional neurotic principle of Ignatian indifference would reassure the DC of their historical function as mediator of conflicts and overseer of postwar reconstruction and the subsequent period of economic growth, now it only puts into relief the absence of any providential design. In the opening of the film, an intertitle informs us that spiritual exercises have been used as an educational tool for the economic and political establishment since the sixteenth century, providing the religious guarantee of a link between divine will and the mundane exercise of power. *Todo Modo* shows what happens when this link is severed. The silence of divine (historical) will reduces sovereignty to an endless practice of scheming and plotting, aimed solely at retaining power in the absence of any transcendental legitimation. This is where the Jesuit ethics of obsessional neurosis meets the Benjaminian figure of the intriguer. With the moment of Ignatian election incapable of yielding any indication of what God wants, the intriguer alone can attempt to stave off catastrophe by way of what we might call a conspiratorial management of decline.

Decline, however, remains inevitable. "It's nothing more than a long downfall" for the party, don Gaetano admits, then adds, "We are the dead burying the dead." This evocative formulation has a long history that links the Gospel of Matthew ("Jesus said to him, 'Follow me, and leave the dead to bury their own dead'" [8:22]) to Marx, who was fond of the expression and used it repeatedly.[32] In Matthew, this is an exhortation to break with the past addressed to a disciple beholden to his duty to bury his dead father. In Marx, the appeal similarly indicates the need to loosen the grip that the dead have over the living, so that the new of the revolution can be born. In *Todo Modo*, however, the famous phrase assumes a more diagnostic tinge. Don Gaetano compares the DC establishment, the representative of the state (district attorney Scalambri [Renato Salvatori]), and himself to the "dead burying the dead," all but acknowledging their shared obsolescence. The string of mysterious assassinations that punctuate the film—the dead to be buried—is then to be understood not as an intraparty feud or a targeted intimidation, but rather as the ratification of a general state of affairs that marks as already dead the living representatives of political, economic, and religious power.

In this sense, if there is a manifestation of divine will in the film, it is to be found in the cryptic message sent by the assassinations themselves. As the President explains to Scalambri, the acronyms of the public companies chaired by the victims come together to form a sentence: "Todo modo para buscar la voluntad divina." The Ignatian dictum is uttered again moments later, when don Gaetano asks the President, mystified as to what this divine will could be, if he would be ready to renounce power. This is what history asks of the President and the DC establishment: accepting obsolescence and exiting the political stage. One is here reminded again of Pasolini's scathing critique of the DC elite as "death masks" in his 1975 article "The Void of Power in Italy," discussed in chapter 6. In *Todo Modo,* just as in Pasolini's description, the DC is presented as suffering from an utterly deluded grasp of its own historical role and unable to come to terms with its own decrepit conditions.

The film's ending seals the fate of this political class. The camera follows the President wandering a hotel estate littered with the corpses of his fellow party members and heaps of incriminating documents from don Gaetano's archive, just before he is himself shot to death. If revolutions, as Marx says, must "let the dead bury the dead" in order to come into their own, what is alluded to in *Todo Modo* is nothing other than the revolution of capital in the 1970s, with the prominence gained by processes of deindustrialization, overproduction, and falling rate of profits in the manufacturing sector, and the consequent migration of capital to the financial sector. In Italy as elsewhere, to accomplish this revolution, it was necessary to let the death masks of power bury their dead, and continue to seek the divine will of capitalism by other means.

Ad Nauseam: Martyrs of the Unconscious in *La Grande Bouffe*

To recapitulate: with *Salò* and *Todo Modo,* we see the articulation of two distinct figures—the tyrant and the intriguer, respectively—grounded in a crisis of sovereignty. The tyrant coincides with the position of the pervert, who disavows the lack in the Other and construes law as omnipotent, while the intriguer corresponds to the obsessional neurotic, who recognizes the lack in the Other and assumes onto himself the burden of propping up a symbolic order on the verge of collapse. With *La Grande Bouffe,* a new figure comes onto the stage: the martyr. There is, according to Benjamin, a specularity between the tyrant and the martyr: "In the baroque the tyrant and the martyr are but the two faces of the monarch. They are the necessarily extreme incarnation of the princely essence."[33] The martyr's extremism is the obverse of the tyrant's; whereas the latter exercises his despotic rule in the absence of any transcendental guarantee of his sovereignty, the former shows the inherent self-destructiveness of such efforts.

As a subset of the *Trauerspiel,* martyr dramas revolve around an insane act of self-annihilation that is specifically thematized as bodily torment, for in baroque drama, "the only response to the call of history is the physical pain of martyrdom."[34] "Martyr" is then returned to its etymological meaning of "witness": a form of suffering that bears the mark of, and thus implicitly announces, a truth. (In the case of baroque drama, this truth is the historical crisis of sovereignty.) The two intertwined aspects of self-destructive madness and physical pain as responses to the "call of history" are absolutely central to Ferreri's film, as the only reaction to this call that the four friends can muster is self-imposed agony. But what is the truth that they bear witness to? If in *Salò* we saw a bourgeoisie intent on supplementing the crisis of its own sovereignty with a surplus of authoritarianism, and in *Todo Modo* we saw the downfall of the political establishment designated to defend the bourgeoisie's interests, then in *La Grande Bouffe* we see the annihilation of the order established by the bourgeoisie in the wake of World War II.

In Ferreri, the four martyrs in *La Grande Bouffe* literalize their own historical condition of obsolescence by way of a psychotic *passage à l'acte*. It is useful to revisit here one of the ways in which Lacan defines the difference between neurosis and psychosis in his late teaching: "The difference between believing *in* the symptom and believing *it* is obvious. It is the difference between neurosis and psychosis. In psychosis, not only does the subject believe in the voices, but he believes them. Everything rests on that borderline."[35] The neurotic believes *in* the symptom in the sense that he acknowledges the existence of the symptom as the sign of a lack in the Other. The psychotic is defined by a further dimension of this belief. He believes the symptom *itself* in the sense that he takes it not as the signifier of a lack, but as the real directly interpellating him. If the Other for the neurotic remains silent and inaccessible, for the psychotic, it never stops speaking; the Other and the psychotic are in a relationship that knows no lack but only imaginary plenitude.

It is in this sense that psychosis can be read as the most radical consequence of the "evaporation of the father" we previously discussed as the psychohistorical situation that the triptych tries to grapple with. As we have seen, the "separation" that Lacan associates with this "evaporation" takes in the triptych the form of seclusion. In *La Grande Bouffe,* this seclusion coincides with a foreclosure—a foreclosure of the Name of the Father as the principle of prohibition that mediates and makes possible the subject's entrance into the symbolic. The four friends set up a situation in which they can experience enjoyment without prohibition. Yet at the same time the film is also marked by a sense of paralysis, as though the negation of the limit paradoxically ends up conjuring the most inescapable of constrictions. This condition is emblematized in the scene in which Marcello launches a Bugatti race car at full speed toward the closed gate with Andrea, the schoolteacher, sitting at his side, as if ready to go for a joyride—only to then stop, back up into the driveway, and do it again. It is what Lacan calls *plus-de-jouir:* in the circuital repetition of the drive, surplus enjoyment coincides with no more enjoyment.

One is here reminded of Lacan's formulation in book 3 of the *Seminar:* "The psychotic is a martyr of the unconscious."[36] Referencing the etymology of the word "martyr," Lacan claims that the psychotic provides an "open testimony" about the existence of the unconscious, whereas the neurotic can only give "a closed testimony that needs to be deciphered."[37] The latter may be able, through analysis, to name the meaning of her testimony; this possibility, however, is precluded to the former: "The psychotic . . . seems arrested, immobilized in a position that leaves him incapable of authentically restoring the sense of what he witnesses and sharing it in the discourse of others."[38] We can discern this deadlock in Marcello's jubilant howling when he succeeds in repairing the Bugatti, in Michel's cries of sorrow when Marcello is found dead, and in Ugo's uncontrollable laughter after a sewage explosion—all nonlinguistic attempts to communicate the psychotic martyrs' experience of the unconscious, tinged with the ambiguous nuances of enjoyment.

Ferreri underlines this ambiguity throughout the film, but it is nowhere more evident than in one of the scenes set in the garden. The scene is composed of two shots. The first is a long shot of the group of friends sitting around a roasting pit, which depicts one of the prostitutes, Gita (Solange Blondeau), bidding Marcello goodbye after complaining that she threw up all night. The second is a medium shot of Ugo standing next to the pit and exhorting his companions to have fun (*"Allegria! Allegria!"*). But his appeal falls flat, and his forced smile is immediately followed by a forlorn stare at the roasting meat (Figure 23).

The contrast in the scene is apparent, as Ferreri juxtaposes the self-preserving dictate of the pleasure principle embodied by Gita to Ugo's extreme and self-destructive drive toward a *plus-de-jouir*. Gita acknowledges that she has reached the outer limit of her enjoyment and leaves in observance of her own instinct of self-preservation, while Ugo's plea and subsequent hesitation signal

Figure 23. Ugo stares at roasting meat in the villa's garden in *La Grande Bouffe* (1973).

the excessive and ultimately deadly nature of the four friends' pursuit of enjoyment.

The four friends are shown as hardly taking any pleasure in the gourmandizing and the fucking, as they chew and swallow their food in as mechanical a manner as they have sex. This kind of automatism of consumption implies that the motivation of this behavior does not originate in any given human need but rather in a self-internalized imperative to enjoy. Ugo's *"Allegria! Allegria!"* and Marcello's reminder to keep eating at all costs when Michel falls ill (*"Il faut manger . . . Il faut manger!"*) are the voice of this imperative in the film—an imperative that disregards any measure of the good and the useful, and that transcends the human limitations of the protagonists' bodies. When Marcello's and Michel's bodies finally give up, they are transferred to the kitchen. Stored in the refrigerating room–turned-morgue, the two corpses keep participating in the feast, visible at all times in the depth of field and staring at their remaining companions. Giving in to the drive and following its trajectory to the ultimate point of self-annihilation means realizing that the drive is the undead, a force of negativity that persists, uncannily, even after death.

The death drive tearing through the bodies of the four protagonists reveals the psychotic freedom of martyrdom as an optical illusion. In a brilliant investigation of the "discourse of freedom" in Pasolini and Lacan, Lorenzo Chiesa argues that the martyr's pursuit of an absolute freedom from castration and the Name of the Father results in the impossibility of actually achieving any liberation: "The martyrs of the unconscious sacrifice the emancipative possibility of acquiring meaning against the background of a more general meaninglessness of human life (that is, in short, a life that language deprives of freedom) in the name of being absolutely free. In doing so, they miscalculate that the mirage of such a freedom is a lure of the Imaginary."[39] The defining paradox here is that of a call for total freedom that comes to coincide with its opposite—that is, an absolute imperative—as exemplified by Marcello screaming "I have to do it!" when he cannot manage to have sex with Andrea.

The psychotic foreclosure of the Name of the Father in *La Grande Bouffe* sets up an even more tyrannical principle of authority grounded not in prohibition but in the imperative to enjoy without restraint. It is hardly surprising that the first martyrs of this new configuration would be the representatives of the bourgeoisie that instated the old order in the aftermath of the Second World War. In a curious short-circuit of representation, the actors in *La Grande Bouffe* play themselves while at the same time evoking obvious bourgeois types: Ugo is the self-made man, who left his small Italian hometown after the war to become a business owner in Paris; Michel represents mass media, which played a crucial part in building the social and political identity of European countries after the war, while also providing ideological legitimation for the rule of the bourgeoisie; the globe-trotting Marcello is the icon of a budding cosmopolitanism in an expanding world market; and the magistrate Philippe conjures the institutions of the bourgeois state. The historical sequence of 1968 took aim at all these, providing forceful critiques of the myth of hard work and meritocracy, the role of media in manufacturing consent, the beginning of globalization, and the state's collusion with capital. Sensing the impending undoing of their social roles, the four friends try to be contemporary to their own time, and they do so by shedding their types in the secluded environment of the villa (as time goes on, the characters start wearing each other's clothes) and fully submitting to the new psychotic arrangement of jouissance.

But the historical gap haunts them at every turn. This gap is already suggested in one of the opening scenes, when Michel meets his daughter (played by Piccoli's real-life daughter, Cordelia) at the TV studio to say good-bye and give her the keys to his apartment—a gesture of withdrawal accompanied by a send-up to paternal authority ("Autorité paternelle de merde!"), which, when uttered by Michel, rings hollow, like the ridiculous affectation of a man out of step with the times. Even the chosen setting of the film signifies the obsolescence of the four bourgeois men. The house, owned by Philippe's family and thus part of the old bourgeoisie's heirloom, is itself a museum-like space saturated with old furniture, paintings, and elaborately staged stuffed animals, along with the vintage race car from the 1920s sitting in the garage and the linden tree under which seventeenth-century poet Boileau used to rest and look for inspiration. Even when the characters play with unequivocal signifiers of contemporary culture, they are still haunted by their own anachronism. It seems indicative that Ugo, of all film icons, would offer an impression of don Vito Corleone in *The Godfather* (Francis Ford Coppola, 1972), with Brando's character being the ultimate emblem of the nostalgic longing for a vanishing world.

Lacan's formulation that psychotics are "martyrs of the unconscious" thus receives in Ferreri a more precise historical acceptation. The four friends are "martyrs of the unconscious" in the sense that they give an "open testimony" about a new social arrangement of enjoyment by succumbing to it. Their suffering and death elucidate the logic of this new form of tyrannical sovereignty of the freedom to enjoy while at the same time sealing the end of the old bourgeoisie's rule over postwar society. The character of Andrea, in this sense, offers the perfect contrast to the protagonists' martyrdom. She is the only one in the villa who seems to genuinely enjoy the food and sex. Her appetite for both is voracious, far outpacing that of her four companions. While the protagonists die one by one, she continues to eat, cook, and have sex with them. As an almost otherworldly entity that knows no fatigue nor satiety, she embodies the drive itself, but in an idealized form. With Andrea, the link between surplus enjoyment and the drive is refigured to elide the principle that every drive is a death drive. By embodying the possibility of an enjoyment without limits, she is the ideal subject of the discourse of freedom in the long '68—the discourse whose toll the four bourgeois men cannot withstand. Andrea is identified by specific attributes: she is young (Ferréol was twenty-six at the time of release) and middle class (schoolteacher being one of the prototypical petty bourgeois professions), thus suggesting the rise of a new social type from the ashes of the old bourgeoisie. In this sense, she is no martyr. Her *plus-de-jouir* is an inexhaustible surplus that seems to never turn into suffering; it testifies to nothing if not the fantasy of an enjoyment without negativity, without repression, and ultimately without unconscious.

Commentators have identified in the film's emphasis on the relentlessness of consumption a critique of consumerism, and there is certainly some validity to that claim.[40] Yet consumerism has primarily to do with desire. It is the capitalist's promise to fill the constitutive lack of the subject with a series of objects, each announcing itself to be "it" yet invariably failing to fulfill that promise, and forcing the subject to move on to the next object. In the film, however, it is not simply a matter of consumption, or even overconsumption. It is also a matter of that which exceeds consumption altogether. The four friends are not seeking reprieve from their own lack in the succession of gourmet dishes; there is never a sense that they believe that the next item on the menu will finally be it, or that any kind of homeostasis between desire and satisfaction can be achieved. On the contrary, the drive ignores the human limitations of consumption and reveals its exorbitant nature, confirming that it is at the level of the drive and its relationship to surplus enjoyment—an enjoyment literally enjoyed by nobody—that the deeper significance of the film rests. The film's ending, in this sense, is telling (Figure 24). It is a long shot of the garden, festooned with carcasses, dogs running around, as large quantities of fresh meat and poultry are being delivered to the villa even after the four friends' death—an image of the uncanny persistence of the drive beyond any notion of what is useful or needed for consumption, and beyond death itself.

Figure 24. Fresh meat abandoned in the garden after the four friends' deaths in *La Grande Bouffe* (1973).

Facies Hippocraticae: From Figure to Allegory

We have seen how in the three films under consideration the crisis of bourgeois sovereignty in the long '68 is registered by three different figures, each marked by a distinct pathological relationship to this crisis. In reacting to the crisis, each figure crystallizes a specific excess: the libertines in *Salò* resort to an excess of authoritarianism; the DC establishment in *Todo Modo* mounts an exaggerated performance of political intrigue; and the martyrdom of the four friends in *La Grande Bouffe* testifies to the deadly and unavoidable presence of a surplus of enjoyment. Yet this psychopathology of the bourgeoisie after 1968 should have us question whether, in fact, the tyrant, the intriguer, and the martyr are figures at all. Throughout this book, I have relied on a definition of the figure as the embodiment of a dialectical relation between two elements: an existing structure and the antagonistic force born within it. The differences among the various figures we have encountered are due to the variations in the contents and parameters of this relation. Now, the three figures analyzed in this chapter hardly convey any sense of an antagonistic force at work—nor, for that matter, of a structural status quo to be overturned. Rather, they are reactive entities that register the collapse of the structure through pathological practices—torturing, conspiring, overeating—that hardly qualify as force because no real antagonism is discernible in them.

What are these figures without structure and without force, then? To describe the appearance of history as decay, Benjamin uses the Latin term *facies Hippocratica,* the emaciated, sunken facial features of the dying.[41] The tyrant, the intriguer, and the martyr are all versions of the Hippocratic face. They are exhausted figures, staring at the spectator with the cloudy eyes of the moribund. Benjamin further specifies that it is with the concept of allegory born in the baroque that history appears in the form of the Hippocratic face, for the allegorical alone can capture the peculiar temporality of historical transience and decay. A tension, then, comes to the surface. Are the Hippocratic faces in *Salò, Todo Modo,* and *La Grande Bouffe* still figures, or have they crossed over into the territory of allegory? More fundamentally, how can we conceive of the difference between the two?

Like figures, allegories dance; in allegory, writes Benjamin, truth is "bodied forth in the dance of represented ideas."[42] Defined by a taste for the theatrical, allegories appear on a stage, putting up performances in the register of the "as if" that make legible the dynamics of history. In the triptych, this theatricality emerges in the artificiality of the settings, the staged rituals of torture, penance, and consumption, the importance accorded to performance, and the ability—or lack thereof—to play one's assigned role. But, in contrast to the figure, allegory pursues its experiments of legibility according to a logic of representation (a "dance of represented ideas"): allegory lets the truth of an obscure historical situation shine through its own representation of it. Commenting on the *Trauerspiel* book, Fredric Jameson puts into focus this representational aspect of allegory: in a world that has become enigmatic, the signs of a fragmented reality are arranged and displayed so as to project a modicum of coherence and meaning. Allegories "are the fragments into which the baroque world shatters, strangely legible signs and emblems nagging at the too curious mind, a procession moving slowly across a stage, laden with occult significance. In this sense, for the first time it seems to me that allegory is restored to us [. . .] as a pathology with which in the modern world we are only too familiar."[43] In the baroque, as in modernity, the world of allegory is a world of signs in which the meaning of what one experiences in everyday life resides elsewhere and functions according to a logic that is far from immediately apparent. Allegory, in other words, is a fictional way of representing a world of signs whose true meaning escapes the grasp of the individual's lived experience. The constitutive inauthenticity and theatricality of allegory, then, reflects a generalized situation in which lived experience itself can no longer be considered authentic. This is why for Jameson allegory is a "pathology" that is "only too familiar" to us moderns. Insofar as the totality of contemporary capitalism does not lend itself to comprehensive depictions, allegory stands as the last aesthetic resort to register, at a minimum, this representational difficulty itself.

Salò, Todo Modo, and *La Grande Bouffe* grapple with a similar problematic of allegorical representation: how to convey the sense of an epochal shift that reshapes class relations, geopolitical scenarios, and the very structure of sovereignty after 1968? This shift can hardly be represented in all its social, economic, and political complexity, so the films resort to figures characterized by a pronounced allegorizing tendency. As "strangely legible signs," they project the semblance of a historical meaning on an otherwise enigmatic situation. "A procession moving slowly across a stage" is admittedly more than a few steps removed from a "dance of figures." The dialectical movement that characterized the figures I have discussed so far in this book does not seem to obtain with the tyrant, the intriguer, and the martyr. More than creatively exploring the possibilities and impossibilities of a given historical sequence, these figures aim to represent the truth of a historical situation. The motif of seclusion is central to this operation. It is motivated by the three figures' desire to stage a performance of sovereignty undisturbed by the rumblings of historical change, yet it is precisely by way of the secluded performance of the figures—and the pathologies that underpin it—that historical change is allegorized in the films.

But in a way, this is all these figures can do. They register their own obsolescence in a failing symbolic order, but they do so exclusively in the form of a representation of crisis. The break of subjectivation that we saw with the worker in *The Working Class Goes to Heaven* or the housewife in *A Special Day* never obtains for the tyrant, the intriguer, or the martyr. What emerges instead is the depiction of a purely structural situation in which subjectivity is reduced to the stillness of pathological positions (the pervert, the obsessional neurotic, the psychotic). To borrow a formulation from Alain Badiou, these figures show no "mastery of loss."[44] They can capture allegorically the undoing of a social class, but only as a consequence of changing structural conditions—never as the opening of a gap in the existent where a new subject can take hold. In this sense, allegory names the outer limit of the figure; it marks the point where the figure falls back into a logic of representation, however mediated and enigmatic this representation may be.

The movement registered by the triptych, then, is one of erosion of the figural into the allegorical. If figures, as the by-product of cinema's inventiveness, provide a dramatization of the subjective conditions of a given historical sequence, allegory can only register the objectivity of decay by representing history as a landscape of mysterious ruins. Among these ruins, the tyrant, the intriguer, and the martyr hesitantly perform the last steps of the dance of figures this book has attempted to choreograph.

Epilogue
The Cinema of '68, the '68 of Cinema

> It is great, or called to greatness, only that historical movement, or that political subject, capable of translating the content of that which was into the forms of that which is to come, and always, always, always, against the present.
> —Mario Tronti, *La politica al tramonto*

How does a dance of figures end? If political cinema, as I have argued, is the name of a set of films that improvise their way through the nonrelation between cinema and politics by way of figures, then there is no reason to believe this set would be somehow limited in advance. Insofar as the nonrelation is never solved once and for all but persists as a condition of every new political film, the number of singular instances of political cinema is potentially infinite.

If not an end, a periodization, then, conjured by a multiplicity of films. But the meaning of these two terms (periodization and multiplicity) and the nature of the relation that binds them (periodization through multiplicity) are far from obvious. One temptation would be to read these films as a series of fragmentary expressions of a supposed essence of the long '68. In this case, the act of periodization takes place outside of cinema per se. The multiplicity of films, juxtaposed to one another like tesserae of a mosaic, becomes one partial representation among many others of the spirit of the sequence. This is, in many ways, the trope of the so-called cinema of '68, which presupposes that the set of ideological signifiers floating in the social, cultural, and political milieu of the time were captured and thematized by its contemporary cinema. According to this trope, what films return to the spectator of yesterday and today is a reified image of the long '68 as a historical sequence defined by unity and internal coherence: clear-cut chronological boundaries, linear historical trajectories, transparent politics, a lasting but exclusively cultural influence—and, to explain it all, frameworks that are vague enough to be mistaken for exhaustive, like the ever-present Oedipal archetype, or the myth of innocence lost that connects, in one fell swoop, the good student protests of '68 to the evil excesses of '77 and then the rise of terrorism.

Narratives like these are by no means unique to the Italian context. As Kristin Ross observes in her pathbreaking account of the French May, these narratives aim to nullify the eventual character of what took place as well as the complexity of the sequence as a whole, which, she argues, can hardly be reduced to the punctiform occurrence of the student protests in the Latin Quarter in Paris, and must be understood instead within the context of French colonialism in Algeria and the country's history of worker struggles. Indeed, Ross explicitly indicates the worker and the colonial militant as two crucial "figures" for understanding the French May and its "pre-history." Ross's concept of the figure is far more general than the one presented in this book, and it embraces a spectrum that extends from "historical actors" to "objects of fictional and theoretical representation."[1] Yet the fundamental gesture of Ross's figures resonates with that of the figures traced in these pages—namely, a diagnosis of '68 as a time of crisis. The introduction of the worker and the colonial militant as figures in the historiographic landscape of the French May has the effect of unsettling the received wisdom about that historical moment as dominated by the figure of the student—a wisdom, Ross explains, peddled for decades by sociologists and student leaders who managed to shape the discourse around *le Mai* and its significance with relentless revisionism. As a result, "the official story that has been encoded, celebrated publicly in any number of mass media spectacles of commemoration, and handed down to us today, is one of family or generational drama, stripped of any violence, asperity, or overt political dimensions—a benign transformation of customs and lifestyles that necessarily accompanied France's modernization from an authoritarian bourgeois state to a new, liberal, financier bourgeoisie."[2]

This "benign transformation" is a far cry from '68 as "a time of crisis and transition," and herein lies the point: tension-figures make crisis visible; they reveal the holes and hollow spaces of history beneath the veneer of coherence and inevitability of ex post facto historical narratives. In the case of the French May, the reintroduction of the worker and the colonial militant onto the stage forces the student to end his monologue and start dancing with them. In fact, the figures singled out by Ross are not found only in the streets or in the minds of revolutionaries and reactionaries but also at the movie theater. *Tout va bien* (Groupe Dziga Vertov, 1972) and *The Battle of Algiers* (*La battaglia di Algeri*, Gillo Pontecorvo, 1966), to cite but two obvious examples, invent their own respective versions of the figure of the worker and the colonial militant, thinking in cinematic form the alliance of intellectuals, students, and workers in the anticapitalist struggle (in the case of *Tout va bien*); the return of the repressed of French colonial violence in the guise of a militarization of the police in the motherland (in *The Battle of Algiers*); and the emergence of an internationalist dimension of the struggle for liberation (in both). One wonders what other figures would be unearthed by an inquiry into French cinema similar to the one undertaken in this book. (Indeed, thinking beyond national borders, what would a figural history of political cinema look like on a global scale? How would it redraw boundaries between different national cinemas and genres? What lessons about cinema and politics would it teach us?)

But figures do not limit themselves to unsettling traditional periodizations; they establish their own. The figures of Italian political cinema think the long '68 in their own way. As experiments of legibility of a given historical moment, they redefine continuities and displace cesurae, opening up the possibility of new periodizations. In this sense, more than the cinema of '68, it would be appropriate to talk about the '68 of cinema. Whereas the former term designates a chronologically and thematically defined set of films that would express the essence of '68, the latter indicates how cinema is able to generate a unique thought of '68 as a time of crisis dramatized through figures. This '68 of cinema is different, for instance, from the '68 of political philosophy and militancy. The two engage similar problems and impasses, and there is no dearth of parallels and even echoes between them, but they give form to the historical sequence as a time of crisis in their own separate ways. This is not a concession to the rhetoric of the many '68s, which often involves a more or less surreptitious (and moralizing) hierarchization—between a violent '68 and nonviolent one, constructive and destructive, influential and forgotten. On the contrary, the emphasis should be on the structuring gap between cinema and politics, and on the different ways in which the same time of crisis has been thought and periodized by the two.

For its part, one of the ways in which politics has periodized the Italian '68 is as the slow, decade-long unfolding of a number of minor collective manifestations of antagonism and revolt interrupted every now and then by pauses and retreats, but always ready to pick up pace again: "Taken individually, many of those events and processes don't remotely rise to the level of a political myth or a narrative of epic temporality; taken together, however, they constitute the blurry articulation of a historical time of crisis and construction alike."[3] It is the trope of *il maggio strisciante* (the creeping May), designed to evoke a contrast to the perceived punctiform occurrence of the French May.[4] The creeping May is one of the names of the historical sequence of the Italian '68 as seen from the standpoint of politics; only politics can think and make legible the lulls and lunges of collective action, and verify their respective viability for a revolutionary strategy. This syncopated diachronic movement of the Italian '68 produced by politics is the correlate of a synchronic dispersion of political agency. With the fading of the hegemonic political subject of modernity—the factory worker—a number of alternative forms of political subjectivity proliferated in the interstices of this "historical time of crisis and construction." The creeping May, then, is the historical conjuncture where the "carnival of subjectivities" we evoked at the beginning of this book makes its appearance.

The '68 of cinema, instead, is not inching toward any particular destination, revolutionary or otherwise; nor does it aim to verify the consistency and resilience of any given political subjectivity across cycles of struggle. Cinema, as we have seen, experiments with figures, and these figures, taken together, engage in their own gesture of periodization. They return to us the image of a time of crisis, but seen from the perspective of cinema. The result is a dance of figures, a tentative exploration of historical possibilities, dramatized in the form of the "as if" and reimagined anew with each film. This dance extends beyond the putative chronological boundaries of the sequence, revealing holes and hollow spaces of history that remained unthought to politics.

It is precisely in this gap, this nonrelation between a carnival of subjectivities and a dance of figures, that a deeper understanding of the historical sequence of the long '68 can arise. When seen from different angles, what is returned to us is the parallax effect of '68 as a time permeated by rifts and ruptures. Indeed, if one can speak at all of an essence of '68 as a historical sequence, this essence can only be understood as crisis. One can interpret the two common revisionisms of '68 mentioned earlier precisely as attempts to mend the torn fabric of history of the sequence itself: on the one hand, the rhetoric of the many '68, which de facto renounces to think '68 as a complex sequence of interconnected events; on the other, the reliance on a univocal narrative that obliterates historical fault lines altogether. The nonrelation between cinema and politics gives us the possibility to think the two together—the unity of a sequence and the discontinuities of a time of crisis. This means that we can name that time and affirm that something did indeed take place then. Something was thought, and cinema and politics can revive the complexity of that thought for us.

At stake is the possibility of restoring the presentness of the past as eventual possibility. As Cesare Casarino puts it, referring to the Italian '68, "Some of us search for, stake a claim on, and elect as our own past that bygone moment when what we desire now was first anticipated and deferred, when what we now want as our future might have taken place but never did."[5] Choosing one's own past is an act of subjective courage. It means deciding that something took place in that past, and that what took place transformed us and the world around us. However, it also means confronting through cinema's figures the possibilities that at one point existed during a time of crisis, and that may not have been seized, or even fully perceived. The parallax view of politics and cinema returns to us the Italian '68 as such a redoubled past: a critical time of events and experiments that still cuts through our present.

Acknowledgments

If it is true, as Benjamin writes, that "the work is the death mask of its conception," then the circumstances of this conception, which are always collective, are inevitably inscribed in the work itself. These circumstances include nothing less than a global pandemic, whose hardships only put further into relief how truly exceptional the support I received while working on this book has been.

The University of Maryland has provided a supportive and invigorating intellectual environment. My research has benefited from the Graduate School Research and Scholarship Award (RASA), which allowed me to focus on writing at a crucial moment. The semester's leave offered by my institutional home, the School of Languages, Literatures, and Cultures, also played a decisive role in the completion of this book, as did the Jonathan Auerbach Cinema and Media Studies Research Award sponsored by the Program in Cinema and Media Studies. Open access for this book was made possible by a generous TOME grant (Toward an Open Monograph Ecosystem) awarded by the University of Maryland Libraries.

At Maryland, I have been fortunate to work with an extraordinary group of colleagues. This book would not exist in its current form without Luka Arsenjuk's patient and careful engagement with the text and our myriad comradely conversations. His sharpness, rigor, and generosity are unmatched, and the singular way he blends the three constitutes a source of continued inspiration for me. He is a master of that unique type of brilliant, cutting critique a writer simply cannot afford to ignore (as much as he would prefer to!). I take it as a testament to his commitment to the work itself beyond any futile narcissism of the authorial ego—and the book is immeasurably better for it. I could hardly be more grateful for his and Lindsey Muniak's friendship, which provided much-needed respite from the struggles of writing on more occasions than I can count. Hester Baer has been a mentor and a friend. Her advice on all matters has been invaluable, and I take her constant presence and support as an exemplar of what mentorship in academia should look like. I can only hope to live up to the high standard she has set. Eric Zakim witnessed the exhilarating confusion of this project in its early days and has unwaveringly supported its development ever since. Saverio Giovacchini has provided crucial historical insight; in particular, his comments on the contested legacy of neorealism in Italian political cinema have been illuminating.

My appreciation goes to all my colleagues in the School of Languages, Literatures, and Cultures, its leadership and administrative staff. In particular, I wish to thank my colleagues in the Program in Cinema and Media Studies for their engagement with my work at various points: Valerie Anischenkova, Mércedès Baillargeon, Caroline Eades, Oliver Gaycken, Jason Kuo, Valérie K. Orlando, and Elizabeth A. Papazian. My gratitude also goes to my colleagues in the Italian program: Giuseppe Falvo, who since the very beginning of my time at Maryland did everything in his power to make me feel welcome and make my job as easy as possible; Stefania Amodeo, whose witty one-liners and gentle poking ("Allora, hai finito 'sto libro?") have been one of the soundtracks of my writing; and Valeria Federici, with whom I share an interest in the art and politics of the Italian long '68. Several of the arguments presented in this book were originated or verified in class, and I am immensely thankful to the students in my undergraduate courses on the history of Italian cinema and the cinema of the long '68. They weathered my lectures on Italian radical politics and history with heroic fortitude, and offered sharp and passionate commentaries of the assigned films. Their brilliance and steadfast commitment to imagining a better world never cease to amaze me.

Parts of this book have been presented at conferences and invited talks at the Cinema Studies Institute at the University of Toronto; the John Hope Franklin Humanities Institute at Duke University; and the University of Massachusetts, Boston. My deepest gratitude goes to Brian Price and Meghan Sutherland, dear friends and true believers in the collective nature of intellectual endeavors. They supported my work with uncommon kindness and enthusiasm, and for that I am humbled. Roberto Dainotto, Cesare Casarino, Rijuta Mehta, Antoine Traisnel, and Anna Fisher offered comments and encouragement at crucial junctures of the writing process. Many thanks to Marco Natoli, one of the last true cinephiles roaming this earth. My conversations with him were instrumental in establishing the corpus of films discussed in these pages, and without his help in securing copies of the most elusive ones, this book may not have been written at all.

I thank Leah Pennywark, Jason Weidemann, and Anne Carter at the University of Minnesota Press for their help and support during an impossibly difficult time. My gratitude also goes to Eric Lundgren for guiding me through the process to obtain open access for the book, and to Karen Hellekson for her careful, eagle-eyed copyediting. The book was improved by the thoughtful comments of two anonymous readers.

Welcome interruptions to the solitary regime of writing were provided by friends old and new, near and far. I thank them all, in particular Andrea Bellavita, who kindly invited me to give a lecture at the Università dell'Insubria in Varese; Eric Doyle; and Christian Massari and Elisa Chierici, who made me feel at home as I was starting to write this book on a summer stay in Perugia. I am grateful for my comrades in the *Capital* reading group: Josh Kiner, Luka Arsenjuk, and my brother, Fabio Resmini. Fabio is one of my most perceptive readers, and his humor has been a panacea through hard times. A special *grazie* to my uncle, Sergio Gualano, who graciously made time to talk to me about his experience on the front lines of radical leftist struggle in Milan in the 1970s.

My parents, Lia e Renato Resmini, have been hearing about this book for years on end. They may think that their contribution is limited to storing in their apartment piles of newly purchased Italian books for me. Not so. Their support, both material and immaterial, extends far beyond, and I am thankful for it.

Finally, my gratitude goes to Viviana Maggioni. Without her, this book would read much differently: less lively, less lucid, and—I have no doubt—less finished. She tirelessly reminded me how crucial clarity is, against the temptation of an obscurity often mistaken for complexity. She is truly an engineer of the rarest ilk: one who values pragmatism but is also eager to improvise—and improvise she did, her support and encouragement coming in countless ways. All the *poroi* through the many impasses I encountered in writing this book are inflected by her poise and creativity. Sometimes it was the result of our wandering and musing through city streets or mountain trails. Others, it was simply about her showing me that the possibility of a way through was indeed there: one just had to invent it.

Notes

Introduction

1. Italian political cinema of the 1960s and 1970s constitutes one of the most understudied topics in the field of film studies, and recent work has by and large relinquished the ambition to engage in a comprehensive theorization of the relationship between politics and cinema. For a pioneering attempt to articulate a wide-ranging argument about the ontology of political cinema, see Ciriaco Tiso, *Cinema Poetico-Politico* (Rome: Partisan, 1971). More recently, Maurizio Grande has attempted to revive the discussion around the concept of political cinema starting from a specific set of Italian films from the 1960s and 1970s. See Maurizio Grande, *Eros e politica. Sul cinema di Bellocchio Ferreri Petri Bertolucci P. e V. Taviani* (Siena: Protagon 1995), esp. 14–44. For contemporary studies of Italian political cinema in the long '68, see Luana Ciavola, *Revolutionary Desire in Italian Cinema* (Kibworth, U.K.: Troubador Italian Studies, 2011); and Alberto Tovaglieri, *La dirompente illusione: Il cinema italiano e il Sessantotto, 1965–1980* (Soveria Mannelli, Italy: Rubbettino, 2014). For an exhaustive overview of the contemporary situation of Italian political cinema, see Giancarlo Lombardi and Christian Uva, eds., *Italian Political Cinema: Public Life, Imaginary, and Identity in Contemporary Italian Film* (Bern: Peter Lang, 2016).

2. "Today, the most politically advanced cinema is very rarely a cinema *on* politics. In fact, the films that deal with politics fill up the filmographies of mediocre and mystifying directors, dozens of Vancinis, Petris, Lizzanis, Pontecorvos, Puccinis, etc." Enzo Ungari, "Nosferatu '70: Una sinfonia del disordine," *Cinema&Film*, no. 7–8 (1969), reprinted in *Barricate di carta. "Cinema&Film," "Ombre rosse," due riviste intorno al '68*, ed. Gianni Volpi, Alfredo Rossi, and Jacopo Chessa (Milan: Mimesis 2013), 115.

3. Lorenzo Pellizzari, "Rosi, Petri, Maselli e altri: Il 'vero' e 'falso' politico," in *Storia del cinema: Italia anni settanta e le nuove cinematografie*, ed. Adelio Ferrero (Padua: Marsilio 1981), 84.

4. Claudio Bisoni, *Indagine su un cittadino al di sopra di ogni sospetto* (Turin: Lindau, 2011), 15.

5. This shared gesture has also the specific effect of normalizing Petri's

cinema as either not political enough or only tangentially political. One of the purposes of this book is precisely to dispel such a misunderstanding. There is hardly anything average about Petri's filmmaking, and the central position his films occupy in most of the following chapters will, I hope, attest to that.

6. This perspective resonates with Alain Badiou's interrogation of the paradoxes of cinema as a "mass art"—that is, as both art and nonart, aristocratic and democratic, cinema presents itself as inherently impure. See Alain Badiou, "On Cinema as a Democratic Emblem," in *Cinema*, trans. Susan Spitzer (Malden, Mass.: Polity, 2013), 233–41.

7. The perceived complicity of *cinema politico* with the status quo was summed up under the disparaging label of "Rosi-Petrism" (*rosipetrismo*), with "generalized Petri-clasty" (*Petriclastia generalizzata*) as its attendant and opposite reflex. The terms appear, respectively, in Michele Guerra, "Impegni improrogabili: Le forme 'politiche' del cinema italiano anni settanta," in *Anni '70: L'arte dell'impegno. I nuovi orizzonti culturali, ideologici e sociali dell'arte italiana*, ed. Cristina Casero and Elena di Raddo (Milan: Silvana Editoriale, 2009), 181; and Callisto Cosulich, "Tavola rotonda. Cinema politico, film politologico?," *Vita e Pensiero*, no. 3–4 (1973): 22, qtd. in Guerra, "Impegni improrogabili," 181. For a scathing critique of *rosipetrismo*, see the work of Goffredo Fofi, esp. *Il cinema italiano: Servi e padroni* (Milan: Feltrinelli, 1971).

8. Goffredo Fofi, *Capire con il cinema: 200 film prima e dopo il '68* (Milan: Feltrinelli, 1977), 264, qtd. and transl. in Evan Calder Williams, "The Fog of Class War: Elio Petri's *The Working Class Goes to Heaven* Four Decades On," *Film Quarterly* 66, no. 4 (2013): 50–59, 56.

9. Jacques Derrida, "Finis," in *Aporias*, trans. Thomas Dutoit (Stanford, Calif.: Stanford University Press, 1993), 20.

10. George Didi-Huberman, *Fra Angelico: Dissemblance and Figuration*, trans. Jane Marie Todd (Chicago: University of Chicago Press, 1995), 89.

11. Nicole Brenez, *De la figure en général et du corps en particulier. L'invention figurative au cinéma* (Brussels: De Boeck, 1998), 13.

12. Badiou cites Brecht's play *Life of Galileo* (performed 1943) and Orson Welles's film *Mr. Arkadin* (1955) as examples of this logic. In both instances, the regime of character creation is superseded by "a sort of fragmentation and constant delocalization" that gives rise to "something else": a figure. Alain Badiou, "Thinking the Emergence of the Event," interview with Emmanuel Burdeau and François Ramone, in Badiou, *Cinema*, 105–28, 128.

13. See Erich Auerbach, "Figura," in *Scenes from the Drama of European Literature* (New York: Meridian, 1959), 9–76, 23. For a critical assessment of the role of the figure in Benjamin's thought, see Carlo Salzani, *Constellations of Reading: Walter Benjamin in Figures of Actuality* (Bern: Peter Lang, 2008).

1. "A Dance of Figures"

1. Derrida, "Finis," 15.
2. This is the position eloquently argued by Badiou, who sees art (including cinema, with its own singular status as the "plus-one" of the arts) and politics as separate and independent truth procedures that, along with science and love, operate according to their own set of practical and conceptual schemata. One could go as far as claiming that for Badiou political cinema per se does not exist. There is politics, and there is cinema. No hierarchy is posited between them, nor is excluded the possibility of intersections, but they remain autonomous with respect to each other. On politics, see Alain Badiou, "Politics as Truth Procedure," in *Metapolitics,* trans. Jason Barker (New York: Verso, 2012), 141–52. On art, see Alain Badiou, *Handbook of Inaesthetics,* trans. Alberto Toscano (Stanford, Calif.: Stanford University Press, 2004). Among the most influential theorizations that reject this reciprocal autonomy, Jacques Rancière's conceptualization of the correspondence between aesthetics and politics stands out. For Rancière, both domains are concerned with the "distribution of the sensible" of a given historical moment—that is, the perceived organization of social hierarchies among different groups and the forms of inclusion and exclusion that enforce it. In the case of the "aesthetic regime of arts" that began at the end of the eighteenth century and still defines the distribution of the sensible of our present moment, we witness the overthrow of hitherto enforced artistic conventions and hierarchies in the name of a radical egalitarianism of all art forms. Rancière considers this egalitarian impulse as analogous to militant political action against established social hierarchies, which also aims at reconfiguring the distribution of the sensible. In an interview, Rancière argues that in spite of theorizations to the contrary (like Badiou's), aesthetics and politics "intermix in any case: politics has its aesthetics, and aesthetics has its politics. But there is no formula for an appropriate correlation. It is the state of politics that decides that Dix's paintings in the 1920s, populist films by Renoir, Duvivier or Carné in the 1930s, or films by Cimino and Scorsese in the 1980s appear to harbor a political critique or appear, on the contrary, to be suited to an apolitical outlook on the irreducible chaos of human affairs or the picturesque poetry of social differences." Jacques Rancière, "The Janus-Face of Politicized Art: Jacques Rancière in Interview with Gabriel Rockhill," in *The Politics of Aesthetics,* trans. and with an introduction by Gabriel Rockhill (London: Continuum, 2006), 49–66, 62. The politics of art is therefore a matter of interpretation, which is entirely determined by the state of politics at any given point in history. Rancière's ultimately historicist account solves the problem of political cinema by taking the relation between the two terms as given, then locating the guarantee of this relation in neither art nor politics but rather in history.

3. Sarah Kofman, "Beyond Aporia?," trans. David Macey, in *Poststructuralist Classics*, ed. Andrew Benjamin (New York: Routledge, 1988), 7–44, 10.

4. Kofman, "Beyond Aporia?," 23.

5. Alberto Farassino, "Comunicazione di *Cinegramma*," in "1968–1972: Esperienze di cinema militante," ed. Faliero Rosati, *Bianco e Nero*, no. 7–8 (1973): 111–14, 112. Farassino further observes that "The notion of political cinema is one of those objects, built not through theoretical work, but through an analogical synthesis that brings about a whole host of misunderstandings" (112).

6. Jean-Louis Comolli and Jean Narboni, "Cinema/Ideology/Criticism" (1969), in *Film Theory and Criticism: Introductory Readings*, ed. Leo Braudy and Marshall Cohen (Oxford: Oxford University Press, 1999), 752–59, 755.

7. The essay, together with the subsequent work published by the *Cahiers* in the 1970s, also had a crucial impact on anglophone film theory. The journal *Screen* in particular welcomed Comolli and Narboni's militant and theoretical impetus. *Screen* published translations of a number of articles from French (including "Cinema/Ideology/Criticism"), while theorists such as Laura Mulvey, Elizabeth Cowie, Stephen Heath, and Colin MacCabe further solidified an approach to cinema that was equally indebted to Marxism and psychoanalysis.

8. Comolli and Narboni, "Cinema/Ideology/Criticism," 754.

9. Comolli and Narboni, "Cinema/Ideology/Criticism," 755.

10. Comolli and Narboni, "Cinema/Ideology/Criticism," 755.

11. These two modes of approaching political cinema have, of course, proper historical names and illustrious genealogies. The militant discourse as a project was born with the Soviet avant-garde of the 1920s and 1930s, then renewed by the leftist film criticism of the late 1960s and 1970s (in journals like *Cahiers* and *Positif* in France and *Ombre rosse* in Italy) and by radical filmmakers the world over. The second discourse has its roots in the intellectual tradition of cultural studies, from its inception with Stuart Hall in Birmingham in the 1960s to its global turn in the 1980s and 1990s.

12. Comolli and Narboni, "Cinema/Ideology/Criticism," 757.

13. Comolli and Narboni, "Cinema/Ideology/Criticism," 757.

14. Comolli and Narboni, "Cinema/Ideology/Criticism," 757, 757, 758.

15. Auerbach, "Figura," 9–76, 12. The nuances become more precise from author to author, in the literary and scholarly uses of the word. "Dream image" or "ghost" (Lucretius), "constellation" (Manilius), "hidden allusion" (Quintilian), and "presage" (Tertullian) are just a few of the examples listed by Auerbach.

16. See Brenez, *De la figure*; and Didi-Huberman, *Fra Angelico*.

17. Brenez, *De la figure*, 44.

18. Brenez, *De la figure*, 55.

19. The figure as an operation of figurative undoing has been studied within a somewhat heretical intellectual lineage that connects, in addition to the aforementioned Brenez and Didi-Huberman, the likes of Georges Bataille, Jean-François Lyotard, and Gilles Deleuze.

20. Jacques Aumont, *À quoi pensent les films?* (Paris: Séguier, 1996), 156.

21. Aumont, *À quoi pensent,* 170.

22. Of course, a figure still relies on representational elements. To be recognized as a worker or a housewife, a figure must display a modicum of features that are characteristically associated with them. This, however, is a necessary but insufficient condition. A figure solely defined by its recognizable traits would not be a figure at all but something more akin to a type in the Lukácsian sense. For György Lukács, the typical weds the concrete existence of an individual, with all its real-life details, to the evocation of the universal dynamics of an individual's historical situation. Yet contrary to the figure, the Lukácsian type still obeys to a logic of representation: as the mediator between individuality and universality, the type expresses history. For an overview of the concept of the type in Lukács, see Béla Királyfalvi, *The Aesthetics of György Lukács* (Princeton: Princeton University Press, 1975), 78–83.

23. Brenez, *De la figure,* 84; Gilles Deleuze, *Francis Bacon: The Logic of Sensation,* trans. Daniel W. Smith (Minneapolis: University of Minnesota Press, 2005), 12.

24. Deleuze associates this temptation with what he calls the "cliché": "One can only fight against the cliché with much ruse, perseverance and prudence: it is a task perpetually renewed with every painting, with every moment of every painting. It is the way of the Figure." Deleuze, *Francis Bacon,* 79.

25. Kaja Silverman, "Figuration and Female Subjectivity in *Tess of the d'Urbervilles,*" *Novel* 18, no. 1 (1984): 5–28, 15. See also Auerbach, "Figura."

26. Ernst Bloch, "The Problem of Expressionism Once Again," in *Heritage of Our Times,* trans. Neville and Stephen Plaice (Cambridge: Polity, 1991), 251–53.

27. Bloch, "Problem of Expressionism," 251 (emphasis added).

28. Bloch, "Problem of Expressionism," 252.

29. Ernst Bloch, "Foundation of Phenomenology," in *Heritage of Our Times,* 275–6.

30. Alain Badiou calls these two processes, respectively, subjectivization and subjective process. See Alain Badiou, *Theory of the Subject,* trans. and with an introduction by Bruno Bosteels (London: Bloomsbury, 2013).

31. Didi-Huberman, *Fra Angelico,* 56.

32. This figure *of* crisis has important continuities, as well as differences, with what Luka Arsenjuk has defined as the figure *in* crisis in the artistic and theoretical work of Soviet filmmaker Sergei Eisenstein. We

both understand the figure as critical in Didi-Huberman's sense, but we emphasize different aspects. For Arsenjuk, the figure in crisis points to the self-division and becoming dialectical of forms of movement in Eisenstein; in this book, the figure of crisis is invented by cinema to give body to the holes and hollow spaces of history. See Luka Arsenjuk, *Movement, Action, Image, Montage: Sergei Eisenstein and the Cinema in Crisis* (Minneapolis: University of Minnesota Press, 2018), 23–64.

33. When cinema tries to foreclose this nonrelation, as we have seen, it lapses back into an operation of mere representation of political content. But the dangers of this foreclosure are just as significant for politics. The example of the worker is in this sense paradigmatic. While cinema invents the figure of the worker to make legible a certain historical situation of crisis, a politics of the figure of the worker would disavow the unavoidable complexity of collective processes of subjectivation under the pretense of a straightforward identification with a type. The temptation of a politics of figures, then, is that of reifying the process of political subjectivation into the static form of a figure to be held up as an identitarian fetish. For a theorization of the politics of the figure of the worker that avoids these pitfalls, see Sylvain Lazarus, *Anthropology of the Name,* trans. Gila Walker (London: Seagull, 2015).

34. Bloch, "Problem of Expressionism," 252.

35. Two essential historical accounts of collective movements in the Italian long '68 are Robert Lumley, *States of Emergency: Cultures of Revolt in Italy from 1968 to 1978* (London: Verso, 1990); and Luisa Passerini, *Autobiography of a Generation: Italy, 1968,* trans. Lisa Erdberg, with a foreword by Joan Wallach Scott (Middletown, Conn.: Wesleyan University Press, 1996). For a contemporary reassessment of the vicissitudes of political militancy in that period, see Giovanni De Luna, *Le ragioni un decennio: 1969–1979. Militanza, violenza, sconfitta, memoria* (Milan: Feltrinelli, 2011).

36. For an overview of the period from the perspective of labor history, see Stefano Musso, *Storia del lavoro in Italia: Dall'unità ad oggi* (Venice: Marsilio, 2002), 229–66.

37. See Antonio Negri, "Proletarians and the State: Toward a Discussion of Workers' Autonomy and the Historic Compromise," in *Books for Burning: Between Civil War and Democracy in 1970s Italy,* trans. and ed. Timothy S. Murphy, trans. Arianna Bove, Ed Emery, Timothy S. Murphy, and Francesca Novello (London: Verso, 2005), 118–79; and Sergio Bologna, "The Tribe of Moles," trans. Red Notes, in *Autonomia: Post-political Politics,* ed. Sylvère Lotringer and Christian Marazzi (Los Angeles: Semiotext(e), 2007), 36–61. For a militant account of the political experiment of the Autonomia and its ongoing influence, see Marcello Tarì, *Il ghiaccio era sottile: Per una storia dell'Autonomia* (Rome: DeriveApprodi, 2012).

38. Paolo Virno, interview in *Gli Operaisti. Autobiografie di cattivi maestri,*

ed. Guido Borio, Francesca Pozzi, and Gigi Roggero (Rome: DeriveApprodi, 2005), 308–25, 312.

39. Auerbach, "Figura," 17.

2. The Worker

1. Despite being arguably more attentive than other national cinemas to the plight of the working class, Italian cinema has by and large steered clear of factories, so much so that its rare depictions remain etched in the national and, dare we say, global imaginary: the shop floor where a Simone Weil-esque Ingrid Bergman replaces a worker in Roberto Rossellini's *Europe '51* (*Europa '51*, 1952); the steel mill in Eduardo De Filippo's *Neapolitans in Milan* (*Napoletani a Milano*, 1953); the glimpses of the Alfa Romeo auto plant in Milan where Luchino Visconti's *Rocco and His Brothers* (*Rocco e i suoi fratelli*, 1960) ends; the images of the assembly line that bookend Alberto Lattuada's *Mafioso* (1962); the late-nineteenth century textile factory in Turin in Mario Monicelli's *The Organizer* (*I compagni*, 1963), to name but a few well-known examples. For an overview of the cinematic explorations of the factory in Italian cinema, see Carlo Carotti, *Alla ricerca del paradiso: L'operaio nel cinema italiano, 1945–1990* (Genoa: Graphos, 1992); and Ruth Ben-Ghiat, "The Italian Cinema and the Working Class," *International Labor and Working Class History* 59 (2001): 36–51.

2. For an overview of the historical sequence that culminated in the *Biennio Rosso*, see Paolo Spriano, *Storia del Partito comunista italiano. I. Da Bordiga a Gramsci* (Turin: Einaudi, 1967), 3–122; and Gwyn A. Williams, *Proletarian Order: Antonio Gramsci, Factory Councils, and the Origins of Italian Communism, 1911–1921* (London: Pluto Press, 1975).

3. In two essays from 1971 and 1973, within the context of a discussion of forms of working-class organization in the twentieth century, Antonio Negri posits a similar distinction between these different types of the worker and their attendant party formations. See Antonio Negri, "Crisis of the Planner-State: Communism and Revolutionary Organization," 1–50, 11–20, and "Workers' Party against Work," 51–117, 94–100, both in Murphy, *Books for Burning*.

4. See Bloch, "Problem of Expressionism."

5. The anecdote is told in Alfredo Rossi, *Elio Petri e il cinema politico italiano: La piazza carnevalizzata* (Milan: Mimesis, 2015), 110–11.

6. See Badiou, *Theory of the Subject*, 241–74.

7. Jacques Lacan, *The Seminar, Book 10: Anxiety*, ed. Jacques-Alain Miller, trans. A. R. Price (Cambridge: Polity, 2014), 116.

8. Alenka Zupančič, *What Is Sex?* (Cambridge, Mass.: MIT Press, 2017), 33.

9. Zupančič, *What Is Sex?*, 33.

10. Karl Marx, *Capital: A Critique of Political Economy*, vol. 1, trans. Ben Fowkes (London: Penguin Books, 1992), 1:271.

11. The irruption in the film of these two gestures of refusal of labor (speech and riot) within the context of class struggle in Italy in the 1960s provides further evidence of the transition from the older typology of the worker to the new one. While the previous type of labor was elevated to a defining element for the worker's identity and a reason for pride, the new worker rejects labor altogether as the primary tool of capitalist oppression over everyday life. The political gesture of refusal of work has a long history in Italian postwar radical thought and praxis, from the wildcat strikes of the early 1960s to Mario Tronti's theorizations a few years later, from the autonomist struggles of the 1970s to the ongoing relevance of the concept for contemporary postworkerist thinkers such as Paolo Virno, Maurizio Lazzarato, Tiziana Terranova, and Bifo Berardi.

12. Badiou, *Theory of the Subject*, 127. Badiou here paraphrases Lacan's famous dictum that "there is no such thing as a sexual relationship." Jacques Lacan, *The Seminar, Book 17: The Other Side of Psychoanalysis*, ed. Jacques-Alain Miller, trans. Russell Grigg (New York: Norton, 2007), 116 (translation modified).

13. Theodor Adorno, *Minima Moralia*, trans. E. F. N. Jephcott (London: Verso, 1978), § 151, pp. 238–44, 239.

14. Badiou, *Theory of the Subject*, 168.

15. Marx, *Capital*, 1:128.

16. Williams, "Fog of Class War."

17. Negri first introduced the concept in 1975 in "Proletarians and the State: Toward a Discussion of Workers' Autonomy and the Historic Compromise," in Murphy, *Books for Burning*, 118–79. For Negri's assessment of his theorization of the "social worker" some thirty years later, see the interview in *Dall'operaio massa all'operaio sociale. Intervista sull'operaismo*, ed. Paolo Pozzi and Roberta Tommasini (Verona: Ombre Corte, 2007).

18. See, e.g., *Linea di montaggio* (Assembly line; Ansano Giannarelli, 1972), where images of the assembly line at the FIAT Mirafiori plant in Turin are coupled with a voice-over reciting passages from *Capital*.

19. Lazarus, *Anthropology*, 26.

20. The three moles can be read as a nod to the geographical shape of Sicily, known in ancient times as Trinacria, from the Greek *tri-* (three) and *akra* (capes).

21. In particular, she draws on Pietro Germi's Sicilian diptych, *Divorce Italian Style* (*Divorzio all'italiana*, 1961) and *Seduced and Abandoned* (*Sedotta e abbandonata*, 1964), as premier examples of these uneasy anachronies.

22. For a discussion of the trope of revenge in cinema and its relation to the logic of debt, see Jean Ma, "Circuitous Action: Revenge Cinema," *Criticism* 57, no. 1 (2015): 47–70.

23. The English word normally used to translate the Italian *padrone* is "owner." *Padrone,* however, is endowed with a larger semantic range. It denotes not just ownership or possession but also the extension of a certain rule and control over the worker. It therefore contains in itself also "boss" and even "master." As an example, the "master" *(Herr)* in Hegel's master–slave dialectic in the *Phenomenology of the Spirit* is usually translated in Italian as *padrone.* For this reason, and mindful of the role the word *padrone* played in the history of leftist struggles in Italy, we will keep the original Italian.

24. It is obviously not by accident that the Italian national anthem, "Fratelli d'Italia" (Brothers of Italy), plays in the background whenever Ferro's characters appear on screen.

25. Friedrich Nietzsche, *On the Genealogy of Morals,* ed. Walter Kaufman, trans. Walter Kaufman and R. J. Hollingdale (New York: Vintage, 1989), 62.

26. Maurizio Lazzarato, *The Making of the Indebted Man,* trans. Joshua David Jordan (Los Angeles: Semiotext(e), 2012), 47.

27. Lazzarato, *Making,* 45–46.

28. Sicily, where the unfinished project of Italian modernity casts the sharpest chiaroscuro, seems to offer a particularly fitting stage for these theatrics, and a long lineage of Sicilian literature (from Luigi Pirandello to Vitaliano Brancati, from Leonardo Sciascia to the more recent work of Giorgio Vasta) dealing with a certain illegibility of the structures of power attests to nothing if not that.

29. Shot between 1971 and 1972, *Trevico-Turin* was produced by a small company controlled by the PCI, Unitelefilm, which provided a small crew and organized a limited release in a few selected theaters.

30. Goffredo Fofi, "Qualche film," *Quaderni piacentini,* no. 50 (1973): 197–208.

31. Lino Micciché, "*Trevico-Torino: Viaggio nel Fiat-Nam* di Ettore Scola," in *Cinema italiano degli anni '70: Cronache 1969–1979* (Venice: Marsilio, 1980), 162–64.

32. Alain Badiou, "The Factory as Event Site," *Prelom* 8 (2006): 171–76.

33. Marx, *Capital,* 1:388.

34. Paolo Virno, *A Grammar of the Multitude: For an Analysis of Contemporary Forms of Life,* trans. Isabella Bertoletti, James Cascaito, and Andrea Casson (Los Angeles: Semiotext(e), 2004), 29–46.

35. Gilles Deleuze, *Cinema 2: The Time-Image,* trans. Hugh Tomlinson and Robert Galeta (Minneapolis: University of Minnesota Press, 1989), 5.

36. Deleuze, *Cinema 2,* 2.

37. Deleuze, *Cinema 2,* 1.

38. Gilles Deleuze, seminar on cinema at the Université Paris 8 Saint-Denis, lecture of March 2, 1982, *La voix de Gilles Deleuze en ligne*

(www2.univ-paris8.fr/deleuze, accessed June 26, 2018), transcribed by Jerôme Letourneur, my translation.

39. The spatial dialectic presented in the film between what is present (the abandoned infrastructures) and what is absent (the factory) points to a certain limitation in Deleuze's conceptualization of the any-space-whatever as an empty place of pure potentiality, for this potentiality is always determined by what that space excludes or hides.

40. Unknown author, review of *Trevico-Turin,* typewritten document, Archivio Audiovisivo del Movimento Operaio e Democratico, Rome (in French, my translation).

41. Fredric Jameson, *Representing Capital: A Reading of Volume 1* (New York: Verso, 2014), 71.

42. See Mario Tronti, "A New Type of Political Experiment: Lenin in England," in *Workers and Capital,* trans. David Broder (New York: Verso, 2019), 65–72.

43. For a critical approach to the figure of the victim, see Daniele Giglioli, *Critica della vittima. Un esperimento con l'etica* (Rome: Nottetempo, 2014).

3. The Housewife

1. For a wide-ranging overview of the history of feminist thought on social reproduction, see Susan Ferguson, *Women and Work: Feminism, Labor, and Social Reproduction* (London: Pluto, 2020). A highly influential assessment of the Marxist legacy within feminism can be found in Lise Vogel, *Marxism and the Oppression of Women: Toward a Unitary Theory* (Chicago: Haymarket, 2013).

2. See Claudia Jones, "We Seek Full Equality of Women" (1949), *Viewpoint Magazine,* February 21, 2015, viewpointmag.com; Angela Davis, *Women, Race, and Class* (New York: Vintage, 1983); "The Combahee River Collective Statement," Combahee River Collective, 1977, combaheerivercollective.weebly.com (accessed November 24, 2020); Shulamith Firestone, *The Dialectic of Sex: A Case for Feminist Revolution* (New York: Farrar, Straus & Giroux, 1970); and Kate Millett, *Sexual Politics* (New York: Columbia University Press, 2016).

3. For a detailed historical and conceptual overview of Wages for Housework written by a former member, see Louise Toupin, *Wages for Housework: A History of an International Feminist Movement, 1972–77* (London: Pluto Press, 2018). On the legacy of *operaismo* in Wages for Housework, see the interviews with Mariarosa Dalla Costa and Alisa Dal Re in Borio, Pozzi, and Roggero, *Gli operaisti,* 121–31 and 144–54.

4. Silvia Federici, "Wages against Housework," in *Revolution at Point*

Zero: Housework, Reproduction, and Feminist Struggle (Oakland, Calif.: P. M. Press, 2012), 15–22, 17.

5. Federici, "Wages against Housework," 19.

6. "The left's proposal for the social struggle was simply the mechanical extension and projection of the factory struggle: the male worker continued to be its central figure. The women's liberation movement considers the social level to be first and foremost *the home,* and thus views the figure of *the woman* as central to social subversion." Mariarosa Dalla Costa, "Preface to the Italian Edition of Women and the Subversion of the Community (March 1972)," in *Women and the Subversion of the Community: A Mariarosa Dalla Costa Reader,* ed. Camille Barbagallo, trans. Richard Braude (Oakland, Calif.: P. M. Press, 2019), 13–16, 16.

7. Silvia Federici, "Marx and Feminism," *tripleC: Communication, Capitalism, Critique* 16, no. 2 (2018), www.triple-c.at.

8. Mariarosa Dalla Costa, interview in the afterword of Toupin, *Wages for Housework,* 220–40, 222.

9. Cesare Casarino, "Images for Housework: On the Time of Domestic Labor in Gilles Deleuze's Philosophy of the Cinema," *differences* 28, no. 3 (2017): 67–92, 74.

10. See Giuliana Minghelli, "Haunted Frames: History and Landscape in Luchino Visconti's *Ossessione,*" *Italica* 85, no. 2–3 (2008): 173–96.

11. Federici, "Wages against Housework," 16.

12. This displacement of colonialism—a motif that returns in Ferreri's subsequent work—seems to speak to the specificity of the Italian colonial experience as something that can only be represented by something else (an apostolate, an exploration), thus evoking the country's largely unresolved relation to its own history of imperialist violence.

13. Mary Ann Doane, "Film and the Masquerade: Theorising the Female Spectator," *Screen* 23, no. 3–4 (1982): 74–87, 81.

14. Juliet Mitchell, *Woman's Estate* (New York: Verso, 2015), 146–47.

15. "What does our oppression within the family do to us women? It produces a tendency to small-mindedness, petty jealousy, irrational emotionality and random violence, dependency, competitive selfishness and possessiveness, passivity, a lack of vision and conservatism. These qualities . . . are the result of the woman's objective conditions within the family—itself embedded in a sexist society." Mitchell, *Woman's Estate,* 162.

16. Mariarosa Dalla Costa, "The Power of Women and the Subversion of the Community," in Barbagallo, *Women and the Subversion of the Community,* 17–49, 38.

17. Kathi Weeks, *The Problem with Work: Feminism, Marxism, Antiwork Politics, and Postwork Imaginaries* (Durham, N.C.: Duke University Press, 2011), 134.

18. Weeks defines the practice of demand as an attempt at cognitive mapping. See *Problem with Work*, 130–31.

19. Weeks, *Problem with Work*, 131.

20. Weeks, *Problem with Work*, 134.

21. Silvia Federici and Nicole Cox, *Counterplanning from the Kitchen* (New York: New York Wages for Housework Committee and Falling Wall Press, 1977), 1–15, 6. Curiously, this quote has been excised from the recent reprint of the essay in Federici, *Revolution at Point Zero*, 28–40.

22. Casarino, "Images for Housework," 78–79.

23. Casarino, "Images for Housework," 78

24. Casarino, "Images for Housework," 85–86.

25. Domietta Torlasco, "Philosophy in the Kitchen," *World Picture Journal*, no. 11 (2016), worldpicturejournal.com.

26. Cesare Casarino, "Images for Housework," 89n1.

27. Leopoldina Fortunati, *The Arcane of Reproduction: Housework, Prostitution, Labor, and Capital,* ed. Jim Fleming, trans. Hilary Creek (Brooklyn, N.Y.: Autonomedia, 1995), 165 (original entirely in italics).

28. "With the advent of *capitalism,* all labor power was 'freed.' Unlike any preceding mode, the new mode of production *formally* established a *different* production relation with *men* from that which it established with *women.* The sexual division of labor developed to such a degree that the work subject of *reproduction* was separated off from that of *production;* the two processes became separated by *value.* The man—as the primary work-subject within production, was obliged to enter the *waged-work relation.* The woman—as the primary work-subject within reproduction, was obliged to enter the *non-waged-work relation.*" Fortunati, *Arcane of Reproduction,* 30–31.

29. Fortunati, *Arcane of Reproduction,* 108.

30. Federici and Cox, *Counterplanning,* 35.

31. Alain Badiou, *Theory of the Subject,* trans. Bruno Bosteels (London: Bloomsbury, 2013), 202.

32. This humiliating exchange between Antonietta and Emanuele reminds us of Juliet Mitchell's acute observation that the housewife-mother's "work is private and *because it is private,* and for no other reason, it is unsupervised. This is the source of that complacent 'your time's your own, you are your own boss' mystifying build-up that housewives are given." Mitchell, *Woman's Estate,* 161.

33. Badiou, *Theory of the Subject,* 127.

34. This position has been variously articulated by, among others, Pier Paolo Pasolini, who sees in the film an example of the "free indirect point-of-view shot" ("The 'Cinema of Poetry,'" in *Heretical Empiricism,* trans. Ben Lawton and Louise K. Barnett [Washington: New Academia Publishing, 2005], 167–86, 178–80); Sandro Bernardi, who emphasizes a certain indis-

cernibility of subjectivity and objectivity in the film (*Il paesaggio nel cinema italiano* [Venice: Marsilio, 2002], 180–88); and Giorgio Tinazzi (*Michelangelo Antonioni* [Milan: Il Castoro Cinema, 1995], 102–7).

35. Angela Dalle Vacche highlights Antonioni's eclectic painterly influences, citing Art Informel (Alberto Burri, Jean Dubuffet, Jean Fautrier), futurism, Giorgio De Chirico, Piet Mondrian, and Mario Sironi as some of the visual inspirations for *Red Desert*. See Angela Dalle Vacche, *Cinema and Painting: How Art Is Used in Film* (Austin: University of Texas Press, 1995), 43–80.

36. Louis Althusser, "Cremonini, Painter of the Abstract," in *Lenin and Philosophy and Other Essays*, trans. Ben Brewster (New York: Monthly Review Press, 2001), 157–66, 163, 160.

37. Althusser, "Cremonini," 158.

38. Karl Marx, *Grundrisse. Foundations of the Critique of Political Economy*, trans. Martin Nicolaus (London: Penguin, 1993), 164.

39. This is the Stirnerian position demolished by Marx with Engels in *The German Ideology* (1846). Without wishing to retrace the complex Marxist debate around the subject, it will suffice to say that the central issue, what Alberto Toscano aptly calls "the open secret of real abstraction," is not that the two opposites—concreteness and abstraction—present themselves ambiguously, so that one can't definitively decide which is which. Rather, the problem is that they are one and the same, two sides of the same coin. See Alberto Toscano, "The Open Secret of Real Abstraction," *Rethinking Marxism* 20, no. 2 (2008): 273–87.

40. Althusser, "Cremonini," 164.

41. This is the crux of the conversation between Corrado and Giuliana on the oil rig, where the former—as capital personified—explains that he must chase lucrative investments wherever they may present themselves, while the latter confesses that she cannot imagine leaving everything behind.

42. This is why, in light of *Red Desert*, one should question the omnipresence of the term "alienation" in discussions of Antonioni's work of the early 1960s. In Marx, particularly in his early writings, alienation presupposes the existence of an essence of the human to be reappropriated with the demise of the capitalist mode of production. On the contrary, *Red Desert* invites us to reinterpret the existential agony of the bourgeoisie through a decidedly more antihumanist lens, one privileging the concept of abstraction to that of alienation.

43. Tithi Bhattacharya, "How Not to Skip Class: Social Reproduction of Labor and the Global Working Class," in *Social Reproduction Theory: Remapping Class, Recentering Oppression*, ed. Tithi Bhattacharya (London: Pluto, 2017), 68–93, 82.

44. In a surprising choice, the English translators render the original

French *Image-pulsion* with "impulse-image," all but obscuring its crucial psychoanalytical reference to the drive. We will maintain the modified translation ("drive" for *pulsion*) throughout our discussion.

45. Gilles Deleuze, *Cinema 1: The Movement Image,* trans. Hugh Tomlinson and Barbara Habberjam (Minneapolis: University of Minnesota Press, 2003), 128.

46. Deleuze, *Cinema 1,* 123.

47. Deleuze, *Cinema 1,* 129.

48. Daniele Rugo, "Marco Ferreri: The Task of Cinema and the End of the World," *Journal of Italian Cinema and Media Studies* 1, no. 2 (2013): 129–41, 138.

49. Alberto Scandola, *Marco Ferreri* (Milan: Il Castoro Cinema, 2003), 76. Similar to *Red Desert,* this is achieved mainly through the use of color. Glauco's white shirt rhymes with the living room walls and the immaculate room divider, while his apron echoes the red and white decoration of the gun. See Scandola, *Marco Ferreri,* 75–76.

50. Althusser, "Cremonini," 164.

51. Tithi Bhattacharya, "Mapping Social Reproduction Theory," introduction to *Social Reproduction Theory,* 1–20, 11.

52. Marx, *Capital,* 1:719.

53. Scandola, *Marco Ferreri,* 78.

54. Deleuze, *Cinema 1,* 126.

55. Althusser, "Cremonini," 165. The Marxian echo is apparent: "The Roman slave was held by chains; the wage-laborer is bound to his owner by invisible threads." Marx, *Capital,* 1:719.

4. The Youth

1. Among the exceptions, let us mention at least Mauro Bolognini's *Chronicle of a Homicide* (*Imputazione di omicidio per uno studente,* 1972), Gianni Amelio's *Blow to the Heart* (*Colpire al cuore,* 1982), and the last episode of the anthology film *Love and Anger* (*Amore e rabbia,* 1969), *Let's Discuss, Let's Discuss* (*Discutiamo, Discutiamo*) by Marco Bellocchio. For a discussion of the latter as emblematic of the politics of 1968, see Mauro Resmini, "Obscurity, Anthologized: Enjoyment and Non-relation in *Love and Anger* (1969)," in *1968 and Global Cinema,* ed. Christina Gerhardt and Sara Saljoughi (Detroit, Mich.: Wayne State University Press, 2018), 199–215.

2. Nanni Balestrini and Primo Moroni, *L'orda d'oro 1968–1977* (Milan: Feltrinelli, 2015), 51.

3. Antonio Negri, "Proletarians and State: Toward a Discussion of Workers' Autonomy and the Historic Compromise," in Murphy, *Books for Burning,* 118–79, 126 (translation modified).

4. See Gilles Deleuze and Félix Guattari, *Anti-Oedipus: Capitalism and Schizophrenia,* trans. Robert Hurley, Mark Seem, and Helen R. Lane, with a preface by Michel Foucault (Minneapolis: University of Minnesota Press, 1983), esp. 1–50.

5. Elvio Fachinelli, "Il desiderio dissidente," in *Al cuore delle cose: Scritti politici (1967–1989)* (Rome: DeriveApprodi, 2016), 29–35, 31–32.

6. See "Uno scambio epistolare Pasolini-Bellocchio," in Pier Paolo Pasolini, *Saggi sulla letteratura e sull'arte,* ed. Walter Siti and Silvia De Laude, 2 vols. (Milan: Mondadori, 1999), 2:2800–15, originally in *I pugni in tasca: Un film di Marco Bellocchio,* ed. Giacomo Gambetti (Milan: Garzanti, 1967), 9–24. The letters were signed by Bellocchio, but it was later revealed that the director, who was twenty-six at the time, thought he was too inexperienced to respond to an established intellectual like Pasolini. So Grazia Cherchi, cofounder and codirector of the journal *Quaderni piacentini,* came to the rescue and penned the responses on his behalf. See Antonio Costa, *I pugni in tasca* (Turin: Lindau, 2007), 58 and 71n6. For a detailed discussion of the epistolary exchange, see Silvia De Laude, "'Cinema di prosa' e 'cinema di poesia,' *tertium datur:* Su Pier Paolo Pasolini e *I pugni in tasca* di Marco Bellocchio," *Engramma* 172 (2020), engramma.it.

7. "Uno scambio epistolare Pasolini-Bellocchio," 2801–2 and 2805. Cherchi also makes a similar point in "L'età verde," *Giovane critica,* no. 12 (1966): 9–12.

8. Italo Calvino, *Rinascita,* no. 15 (April 9, 1966), qtd. in Costa, *I pugni in tasca,* 170.

9. "Uno scambio epistolare Pasolini-Bellocchio," 2805.

10. Grande, *Eros e politica,* 47–48.

11. The faint echoes of Sophocles in the context of the Italian long '68 are markedly different from the ones that reverberate through Germany in the second half of the 1970s. Thanks in particular to the collective film *Germany in Autumn* (Alexander Kluge et al., 1978), the event of the death of the Red Army faction original members in the Stammheim prison in 1976–77 conjures the all-too-palpable specters of Antigone and Creon as emblems of the state's violent repression of dissent. On Antigone's overdetermination in the so-called German Autumn, see Thomas Elsaesser, "Antigone Agonistes: Urban Guerrilla or Guerrilla Urbanism? The Red Army Faction, *Germany in Autumn,* and *Death Game,*" in *Giving Ground: The Politics of Propinquity,* ed. Joan Copjec and Michael Sorkin (New York: Verso, 1999), 267–302.

12. Interview with Liliana Cavani included in the 2014 Blu-ray release of the film by Raro Video.

13. In interviews, Cavani has repeatedly corroborated this interpretation. For a selection of her interventions on the topic, see Ciriaco Tiso, *Liliana Cavani* (Florence: La Nuova Italia, 1975), 66–71.

14. The polymorphic nature of the self in Moretti's oeuvre has been extensively discussed in scholarship, especially in relation to the perceived narcissism of Moretti's persona. See, e.g., Ewa Mazierska and Laura Rascaroli, *The Cinema of Nanni Moretti* (New York: Wallflower, 2004).

15. Sergio Benvenuto, *What Are Perversions? Sexuality, Ethics, Psychoanalysis* (New York: Routledge, 2018), e-book.

16. Jacques Lacan, *Television,* ed. Joan Copjec, trans. Dennis Hollier, Rosalind Krauss, and Annette Michelson (New York: Norton, 1990), 23.

17. Lacan, *Television,* 30.

18. Lacan, *Television,* 30.

19. Colette Soler, *Lacanian Affects: The Function of Affect in Lacan's Work,* trans. Bruce Fink (New York: Routledge, 2016), 81.

20. Soler, *Lacanian Affects,* 82.

21. Éric Laurent, "From Saying to Doing in the Clinic of Drug Addiction and Alcoholism," *Almanac of Psychoanalysis* 1 (1998): 129–40, 139.

22. Jacques Lacan, "On Freud's 'Trieb' and the Psychoanalyst's Desire," in *Écrits: The First Complete Edition in English,* trans. Bruce Fink (New York: Norton, 2007), 722–25, 722.

23. In the film's climactic scene, Michela overdoses at the feet of the monument commemorating Pasolini's murder in Ostia in 1975. It is, first and foremost, an homage to an artist whose influence is palpable in *Toxic Love*. But it is also a highly symbolic choice, implicitly connecting the tragedy of drug addiction in the 1980s to a larger history of the scandalous spectacle of young bodies in Italy, of which Pasolini was inarguably the most acute and most passionate critic. Moretti would visit that same monument twenty years later, riding his Vespa in *Dear Diary*. In these pilgrimages, one can perhaps discern the silhouette of a kinship between Pasolini, Moretti, and Caligari: a shared desire to diagnose the political potentialities and contradictions of a historical moment, which, in different ways, the figure of the youth crystallizes for all three of them.

24. It is worth noting that in the 1970s, the criminalization of left-wing political activists was one of the most widely used and effective tactics adopted by the repressive apparatuses of the state. Although no explicit political motives are attached to the bank robber's actions, it would not be a stretch to imagine Monicelli relying on the implicit state-sponsored association "radical activist = criminal" to throw into relief the opposition between the two faces of the youth in the film, with the series law-abiding/middle-class/apolitical on the side of Mario and criminal/proletarian/radical on the side of the bank robber.

25. The most spectacular display of this nascent sentiment will be the famous *Marcia dei quarantamila*. On October 14, 1980, in Turin, forty thousand white-collar workers from FIAT took to the streets to protest the ongoing blue-collar strike at the Mirafiori plant. Secretly organized

and promoted by FIAT's upper management, the silent procession provided a funereal response to the tumultuous protests of the previous decade and pushed the unions toward a deal that favored the ownership, thus marking the end of an era of working-class struggle at Mirafiori.

5. The Saint

1. For a critical engagement with the role of the youth in Pasolini's oeuvre, see Simona Bondavalli, *Fictions of Youth: Pier Paolo Pasolini, Adolescence, Fascisms* (Toronto: Toronto University Press, 2015). For a specific focus on the youth in Pasolini's cinema, see John David Rhodes, "Watchable Bodies: *Salò's* Young Non-actors," *Screen* 53, no. 4 (2012): 453–58.

2. Pier Paolo Pasolini, "Repudiation of the *Trilogy of Life*," in *Heretical Empiricism*, trans. Ben Lawton and Louise K. Barnett (Washington, D.C.: New Academia, 2005), xvii–xx, xvii.

3. Pasolini, "Repudiation," xix. Patrick Rumble has offered a compelling reading of the "Abiura" as an ironic recantation in the vein of Boccaccio and Chaucer. However, the sheer existence of a film like *Salò*—and the unfinished project of a trilogy of death—invites us to take Pasolini's repudiation more seriously than not. See Patrick Rumble, *Allegories of Contamination: Pier Paolo Pasolini's Trilogy of Life* (Toronto: University of Toronto Press, 1996), 82–99.

4. Pasolini, "Repudiation," xviii. In his opinion pieces from the early 1970s for the newspaper *Corriere della Sera,* Pasolini had already discussed what he saw as the alarming signs of petty bourgeois conformism in youth counterculture. See esp. Pier Paolo Pasolini, "Il 'discorso' dei capelli," "Acculturazione e acculturazione," "Studio sulla rivoluzione antropologica in Italia," and "Limitatezza della storia e immensità del mondo contadino" in *Scritti Corsari*, collected in *Saggi sulla politica e sulla società,* ed. Walter Siti and Silvia De Laude (Milan: Mondadori, 1999), 271–77, 290–93, 307–12, and 319–24.

5. Pasolini, "Repudiation," xviii.

6. See, e.g., Stefania Benini, *Pasolini: The Sacred Flesh* (Toronto: University of Toronto Press, 2015); *Pasolini e l'interrogazione del sacro,* ed. Angela Felice and Gian Paolo Gri (Venice: Marsilio, 2013); Giuseppe Conti Calabrese, *Pasolini e il sacro* (Milan: Jaca Book, 1994); and Tomaso Subini, *La necessità di morire: Il cinema di Pier Paolo Pasolini e il sacro* (Rome: Ente dello Spettacolo, 2008).

7. The other two obvious instances of the depiction of sainthood in Italian cinema would be Roberto Rossellini's *The Flowers of Saint Francis (Francesco giullare di Dio,* 1950) and Liliana Cavani's 1966 made-for-television film *Francesco d'Assisi* (then remade into *Francesco* for the big screen in 1989). Pasolini had high praise for *The Flowers,* but he considered

Cavani's attempt at depicting sainthood on screen to be a failure. For a discussion of Pasolini's depiction of Franciscanism in his cinema in comparison to Rossellini's and Cavani's, together with Pasolini's assessment of them, see Benini, *Pasolini*, 147–86.

8. Pier Paolo Pasolini, "Elogio della barbarie, nostalgia del sacro," in *Il sogno del centauro. Incontri con Jean Duflot*, collected in Siti and De Laude, *Saggi sulla politica e sulla società*, 1480–90, 1483.

9. Pier Paolo Pasolini, *Teorema* (Milan: Garzanti, 2016), 18.

10. Maurizio Viano, *A Certain Realism: Making Use of Pasolini's Film Theory and Practice* (Berkeley: University of California Press, 1993), 198–213.

11. Pasolini, *Teorema*, 18.

12. It is important to underscore that the members of the family seduce the Visitor, not the other way around. Fabio Vighi has argued that the figure of the Visitor can be identified with the Lacanian *objet a* (the object-cause of desire) and that the characters, confronted with the unsettling proximity of this object, can only resort to sex to placate their anxiety. This argument resonates with Pasolini's own skepticism in "Repudiation": far from a liberating cure-all for the ailments of society, sex would then be nothing more than a reactive defense mechanism to keep anxiety at bay. See Fabio Vighi, *Sexual Difference in European Cinema: The Curse of Enjoyment* (New York: Palgrave Macmillan, 2009), 191–92.

13. See, e.g., Serafino Murri, *Pier Paolo Pasolini* (Milan: Il Castoro Cinema, 2003), 97–104.

14. Pier Paolo Pasolini, "*Teorema:* Come leggere nel modo giusto questo libro," in *Teorema*, vi.

15. Pasolini was planning to direct a film in which Saint Paul's story was to be transposed to World War II. Paul would have been a French fascist hunter of partisans who receives an illumination on his way to Franco's Spain (with Barcelona as a stand-in for Damascus) and as a result joins the resistance. Pasolini wrote an outline for a screenplay, but the project never found financial backing and was ultimately abandoned by the director. See Pier Paolo Pasolini, *Saint Paul: A Screenplay* (London: Verso, 2014). For a systematic discussion of the Pauline legacy in Pasolini, see Benini, *Pasolini*, 187–220; Francesca Parmeggiani, "Pasolini e la parola sacra: Il progetto del 'San Paolo,'" *Italica* 73, no. 2 (1996): 195–214; and Tomaso Subini, "La caduta impossibile: San Paolo secondo Pasolini," in *Il dilettoso monte. Raccolta di saggi di filologia e tradizione classica*, ed. Massimo Gioseffi (Milan: LED, 2004), 227–74. My gratitude goes to Tomaso Subini for sharing a copy of his essay with me.

16. Alain Badiou, *Saint Paul: The Foundation of Universalism*, trans. Ray Brassier (Stanford, Calif.: Stanford University Press, 2003), 2, 66.

17. See Badiou, *Saint Paul*, 23.

18. See Badiou, *Saint Paul*, 74–85; and Jacques Lacan, *The Seminar, Book*

7: The Ethics of Psychoanalysis, 1959–1960, trans. Dennis Porter (New York: Norton, 1992), esp. 83–84.

19. Pasolini, *Teorema*, 106.
20. Pasolini, *Teorema*, 172.
21. Lacan, *Television*, 15–16.
22. See Jacques-Alain Miller, "A Reading of Some Details in *Television* in Dialogue with the Audience," *Newsletter of the Freudian Field* 4, no. 1–2 (1990).
23. Cesare Casarino, "Pasolini in the Desert," *Angelaki* 9, no. 8 (2004): 97–102, 101–2.
24. Benini, *Pasolini*, 200.
25. Lacan, *Television*, 16 (translation modified).
26. Casarino has underlined the inconsequentiality of the Father's gesture: "Clearly, collective ownership of the means of production is no sufficient guarantee against the extraction of surplus value—and against its attendant and constitutive forms of exploitation—if the process of production itself does not undergo radical transformations." Casarino, "Pasolini in the Desert," 100.
27. Lacan, *Television*, 16.
28. Lacan, *Television*, 16.
29. Jacques Lacan, *Le Séminaire, Livre 22. RSI, 1974–5*, ed. Jacques-Alain Miller, seminar of February 18, 1975, *Ornicar?*, no. 4 (1975): 101–6, 106.
30. See Jacques Lacan, *The Seminar, Book 23: The Sinthome, 1975–1976* (Cambridge: Polity, 2016).
31. Lacan, *Television*, 16.
32. Michel Foucault, "Society Must Be Defended," *Lectures at the Collège de France 1975–1976*, trans. David Macey (London: Picador, 2003), 241.
33. It would perhaps not be too far-fetched to suggest that this new regime of accounting of enjoyment might share some traits with Foucault's concept of biopower, especially in relation to the shift from sovereign power and the "right of life and death" over its subjects to biopower as consisting in "making live and letting die." Foucault, in "Society Must Be Defended," reminds us that in ancient times, "death was the moment of the most obvious and most spectacular manifestation of the absolute power of the sovereign" (248). In *Pigsty*, this certainly holds true for the death of the cannibal. But in the era of the Klotzs and the Herdhitzes, death becomes a secretive moment, "when the individual escapes all power, falls back on himself and retreats . . . into his own privacy" (248). Is this not a fitting description of Julian's final demise, which the film refrains from showing? In this new regime, Foucault explains, "power no longer recognizes death. Power literally ignores death." This is exactly what Herdhitze does in the final scene, when he chooses to disregard the news of Julian's suicide out of strategic calculation. Herdhitze, the Nazi

officer turned industrialist, exercises figuratively the power of "making live and letting die" that he had wielded literally during the Holocaust.

34. Lacan, *Television*, 16.

35. For Pasolini, Saint Paul "represents both the knot and the suture between the sacred dimension and the foundation of an institution. On the one hand, at the moment he ascends to the Third Heaven and issues the sacred word, Paul acts as the initiator of a process that over the long term will dismantle the classical world and its institutions, including slavery. On the other hand, it is also Paul who establishes the Church and its rules, rules that determine its relationship to institutional power." Benini, *Pasolini*, 193.

36. See Lorenzo Chiesa, *The Virtual Point of Freedom: Essays on Politics, Aesthetics, and Religion* (Evanston, Ill.: Northwestern University Press, 2016), 17–29.

37. Pier Paolo Pasolini, "Troppa libertà sessuale e si arriva al terrorismo," in Siti and De Laude, *Saggi sulla politica*, 237–41, 238, qtd. in Chiesa, *Virtual Point of Freedom*, 20.

38. The expression appears in Alain Badiou, *Manifesto for Philosophy*, ed. and trans. Norman Maradasz (Albany: State University of New York Press, 1999), 89. Badiou comments on it in "Thinking the Emergence of the Event," interview with Emmanuel Burdeau and François Ramone, in Badiou, *Cinema*, 105–28, 109.

6. The Specter

1. Jacques Derrida, *Specters of Marx: The State of the Debt, the Work of Mourning, and the New International*, trans. Peggy Kamuf (New York: Routledge, 2006), xvii.

2. Fredric Jameson, "Marx's Purloined Letter," in *Ghostly Demarcations: A Symposium of Jacques Derrida's "Specters of Marx,"* ed. Michael Sprinker (New York: Verso, 2008), 26–67, 38.

3. Derrida, *Specters of Marx*, 150.

4. Derrida, *Specters of Marx*, 74.

5. Derrida, *Specters of Marx*, 81.

6. Apart from the geopolitical implications of the oil cartel's monopolistic practices in *The Mattei Affair*, other subjects of Rosi's film inquiries include the ties between politics and real estate speculation in the Italian South (*Hands over the City* [*Le mani sulla città*, 1963]) and the inscrutable alliances between the Italian state, foreign powers, and the Mafia (*Salvatore Giuliano* [1962], *Lucky Luciano* [1973]). Emmanuel Barot has looked at Rosi's film inquiries through the lens of Lukácsian realism; see Emmanuel Barot, *Camera politica: Dialectique du réalisme dans le cinéma politique et militant* (Paris: Vrin, 2009), 57–86.

7. See Fredric Jameson, "Cognitive Mapping," in *Marxism and the Interpretation of Culture*, ed. Cary Nelson and Lawrence Grossberg (Urbana: University of Illinois Press, 1990), 347–60.

8. See Fredric Jameson, "Totality as Conspiracy," in *The Geopolitical Aesthetic: Cinema and Space in the World System* (Bloomington: Indiana University Press, 1995), 9–84.

9. Derrida, *Specters of Marx*, 11.

10. Derrida, *Specters of Marx*, 49.

11. Derrida, *Specters of Marx*, 46.

12. This is a quote from a speech Mattei gave at the Ninth Hydrocarbon Conference in Piacenza in 1960, with many executives of the Seven Sisters attending. See Fulvio Bellini and Alessandro Previdi, *L'assassinio di Enrico Mattei* (Milan: Flan, 1970), 151.

13. The outsized influence Mattei had in political matters was observed with a certain apprehension from across the Atlantic, where the Kennedy administration saw the CEO and his primary political backers (DC notables Giovanni Gronchi and Amintore Fanfani) as the initiators of a possible Italian drift within NATO away from the United States and toward neutrality: "The leitmotiv ... is precisely the intertwining of ENI's business and Mattei's foreign policy strategies, which had a considerable impact on the official Italian position—to the point where the United States became concerned that the situation would lead to a crisis of the entire framework of the Atlantic alliance." Nico Perrone, *Obiettivo Mattei: Petrolio, Stati Uniti e politica dell'ENI* (Rome: Gamberetti, 1995), 104. This more neutralist stance within NATO became known as neo-Atlantism, a current within the DC that began in 1958 with the second Fanfani government.

14. Fofi, *Capire con il cinema*, 261.

15. Leonardo Sciascia, "Nota," in *Il contesto* (Milan: Adelphi, 2006), 113–14, 114.

16. The character of Cres is somewhat reminiscent of other innocent victims of the machinations of state power like anarchists Pietro Valpreda and Giuseppe Pinelli, both erroneously tied to the 1969 Piazza Fontana bombing in Milan. The expression "strategy of tension" first appeared in an article on the bombing in the *Observer* on December 14, 1969.

17. See Robert Brenner, *The Economics of Global Turbulence* (New York: Verso, 2006).

18. Long celebrated as a laboratory of radical politics, the Italian 1960s were just as much a testing ground for covert operations orchestrated by the United States. These include Gladio, a clandestine stay-behind operation designed in the early 1950s to repel a possible invasion of Italy by the members of the Warsaw Pact; the Solo Plan, a preemptive military coup planned in 1964 to neutralize the perceived rise of leftist forces in the country; and the attempted coup of 1970 led by former Fascist Navy

commander Junio Valerio Borghese, parodied by Mario Monicelli in *We Want the Colonels* (*Vogliamo i colonnelli,* 1973). See Mirco Dondi, *L'eco del boato: Storia della strategia della tensione 1965-1974* (Bari: Laterza, 2015); and Aldo Giannuli, *La strategia della tensione* (Milan: Ponte alle Grazie, 2018).

19. It is worth pointing out that the Italian for "rule of law" (*stato di diritto,* from the German *Rechtsstaat*) implies a direct overlap between the law and the state as the institution tasked with defending the rights and liberties of the individual.

20. Sciascia, *Il contesto,* 45.

21. Slavoj Žižek, *In Defense of Lost Causes* (New York: Verso, 2017), 378.

22. See Mary P. Wood, "Revealing the Hidden City: The Cinematic Conspiracy Thriller of the 1970s," *Italianist* 23 (2003): 150-62.

23. Pier Paolo Pasolini, "1 Febbraio 1975. L'articolo delle lucciole," in Siti and De Laude, *Saggi sulla politica e la società,* 404-11, 409.

24. Pasolini, "1 Febbraio 1975," 411.

25. See, e.g., Bisoni, *Indagine su un cittadino;* Rossi, *Elio Petri,* 99-107; and Vito Zagarrio, "La fantasia al potere. Indagine su un film al di sopra di ogni sospetto," in *L'ultima trovata. Trent'anni di cinema senza Elio Petri,* ed. Diego Mondella (Bologna: Pendragon, 2012), 59-66.

26. In the film, this enjoyment attaches itself to specific partial objects. The most conspicuous—and humorous—example is the Chief's socks. Mocked by Augusta because they are too short, the socks are prominently displayed throughout the film, an inadvertent sign of inadequacy barely concealed by his otherwise impeccable suits.

27. Derrida, *Specters of Marx,* 6.

28. Antonio Negri, "The Specter's Smile," in Sprinker, *Ghostly Demarcations,* 12.

29. Karl Marx, "Economic and Philosophical Manuscripts (1844)," in *Early Writings,* trans. Rodney Livingstone and Gregor Benton (London: Penguin, 1992), 279-400, 348-49.

30. Marx, "Economic and Philosophical Manuscripts," 351.

31. Marx, "Economic and Philosophical Manuscripts," 349.

32. Marx, "Economic and Philosophical Manuscripts," 351, emphasis added.

33. Alberto Toscano and Jeff Kinkle, *Cartographies of the Absolute* (Winchester, U.K.: Zero, 2014), 46.

34. Slavoj Žižek, *The Parallax View* (Cambridge, Mass.: MIT Press, 2006), 61.

35. See Samo Tomšič, *The Capitalist Unconscious: Marx and Lacan* (New York: Verso, 2015).

36. See Lacan, *Seminar, Book 17: Other Side of Psychoanalysis,* 177-78.

37. Karl Marx, "On Proudhon: Letter to J. B. Schweizer," in *Karl Marx*

and Friedrich Engels: Selected Works (Moscow: Progress, 1969), marxists .org.

38. Marx, "On Proudhon."
39. Marx, "Economic and Philosophical Manuscripts," 346.
40. Marx, "Economic and Philosophical Manuscripts," 346.
41. See Rossi, *Elio Petri*, 120.
42. Marx, "Economic and Philosophical Manuscripts," 346.
43. Paolo Virno, "The Ambivalence of Disenchantment," in *Radical Thought in Italy: A Potential Politics*, ed. Paolo Virno and Michael Hardt, trans. Michael Turits (Minneapolis: University of Minnesota Press, 1996), 13–36, 13 (translation modified).
44. Mark Fisher, *Ghosts of My Life: Writings on Depression, Hauntology and Lost Futures* (London: Zero, 2014), 18.
45. David Bernard, *Lacan et la honte: De la honte à l'ontologie* (Paris: Éditions du Champ lacanien, 2011), 12.
46. Bernard, *Lacan et la honte*, 12.
47. Lacan, *Seminar, Book 17: Other Side of Psychoanalysis*, 180.
48. See Soler, *Lacanian Affects*, 89–98.
49. Lacan, *Seminar, Book 17: Other Side of Psychoanalysis*, 182.
50. Lacan's mathemes for the master's discourse and the university discourse appear in *Seminar, Book 17: Other Side of Psychoanalysis*, 29.
51. Wendy Brown, "Resisting Left Melancholy," *boundary 2*, 26, no. 3 (1999): 19–27, 26.
52. Derrida, *Specters of Marx*, 88.
53. Derrida, *Specters of Marx*, 86.
54. Alain Badiou, "Of an Obscure Disaster: On the End of the Truth of the State," in *Can Politics Be Thought?*, trans. Bruno Bosteels (Durham, N.C.: Duke University Press, 2019), 111–41, 111. Badiou shares with Derrida the fundamental assumption of the undecidability of a situation ("the condition of decision wherever decision cannot be deduced from an existing body of knowledge as it would be by a calculating machine"; Jacques Derrida, "Marx and Sons," in Sprinker, *Ghostly Demarcations*, 213–69, 240), yet draws from it diametrically opposed conclusions. Where for Derrida this undecidability imposes a political subjectivity of "waiting without expectation" (249), for Badiou it calls forth a subjectivity of courage: politics resides in the wager to act that the subject makes in the context of an undecidable situation.
55. Badiou, "Of an Obscure Disaster," 115.

7. Apocalypse with Figures

1. The vicissitudes of *Salò*'s release are well known. It premiered in Paris in 1975 and was then released in Italy in January of the following

year, only to disappear suddenly, banned by the authorities until 1978, but de facto never screened publicly again until 1985. *Todo Modo,* which portrays a grotesque version of Aldo Moro, president of the DC and prime minister at the time, was banned—and all the negative originals burned—after Moro was murdered by the Red Brigades in 1978. The film resurfaced at festivals and in home video formats well into the 2000s. *La Grande Bouffe* met a relatively more forgiving destiny: it was resoundingly booed at Cannes (where it nonetheless won the critics' prize), and censors slashed it by over fifteen minutes.

2. Pasolini's choice of setting is highly symbolic. Marzabotto was the main theater of one of the bloodiest massacres of civilians orchestrated by the occupying Nazis during the war of liberation, the so-called Massacre of Monte Sole, near Bologna. From September 29 to October 5, 1944, Nazi and Italian collaborationist soldiers summarily executed 1,830 people, including several children.

3. Roland Barthes, *Sade, Fourier, Loyola,* trans. Richard Miller (Baltimore, Md.: Johns Hopkins University Press, 1997), 28. Barthes is referring here to Sade specifically, but his reading can easily be extended to all three films.

4. Gilles Deleuze links this idea of irreversible decay to the drive-image, which he identifies in the work of Ferreri, among others. For a discussion of the drive-image in another film by Ferreri, *Dillinger Is Dead* (*Dillinger è morto,* 1969), see chapter 3.

5. Walter Benjamin, *The Origin of German Tragic Drama,* trans. John Osborne (New York: Verso, 1998), 179.

6. Samuel Weber, "Taking Exception to Decision: Walter Benjamin and Carl Schmitt," *Diacritics* 22, no. 3–4 (1992): 5–18, 9.

7. Weber, "Taking Exception," 9 (emphasis in original).

8. Giorgio Agamben, *State of Exception,* trans. Kevin Attell (Chicago: University of Chicago Press, 2005), 1.

9. Benjamin, *Origin,* 70–71 (translation modified).

10. Agamben, *State of Exception,* 56.

11. Georg [György] Lukács, "On Walter Benjamin," *New Left Review* 1 (1978): 83–88, 84.

12. Benjamin, *Origin,* 55. It is thus no surprise that Benjamin would encounter many of the features of the *Trauerspiel* in modern art, especially in the work of Baudelaire.

13. See Agamben, *State of Exception,* 16–18. Agamben makes explicit reference to the Decreto Moro (Moro decree) of March 28, 1978, as well as the law decree of December 15, 1979. One could also mention the decree of April 11, 1974 (which significantly lengthened preventive detention), and the decree of May 4, 1977, on the matter of maximum-security prisons for terrorists, the so-called *carceri speciali.*

14. Jacques Lacan, "Note on the Father and Universalism," trans. Russell Grigg, *Lacanian Review* 3 (2017): 11.
15. Lacan, "Note on the Father," 11.
16. Lacan, "Note on the Father," 11.
17. Benjamin, *Origin*, 66.
18. Weber, "Taking Exception," 14.
19. Barthes, *Sade*, 167.
20. Barthes, *Sade*, 167.
21. Lacan, *Seminar, Book 23: Sinthome*, 69.
22. Serge Daney, "Notes sur *Salò*," *Cahiers du Cinéma*, no. 268–69 (1976): 102–3.
23. Lacan, *Seminar, Book 23: Sinthome*, 99.
24. Lacan, *Seminar, Book 23: Sinthome*, 47.
25. Weber, "Taking Exception," 17.
26. Barthes, *Sade*, 70.
27. Elio Petri, "Short Tracts on *A ciascuno il suo* and *Todo Modo*," in *Writings on Cinema and Life*, ed. Jean A. Gili, trans. Camilla Zamboni and Erika Marina Nadir (New York: Contra Mundum, 2013), 250–58, 257 (translation modified).
28. Barthes, *Sade*, 45.
29. Barthes, *Sade*, 48.
30. Barthes, *Sade*, 72–73.
31. The President's inadvertent use of *conciliazione* (conciliation) may refer to the formal agreement signed by the fascist government and the Vatican in 1929.
32. Most notably in Karl Marx, "The Eighteenth Brumaire of Louis Bonaparte," in *Surveys from Exile*, trans. Ben Fowkes (New York: Verso, 2010), 143–249. For a discussion of the significance of this expression in Marx's writings, see Mark Neocleous, "Let the Dead Bury Their Dead: Marx and the Politics of Redemption," *Radical Philosophy* 128 (2004), radicalphilosophy.com.
33. Benjamin, *Origin*, 69.
34. Benjamin, *Origin*, 91.
35. Jacques Lacan, *The Seminar, Book 22: RSI, 1974–75*, seminar of January 21, 1975, trans. Jacqueline Rose, in *Feminine Sexuality: Jacques Lacan and the École Freudienne*, ed. Juliet Mitchell and Jacqueline Rose, 162–71, 170 (emphasis added).
36. Jacques Lacan, *The Seminar, Book 3: The Psychoses*, ed. Jacques-Alain Miller, trans. Russell Grigg (New York: Norton, 1997), 132.
37. Lacan, *Seminar, Book 3: Psychoses*, 132.
38. Lacan, *Seminar, Book 3: Psychoses*, 132.
39. Chiesa, *Virtual Point of Freedom*, 30–54, 34.

40. See, e.g., Fabio Vighi, *Traumatic Encounters in Italian Film: Locating the Cinematic Unconscious* (Bristol, U.K.: Intellect, 2006), 94.

41. Benjamin, *Origin*, 166.

42. Benjamin, *Origin*, 29. For a discussion of the representational character of allegory in Benjamin, see Bainard Cowan, "Walter Benjamin's Theory of Allegory," *New German Critique* 22 (1981): 109–22.

43. Fredric Jameson, *Marxism and Form* (Princeton: Princeton University Press, 1974), 72.

44. Badiou, *Theory of the Subject*, 138.

Epilogue

1. Kristin Ross, *May '68 and Its Afterlives* (Chicago: University of Chicago Press, 2002), 10.

2. Ross, *May '68,* 5–6.

3. Evan Calder Williams and Alberto Toscano, "Wrong Place, Right Time: '68 and the Impasses of Periodization," *Cultural Politics* 15, no. 3 (2019): 273–88, 283.

4. Williams and Toscano trace the first scholarly use of the term to Emilio Reyneri, "Il 'maggio strisciante': L'inizio della mobilitazione operaia," in *Lotte operaie e sindacato: Il ciclo 1968–1972 in Italia,* ed. Alessandro Pizzorno (Bologna: Il Mulino, 1978), 49–107.

5. Cesare Casarino, "Surplus Common: A Preface," in Cesare Casarino and Antonio Negri, *In Praise of the Common: A Conversation on Philosophy and Politics* (Minneapolis: University of Minnesota Press, 2008), 1–40, 13.

Index

Accattone (Pasolini), 165
Adorno, Theodor, 45
Agamben, Giorgio, 227–28, 286n13
Agnelli, Giovanni, 103
Althusser, Louis, 20, 112–13, 122
Antonioni, Michelangelo, 3–11 passim, 110, 111, 115, 275n42
Ape Woman, The (Ferreri), 85–93, 119, 125
aporia, 8, 16–19, 21, 24, 27, 31
Arabian Nights, The (Pasolini). See Trilogy of Life
Arsenjuk, Luka, 267–68n32
Auerbach, Erich, 9, 25–26, 266n15
Aumont, Jacques, 26
Autonomia (political movement), 2, 33, 83, 130, 268n37
Autunno caldo (hot autumn), 36
Average Little Man, An (Monicelli), 159–63

Badiou, Alain, 8–9, 12, 37, 43, 68, 109, 131, 171–72, 182, 220, 251, 264n6, 264n12, 265n2, 267n30, 285n54
Balestrini, Nanni, 130
baroque: and allegory, 249–50; architecture, 199; drama, 13, 225–30, 242
Barthes, Roland, 225, 231, 236–38
Battle of Algiers, The (Pontecorvo), 255

Bebel, August, 82
Before the Revolution (Bertolucci), 131–40, 141, 142, 144, 145, 146, 148, 163, 179
Bellocchio, Marco, 3–12 passim, 132, 145, 147, 149, 160, 180, 277n6
Benini, Stefania, 174, 282n35
Benjamin, Walter, 226–29, 231, 234–35, 242, 249–50
Benston, Margaret, 82
Berardi, Franco Bifo, 2
Bertolucci, Bernardo, 3–12 passim, 132, 134, 139, 140, 144, 149, 160, 180
Bhattacharya, Tithi, 120, 123
Bicycle Thieves (De Sica), 128
Biennio Rosso (two red years), 35
Bisoni, Claudio, 5
Bloch, Ernst, 29, 36, 184
Bologna, Sergio, 2
Brenez, Nicole, 8, 26, 27
Brenner, Robert, 194
Bye Bye Monkey (Ferreri), 121

Cahiers du cinéma, 19, 20, 22, 24, 266n7, 266n11
Caligari, Claudio, 6, 153, 155–57, 159, 160, 180, 278n23
Calvino, Italo, 147
Cannibals, The (Cavani), 149–53, 178, 180

Canterbury Tales, The (Pasolini). *See* Trilogy of Life
Casarino, Cesare, 86, 99, 100–101, 108, 174, 257, 281n26
Cavani, Liliana, 3–12 passim, 149, 150, 151, 152, 153, 180, 279–80n7
censorship, 13, 223, 285–86n11
centralità operaia (workers' centrality), 79, 129
Chaplin, Charlie, 52
Cherchi, Grazia, 145–46, 147, 277n6
Chiesa, Lorenzo, 181–82, 245
Children Are Watching Us, The (De Sica), 128
Christian Democrats (Democrazia Cristiana, DC), 6, 187, 200, 216, 218, 224, 236–37, 239–41, 249, 283n13
cinema d'impegno, 1; and medietas, 4–6; and militant leftist critics, 6–7; as *rosipetrismo*, 284n7
cinema verité, 66
Cinema&Film, 7
colonialism, 90–92, 254
Combahee River Collective, 82
Come Play with Me (Samperi), 4, 132, 140–44, 145, 146, 148, 152, 169, 173, 179
Communist Party USA, 82
Comolli, Jean-Louis, 19–24
conspiracy, 1, 12, 63, 185, 188–90, 193–202, 205, 229–30
Cremonini, Leonardo, 112–13, 124

Dalla Costa, Mariarosa, 2, 11, 82, 94
Damiani, Damiano, 1
Daney, Serge, 232
Davis, Angela, 82
debt, 56, 58, 62–66, 270n22
Decameron, The (Pasolini). *See* Trilogy of Life
Deleuze, Gilles, 27–28, 71–72, 73–74, 99, 120–21, 124, 131, 267n24, 272n39

Derrida, Jacques, 8, 12, 16, 183–85, 189–90, 207, 216, 219–20
Didi-Huberman, Georges, 8, 26, 30
Dillinger Is Dead (Ferreri), 85, 109, 118–26, 207
di Palma, Dario, 62
Doane, Mary Ann, 91
drive-image (Deleuze), 120–25

Ecce Bombo (Moretti), 153–59
economic miracle, 32, 85, 110, 128, 174, 200
Engels, Friedrich, 77, 82
ENI (Ente Nazionale Idrocarburi), 186, 189, 191

Fachinelli, Elvio, 133
Farassino, Alberto, 17, 266n5
Federici, Silvia, 2, 11, 82–84, 90, 96
Ferreri, Marco, 3–11 passim, 86, 88, 89, 90, 93, 119, 120, 124, 125, 242, 244, 247, 273n12
FIAT (auto company), 10, 54, 56, 58, 66, 68, 70, 73, 75, 78–79, 103, 270n18, 278–79n25
figure, 2; and allegory, 249–52; in art history, 25; as con-figuration, 7–9; dialectic of, 2, 26–27, 29–32; and history, 28–33; and iconicity, 25; and political subjectivity, 28, 30–33; as tension-figure (Bloch), 29–30, 36. *See also* political cinema
Firestone, Shulamith, 82
Fists in the Pocket (Bellocchio), 131–32, 145–49, 169, 173
Fofi, Goffredo, 7, 191
Fortunati, Leopoldina, 11, 82, 101–2, 274n28
French Communist Party (Parti Communiste Français, PCF), 139

Germany Year Zero (Rossellini), 128, 213

Giordana, Marco Tullio, 13, 186, 213, 214
Giotto, 27
Gospel According to Saint Matthew, The (Pasolini), 165, 168
Grande Bouffe, La (Ferreri), 223–29, 241–48, 249, 251, 285–86n1
Guattari, Félix, 131

Hawks and the Sparrows, The (Pasolini), 168
Heidegger, Martin, 71
Hitler, Adolf, 97, 98

I Am Self-Sufficient (Moretti), 153–59
ideology critique (film studies), 19–24
Ignatius of Loyola, Saint, 224, 237–38, 240–41
Italian Communist Party (Partito Comunista Italiano, PCI), 6, 55, 58, 67, 72, 138–39, 239

James, Selma, 82
Jameson, Fredric, 77, 188–89, 190, 192, 193, 250
Jones, Claudia, 82

Kinkle, Jeff, 209
Kofman, Sarah, 16–18, 27
Kollontai, Alexandra, 82

Lacan, Jacques, 37, 41, 42, 134, 155–57, 159, 172–76, 179, 182, 197, 209, 210, 215–17, 229–31, 234–35, 242–43, 245, 247
Lazarus, Sylvain, 53
Lazzarato, Maurizio, 64
Lizzani, Carlo, 1
Loren, Sophia, 104
Lotta continua (political organization), 67, 213, 217
Lukács, Georg, 228, 267n22

Mafia, 1, 54–56, 63
Mainardi, Pat, 82
Mamma Roma (Pasolini), 165
Manilius, 9
Marx, Karl, 41–42, 44, 48, 77, 90, 113, 120, 122, 123, 207–11, 240–41, 275n42
Mattei, Enrico, 186–92, 283n13
Mattei Affair, The (Rosi), 185, 186–92, 193, 194, 196, 201, 213
metis, 17, 19, 26
Miccicché, Lino, 67
Millett, Kate, 82
Mitchell, Juliet, 92, 273n15, 274n32
Monicelli, Mario, 3, 35, 160
Montaldo, Giuliano, 1
Moretti, Nanni, 6, 153–57, 159, 160, 278n23
Moro, Aldo, 216, 218, 224, 237, 239, 285–86n1
Moroni, Primo, 130
Morricone, Ennio, 39
Morton, Peggy, 82
Mussolini, Benito, 97, 103, 162

Narboni, Jean, 19–24
Negri, Antonio, 2, 51, 130, 269n3
neorealism, 71–72, 100–101, 128, 132
Nietzsche, Friedrich Wilhelm, 60, 63
nonrelation. *See* political cinema

Ombre rosse, 7, 266n11
Omicron (Gregoretti), 35–36
operaio sociale (Negri), 32–33, 51
operaismo (Workerism), 2, 36, 75, 79, 83
Organizer, The (Monicelli), 35
Ossessione (Visconti), 86–89, 99–101, 124

Pasolini, Pier Paolo, 3–12 passim, 145, 147, 165–82, 200–201,

216, 226, 231, 241, 245, 274n34, 278n23, 279n4, 280n15
Paul, Saint, 171–75, 179, 181, 280n15, 282n35
Pellizzari, Lorenzo, 4–5
Petri, Elio, 1–13 passim, 28, 36, 39, 47, 49, 53, 69, 70, 94, 202–12 passim, 226, 237, 263–64n5, 264n7
Pigsty (Pasolini), 12, 167, 168, 176–83, 281–82n33
political cinema: end of, 253; as fetish, 17–18; and the figure, 2, 24–28; and genre, 3; impurity of, 3–7; as nonrelation, 1–2, 15–19, 24; and periodization, 253–58; and the politics of the long '68, 32–33
poros, 16–19, 25
Property Is No Longer a Theft (Petri), 185–86, 206–12, 213, 215, 220

real abstraction, 112–16, 118, 122, 125, 185–86, 206–12, 215–16, 275n39
Red Desert (Antonioni), 85, 109–18, 121, 122, 207
ressentiment, 60–64, 69, 78–80, 161
Ricotta, La (Pasolini), 168
Rome Open City (Rossellini), 128
Rosi, Francesco, 1–12 passim, 187–88, 191, 193, 194, 199, 201, 205, 264n7
Rowbotham, Sheila, 82

Sade, Marquis de, 231, 237
Salò, or the 120 Days of Sodom (Pasolini), 13, 167, 223–35, 241, 242, 249, 251, 285–86n1
Samperi, Salvatore, 7, 132, 140, 142, 144, 149, 160, 180
Sciascia, Leonardo, 193, 194, 224

Scola, Ettore, 2–11 passim, 66–68, 69, 71–72, 75, 98, 99, 100, 101, 104, 107, 109–10
Seduction of Mimì, The (Wertmüller), 3–4, 10, 37, 54–66, 69, 72, 78–80
Seven Sisters (oil companies), 186–87, 188, 190, 191, 192, 202
shame, 186, 214–19
Shoeshine (De Sica), 128
Silverman, Kaja, 29
sinthome (Lacan), 175–76, 235
Soler, Colette, 155–56, 216
sovereignty. *See* state of exception
Special Day, A (Scola), 85, 97–109, 117, 119, 126, 251
stakhanovism, 36, 38; as perversion, 39–41, 43, 44, 56, 75
state of exception, 13, 193, 225, 227–28, 230, 236, 238; in Italy, 286n13
strategy of tension, 63, 193–94, 200, 202, 213, 283n16
Straub, Jean-Marie, 36

Teorema (Pasolini), 12, 165, 167, 168–76, 177, 180, 182, 235
Thompson, William, 82
Todo Modo (Petri), 13, 14, 223–29, 235–41, 242, 249, 251, 285–86n1
To Love the Damned (Giordana), 13, 186, 213–20
Torlasco, Domietta, 124
Toscano, Alberto, 209, 275n39
Tout va bien (Groupe Dziga Vertov), 255
Toxic Love (Caligari), 153–59, 278n23
Trevico-Turin: Voyage in the Fiat-Nam (Scola), 10, 28, 37, 54, 66–81, 118, 271n29
Trilogy of Life (Pasolini), 166
Tronti, Mario, 2, 270n11

Vancini, Florestano, 1
Viano, Maurizio, 170
Virno, Paolo, 2, 33, 71, 212, 214
Visconti, Luchino, 86, 88, 100, 102
Volonté, Gian Maria, 39, 48, 189, 202, 204, 224, 237

Wages for Housework, 11, 82–84, 95–96, 100–101, 110, 117
We All Loved Each Other So Much (Scola), 72
Weber, Samuel, 226, 230
Weeks, Kathi, 95
Wertmüller, Lina, 2, 3, 37, 55–60 passim, 69, 70, 75
We Want the Colonels (Monicelli), 283–84n18
Wheeler, Anna, 82
Working Class Goes to Heaven, The (Petri), 7, 10–11, 28, 36–54, 55, 56, 58, 68, 75, 79, 84, 85, 93, 96, 97, 119, 122, 204, 251

Zetkin, Clara, 82
Žižek, Slavoj, 196
Zupančič, Alenka, 42

Mauro Resmini is associate professor of cinema and media studies and Italian at the University of Maryland, College Park.

Lightning Source UK Ltd.
Milton Keynes UK
UKHW021114291222
414437UK00004B/70